MW00615739

CITY OF NEWSMEN

CITY OF NEWSMEN

Public Lies and Professional
Secrets in Cold War Washington

KATHRYN J. McGARR

The University of Chicago Press

Chicago and London

The University of Chicago Press, Chicago 60637
The University of Chicago Press, Ltd., London
© 2022 by Kathryn J. McGarr
All rights reserved. No part of this book may be used or repro-
duced in any manner whatsoever without written permission,
except in the case of brief quotations in critical articles and
reviews. For more information, contact the University of Chicago
Press, 1427 E. 60th St., Chicago, IL 60637.
Published 2022
Printed in the United States of America

31 30 29 28 27 26 25 24 23 22   1 2 3 4 5

ISBN-13: 978-0-226-66404-0 (cloth)
ISBN-13: 978-0-226-66418-7 (e-book)
DOI: https://doi.org/10.7208/chicago/9780226664187.001.0001

Library of Congress Cataloging-in-Publication Data

Names: McGarr, Kathryn J., author.
Title: City of newsmen : public lies and professional secrets in
    Cold War Washington / Kathryn J. McGarr.
Description: Chicago : The University of Chicago Press, 2022. |
    Includes bibliographical references and index.
Identifiers: LCCN 2022001024 | ISBN 9780226664040 (cloth) | ISBN
    9780226664187 (ebook)
Subjects: LCSH: Foreign news—Washington (D.C.)—
    History—20th century. | Journalists—Washington (D.C.)
    | Journalistic ethics—Washington (D.C.) | Journalism—
    Objectivity—Washington (D.C.) | Cold War—Press coverage—
    Washington (D.C.) | Government and the press—Washington
    (D.C.)—History—20th century. | United States—Foreign
    relations—1945–1989—Press coverage.
Classification: LCC PN4888.F69 M34 2022 | DDC 070.4/33209753—
    dc23/eng/20220304
LC record available at https://lccn.loc.gov/2022001024

♾ This paper meets the requirements of ANSI/NISO Z39.48-1992
(Permanence of Paper).

For my parents, Janie and Cappy

CONTENTS

INTRODUCTION

CHALLENGING THE MEMORIES

On January 7, 1954, just back from a diplomatic trip around the world, Vice President Richard Nixon conferred with a few trusted reporters from mainstream news outlets. The wide-ranging discussion covered everything from British negotiations for Iranian oil to the new French military plan in Vietnam. Concerning Vietnam, the *New York Times'* reporter noted in a memo to his editor, "He is not as optimistic in private as he, the President, and the Secretary of State must be in public. Indeed, he is very concerned, and very pessimistic in private."[1] Throughout the 1940s and 1950s, private conversations—written confidentially in memoranda but not shared with the public—were a commonplace of foreign policy reporting in Washington, DC. The *Washington Post* editor at the Nixon session had written a similar memo for his files, noting that Nixon commented, "I have talked optimistically about Indo China, in public. Must do so, I think because it would be a catastrophe for us to lose it and we have our money on it and must stick with it to the end. At same time must not expect that we are going to be able to deal permanently with situation. May put in 800 million dollars a year but not going to crush Communism as long as Communist China is active and aggressive. Will continue indefinitely to be a problem."[2] In other words, as early as 1954 the press corps in the nation's capital knew the US government's attitude toward Vietnam and the duplicity with which it discussed its position with the American people. The only immediate stories in the *Times* and the *Post* to come from this meeting with Nixon were short front-page articles noting that the vice president had reiterated the Eisenhower administration's initial commitment not to recognize the Peiping (later Beijing) government, ending speculation about a "new look" for China policy.[3] The foreign policy information economy operated through public lies and private understandings.

Washington journalism of the 1940s and 1950s suffers from at least two contradictory misconceptions. The first is that the press used to be trustworthy, and today it is not. The second is that reporters during this period were passive stenographers who trusted whatever people in power said. The Vietnam War and the Watergate scandal, this account holds, lifted a veil from reporters' eyes: they became adversarial, savvier, more willing to question the government's motives.[4] The new generation of baby boomer reporters was too sophisticated to have been taken in by, say, a Henry Kissinger, unlike the gullible Greatest Generation. Of James "Scotty" Reston, who served in the *New York Times*' Washington bureau from 1941 to 1989, the iconoclastic writer Gay Talese wrote, "There was little negativism or doubt in his vision, and thus his America was a positive place for right-thinking people, and God was on our side—it was as it had been during World War II."[5] As we will see, though, Reston expressed frequent doubt about the wisdom of both America and Americans. What went on behind the scenes as Washington newsmen created the *appearance* of consensus was far more complex than Talese allowed. World War II did affect how Reston saw the world, but that was true for almost everyone who lived through it and had seen the rise of totalitarianism in the 1930s. The leading reporters of the 1950s were not somehow collectively more naive than those they recruited from the *Harvard Crimson* to succeed them.[6]

In a July 1993 *New York Times* column on the fortieth anniversary of the Korean armistice, the journalist James L. Greenfield propagated the most widely held view of the midcentury press: "For the most part, the correspondents in Korea were still awash in the patriotic fervor of World War II. For the press in general it was a less questioning, less cynical time."[7] These descriptors should not be treated as mutually exclusive; members of the press could be awash in patriotic fervor at the same time that they were distrustful and cynical. Indeed, the idea of what it meant to be a patriotic newsman usually included the notion that he *would* question the government, though often not in print. The stereotypical cynicism of a 1930s wisecracking reporter only intensified during World War II after so many reporters had disappointing experiences—sometimes as newsmen, sometimes as propagandists—with government information practices and censorship. They were more distrustful and more cynical but also less sure of how best to prevent the next world war.

For most of the newsmen who went on to cover postwar foreign policy, the patriotism of World War II was hardly a flag-waving nationalism. As a cohort, they instead believed in a very conscious internationalism, which for them meant an alignment of the nation's well-being with Western Europe, specifically Great Britain and France. Through their work, they advocated on behalf of an internationalism based in the Atlantic Community.[8] Moreover, in the homogenous world of like-minded white men that they intentionally created across Washington, they constantly reinforced the rightness of their views and developed private spaces in which to work through them.

Still, this period before Vietnam and Watergate is believed to be unique in the annals of press history for its "short-lived patriotic collaborations" during an "era of good feelings," as Max Frankel, a longtime *New York Times* reporter, editor, and columnist put it in his memoir.[9] About the 1960 U-2 spy plane incident, during which an American pilot was captured in the Soviet Union, he wrote that "Washington mindlessly issued the customary cover story" about a weather plane veering off course. "Probably for the last time in the Cold War, American reporters assumed that their government was telling the truth."[10] He—and other journalists who echoed this sentiment in memoirs and oral histories—had it wrong.[11] Reporters in Washington *rarely* assumed their government was telling the truth, nor did they unself-consciously repeat what their government sources told them. In this case, most of the men at the top newspapers had known for years that the United States had spy planes entering Soviet airspace, so they did not believe stories about off-course weather planes or the many other fictitious accounts.[12] This postwar period was not an era of good feelings but one of friction—among reporters and between reporters, editors, publishers, and public officials.[13]

With this book, I venture to add some nuance to our understanding of midcentury foreign policy reporters, who have been treated historically—at times by their own later accounts—as patriotic dupes rather than men who struggled through the problems of covering a world armed with nuclear weapons. Total destruction remained foremost in the minds of the generation that had witnessed the atomic explosions in 1945. Not doing anything to trigger the next war, which could be the final one, was central to journalistic responsibility from 1945 to 1963, when the United States and the Soviet Union negotiated a nuclear test ban treaty.

Reporters did not suffer from the false consciousness so often attributed to them. They constantly discussed the difficulties of reporting the news objectively, an ideal they knew was unattainable. They knew that the official version of events was not always true—that the government, in fact, lied—and readily acknowledged that news about foreign policy came through a filter.[14] In 1952, a *St. Louis Post-Dispatch* reporter based in Washington lamented, "More and more of our foreign news these days is reaching our readers as screened or filtered through either the State Department or the Pentagon. Too few of our correspondents are equipped, or will take the trouble, to go out and get their stuff first-hand."[15] The exigencies of daily reporting, combined with a sense of responsibility for preserving the peace after World War II, determined much of what the public read far more often than any ideological considerations like anticommunism.

Throughout this book, I use the words *men* and *newsmen*. Women populated many Washington spaces, and some of them were journalists. However, the men who covered foreign policy actively excluded women reporters as well as reporters of color. Using their language—*newsmen, newspapermen,* or Times*men,* as those who worked for the *New York Times* called themselves—helps us understand how they thought. Newspapers could not risk assigning a woman to cover the

European Defense Community in 1954 when she would not be able to attend the National Press Club luncheon at which the French premier spoke or gain access to the private "smoker" for him later that evening at the home of Eugene Meyer, the chairman of the board of the *Washington Post*.[16] These newsmen were also white. Since Washington remained segregated, white-owned newspapers would not risk that their reporter might be excluded from a newsworthy event because of his race. News organizations from other countries did assign women to cover the State Department, since as foreigners they would not be included in private sessions, regardless of their sex. When the new secretary of state held a large press reception in February 1961, the guest list was submitted as "the following newsmen," since out of 197 invitees, only 10 were women, 6 of whom worked for international news organizations.[17] Yes, some influential women worked in Washington, but this is not their story—the story of the exceptions to the rule.[18] This is the story of the rule.

We already know that Washington was an elite boys' club—still is, in many ways—and that this clubbiness influenced US foreign policy.[19] But the story we know about policy makers and select members of the press fails to capture the majority of the working reporters in Washington who were middle-class, were educated at public universities, and felt little affinity for blue bloods like Secretary of State John Foster Dulles or the syndicated columnist Joseph Alsop.[20] While many of the elite foreign policy makers may have forged their ideals in the crucible of East Coast preparatory schools and Ivy League colleges and universities, the men who wrote about foreign policy—those responsible for circulating ideas within Washington and transmitting them to people outside the capital—were typically midwesterners who had attended public high schools and land-grant colleges. More Washington correspondents at midcentury were from Indiana and Illinois than any other states.[21] Scotty Reston and one of his friends and competitors, Wallace Deuel, were both from Illinois and attended the University of Illinois. The influential syndicated columnist Marquis Childs was from Wisconsin and attended the state university, where he roomed with Robert Allen, who also became a Washington columnist. From radio, Elmer Davis hailed from Indiana and attended Franklin College in his home state, and Eric Sevareid attended the University of Minnesota. Some newsmen went to elite liberal arts colleges: the *Washington Post*'s Alfred Friendly (from Salt Lake City) and Chalmers Roberts (from Pittsburgh) became close friends at Amherst, and the *Christian Science Monitor*'s Joseph Harsch (from Toledo, Ohio) went to Williams College and then Cambridge University. These men were certainly not monolithic in their upbringings or their beliefs. They came from different parts of the country and different class backgrounds, and they forged their ideas about the world through their travels during World War II and their friendships in Washington. They were weighing heavy life-and-death issues and relied on one another to come to intellectual consensuses about US obligations in a postwar world.

During this period, loyalty and social solidarity, which prevented the public airing of journalistic disputes and ethical anxieties, coincided with the remaking of the international order and a concern that the two recent world wars would be followed by a third. The 1940s and 1950s were also a time of civil rights progress at home and anticolonial revolutions abroad—two changes that most of these journalists would have said they supported in theory. When it came to practice, however, they enjoyed their exclusive clubs and the fact that they could put on skits wearing blackface without critique. Any conversation about anticolonialism or nascent nationalism abroad would have been suffused with the understanding that the country's two greatest allies, France and Britain, depended on the raw materials that former colonies offered.

Like many professionals, reporters in Washington limited their circles to like-minded men and, beginning in World War II, created an information-sharing system that depended on individual responsibility and good fellowship. In doing so, they excluded women, reporters of color, and dissidents, ensuring that their discourse would be the dominant one. The private conversations among the white men of the press, at exclusive meetings of the Overseas Writers group, the Gridiron Club, and the Metropolitan Club, to name just a few important spaces, then perpetuated an us-versus-them conception of nonwhite nations. Maintaining exclusion in news clubs and performing in blackface at the Gridiron Club dinner ensured that a white supremacist vision of the world dominated the foreign policy discourse in white-owned newspapers.

The US government, of course, pushed its propaganda on reporters during the 1940s and 1950s.[22] If we look only at government sources and the published record, reporters' agency or sometimes even their ability to reason can seem dubious. But reporters did not think in black and white; they merely sometimes wrote in it, and not as often as critics seem to believe. Looking behind the printed word to the world they lived in is important to avoid caricaturing the whole group. Viewing more closely their transition from waging war to "waging peace," as Americans called postwar planning, challenges the notion that the government was manipulating the press; instead, a two-way manipulation of and struggle over information took place.

The Atlantic Community orientation of important news outlets and the desire to save Western Europe ultimately led the press to promote the Marshall Plan, the North Atlantic Treaty Organization (NATO), and the internationalist wing of the Republican Party, which in 1952 was led by the man credited with having saved Europe for democracy, Dwight Eisenhower. Such unity of purpose then began to fray with the increasing tendency toward state secrecy during the early 1950s as well as the press's growing discomfort with the secrets and lies of the Eisenhower administration—especially those of the two Dulles brothers, Allen and John Foster, who were running the Central Intelligence Agency and the State Department, respectively. Scotty Reston coined the term *news management* in 1955, the year we start to see the breakdown of government-press cooperation, long before the cynicism of the Vietnam War era set in.

The media scholar Daniel Hallin has found that the world of foreign policy reporters in Washington, from the 1940s through and past Vietnam, constituted a "sphere of consensus," and the sociologist Herbert Gans demonstrates that newsmen shared "enduring values."[23] We still need a better understanding of how the sphere and the values actually formed—how reporters operated under and sometimes created their own physical and ideological constraints, beyond those typically experienced by any social or professional group.[24] We might say that they prized objectivity like other journalists, but objectivity was simply one of many news values of this period—one that this cohort placed below internationalism. While many reporters were willing to prioritize citizenship over scoops, they did so sparingly and knowingly, not as government dupes. Their concern for national security and for not sparking nuclear war did not diminish the skepticism of their government or their agonizing and constant reappraisals of their watchdog function. Only by looking at the archival papers of reporters, editors, and publishers and the private side of the printed conversation can we understand how and why the media acted as they did during this period.[25]

Trust was also an extremely important value *among* newsmen, who needed one another's acceptance more than they needed it by the men in power. Scotty Reston did not trust the men in power. But he also did not raise his mistrust in print until the mid- to late 1950s, not because he was a patriot but because he found that it was counterproductive with readers. As he wrote in 1951 to an editor friend, "The public doesn't give a damn about our newspaper problems and, certainly, doesn't respond to general statements about how we don't trust public officials." He continued, describing exactly what would later be called the credibility gap: "I think the public confidence in the newspapers is no greater, if as great, as it is in public officials and, therefore, it is not effective merely to complain without illustrating precisely what we are complaining about."[26] That precise illustration would not come until the publication of the Pentagon Papers in 1971, but reporters' complaints about credibility had dominated their private debate well before then.[27] Some of the public may have been shocked to learn of the cumulative lies told by multiple administrations with regard to Vietnam, but these newsmen were not.

Nevertheless, journalists' memories of being lied to persisted, maybe to distract from their own complicity in early support for the Vietnam War. A *New York Times* writer, speaking of that war, recalled in the 1980s, "I was brought up with the lessons of World War II. . . . We were being told that this was Communist aggression. . . . The Secretary of State tells me that, and who am I to argue with him . . . that's the view one had at the time. . . . We had not yet been taught to question the President. . . . We had not been taught by bitter experience that our government like any other *in extremis* will lie and cheat to protect itself."[28] Views like this mischaracterized the past, perhaps because of the heavy retrospective shadow of the Vietnam War. Regardless, few reporters in Washington would have thought that total trust in government was among the lessons of World War II.

We also do not have a good understanding of how a figurative boys' club developed in the physical spaces of Washington, DC. Literal boys' clubs—facilitating relationships between members, bonding them through annual rituals, and creating insiders and outsiders—played an important role in establishing newspaper norms and consensuses. They helped in determining what should be reported or withheld, and in deciding what constituted legitimate news. The constant fellowship and togetherness of white male reporters could then inhibit radical thinking and especially radical writing.[29] Much like in the business world, elite reporters used private clubs to maintain control over their profession. In closing these spaces to women reporters, reporters of color, and white men whom they considered outsiders, they reinforced their echo chamber.[30]

A history grounded in archives allows us to see that the Washington information economy was far more complicated than it first seems and often far different from what reporters later said it had been like.[31] Reporters formed not only an "interpretive community" but also a physical one.[32] These men interacted with their subjects and with one another in the lobby of the Mayflower Hotel and in the shared office space of the National Press Building; at the lunch tables of the Metropolitan Club and at Sans Souci restaurant; at the luncheons of the Overseas Writers group, where officials shared information that could not be attributed; at the white-tie banquets of the Gridiron Club; and in the living room of the influential columnist Walter Lippmann.[33] The friendships among these reporters constituted a world of debts and loyalties, shared memories of harrowing wartime experiences, shared frustrations with government censorship and information programs, shared antagonisms, and shared mentors. They built and maintained gendered and racialized spaces and created common loyalties, outlooks, and ideas—and they did so as their country was assuming global leadership. But they lived in a social-professional world about which we know little.

William F. Buckley Jr. critiqued the camaraderie and conformity of the liberal establishment in his 1955 founding statement for the *National Review*: "Drop a little itching powder in Jimmy Wechsler's bath and before he has scratched himself for the third time, Arthur Schlesinger will have denounced you in a dozen books and speeches, Archibald MacLeish will have written ten heroic cantos about our age of terror, *Harper's* will have published them, and everyone in sight will have been nominated for a Freedom Award."[34] Buckley was describing the visible links between visible men, none of whom resided in Washington, DC. The invisible links in the spaces of Washington ran much deeper and more broadly; and while it is almost impossible to say that x encounter led to y opinion, the totality of the informal socializing—grafted onto the more formal background occasions and stag banquets—created a dense communications network of individuals who wrote for newspapers across the country. The editorials of their respective papers, the local news that appeared alongside their reporting, and the politics of statehouses—all of these were different. Only foreign policy reporting was the same, and not because its journalists shared some particular patriotic vision of America; indeed, most were annoyed by her hypocrisy. And certainly not because they shared faith in public officials; most actively distrusted what policy makers told them. It was the same because they reported from Washington. They attended the same background sessions that they were then pressured by one another and their sources to report in specific ways. They remained on good terms with one another so they could attend the Gridiron Club dinner or host the most desirable guests there. They adjusted their work to their publishers' and editors' critiques so they would not get fired. They did not operate within a prefabricated sphere of internationalist consensus; they helped build that sphere and silence its critics. Understanding the contours of this sphere allows us to understand how an internationalist view of foreign policy dominated the press, even as isolationism and resentment of Europe remained at the grass roots.[35]

Attempting to recreate the daily interaction and web of interconnectedness is the only way for us to understand what made postwar Washington an echo chamber for liberal internationalism—specifically, US leadership of and intervention on behalf of what became known as the free world. The constant socializing circulated ideas and created loyalties, debts, and sometimes resentments, all while fostering a closed community. Of course, foreign policy reporters did not agree on what to report simply because they admired Walter Lippmann and depended on him to second their nomination to the Metropolitan Club. Lippmann, in fact, often criticized the State Department's policies, and though he is best remembered for his hostility to the Lyndon Johnson administration, he was extremely critical of Johnson's predecessors as well.[36] But that dense web of interpersonal connections helps us understand how a variety of opinions and information could be filtered into common narratives about the necessity of American leadership abroad. At the supposed height of the era of objective journalism, the news was subjectively and consciously crafted.

This book draws from more than fifty archival collections, mostly those of reporters, editors, and publishers. But the written record is incomplete when we are dealing with what was "in the air." Based only on their published writings or even their private archives, Scotty Reston and Joe Alsop seem to have had a relationship that was distant at best and strained at worst, with little contact. In reality, they saw each other constantly, as I was reminded by a letter that the socially active reporter Kay Halle sent to her close friend, the historian Arthur Schlesinger Jr., in June 1948: "Then yesterday at a wedding Scotty and Jo[e] Alsop and I went over more of the horror" of recent congressional cuts to the Marshall Plan. "Jo[e] is fearfully pessimistic—Scotty with his positive Presbyterian nature is not so much."[37] Schlesinger was planning to come to Washington that month, which he had told Joe Alsop about in a letter (now in the Alsop Papers) informing him of his plans and letting him know he did not need to stay in his guest room on this occasion, but would still see him ("of course").[38] The reporter Wallie Deuel's notes from a 1953 dinner with Secretary of State John Foster Dulles were in his own papers at the Library of Congress, but a memo a week later explaining the circumstances of the dinner to his editor at the *St. Louis Post-Dispatch* was in the columnist Mark Childs's papers at the Wisconsin Historical Society. Deuel's notes described a kerfuffle from that week at the *New York Times*, which I corroborated with a series of memos from the archives of the *Times'* managing editor, Turner Catledge, at Mississippi State University. All this is to acknowledge that like any historian piecing together a world, my method was informed by luck.

Journalism is often seen a first draft of history, so we need to understand how that first draft, which then becomes part of the historical record, gets made. Our understanding of news changes when we interrogate it as we would any other source and examine the process of its creation. Joseph Harsch, a Washington correspondent for the *Christian Science Monitor*, CBS, and NBC, once explained to the historian Henry Steele Commager that if Harsch and his colleagues wrote what they believed, they would have no readers. "The events as I, and I think most of my colleagues see them, sometimes run counter to the current of American folklore. Were I to write the story of Washington today exactly as I see it I would soon alienate much of my audience and in the process, deprive myself entirely of an audience." Harsch continued with a description of false journalistic balance still familiar to journalists today, who usually abhor the practice as much as Harsch did but use it nonetheless: "Sometimes consciously, more often subconsciously, I employ the practice of buying the freedom to say what I want to say. To say something unfavorable about Republicans I first say something unfavorable about Democrats. Often this can be done with full justification. Sometimes, under the pressure of daily journalism, it is done carelessly and with violence to objective fact. The inclination to err on the side of the administration is ever present. The pressure from editors and readers (perhaps in the future from the FBI) is powerful."[39] Harsch was describing a complicated process involving multiple pressures that he and his colleagues carried out daily. Commager replied that he appreciated the insight: "It is a wonderful letter, one that tells more about the real methods of journalism than any number of school of journalism lectures."[40] In the pages that follow, I describe those "real methods of journalism" and that "story of Washington today exactly as I see it" that Harsch and his fellow newsmen sometimes kept from their contemporary readers but preserved in their files for future ones.

1

BUILDING A CITY OF GENTLEMEN

When forty-five-year-old Arthur Krock moved to Washington, DC, to run the *New York Times* bureau there in 1932, he pronounced his job "penal servitude" and immediately began looking for his replacement. Washington was a provincial town, and he found the bureau to be staffed by a "sub-calibre group—lazy, sycophantic, the ways of local rooms forgotten, often stupid, devoted to the 'huddle' instead of original research in the quest for news, intent on radio appearances and Gridiron dinners and wishing to shine in journalistic or capital society." In fact, Washington *made* reporters lazy, Krock thought, since "one dies spiritually as well as professionally here." "The talk in the capital is all of politics and personalities and Gridiron dinners: no breadth of outlook, no acquaintance with books or plays or the great life of the outer world. . . . The newspaper world folds upon itself, and most of its members look inward."[1] Washington reporting was limiting, and Krock—though himself a member of the Gridiron Club—imagined himself a player in a wider world.

Washington would remain insular in many respects, and the Gridiron dinner would remain important. But as the federal government expanded and the nation's capital assumed its position as an internationally important city in the years between the world wars, the mandate for Washington journalism expanded too. Newsmen would begin looking outward for professional influence while also strengthening their ties to one another.

The Gentlemen's Clubs

When in 1790 the US Congress voted to move the seat of government from New York to sparsely inhabited slave plantation land along the Potomac River, it chose isolation and insularity over the urbanity typifying the great capital cities of Europe. The area was not entirely devoid of population, though. Nearby in Georgetown and Alexandria were larger settlements that had displaced the indigenous population more than a century earlier. Further, there was hope that with the addition of the capital, the Potomac could become an important river port— the "emporium of the United States," as George Washington put it.[2] The commercial aspirations for the city did not materialize, however; the main business of the new capital would be government, its primary import congressmen and journalists and its primary export laws and news.

In October 1800, the *National Intelligencer* became the capital's first locally printed newspaper. Its four pages appeared three times per week, cost the princely sum of five dollars per year, paid in advance, and, like all newspapers in the early republic, was intended for the elite who ran the nation's politics and finances. In his introductory letter to readers, the publisher, Samuel Harrison Smith, wrote of the newspaper's lofty goals and emphasized the meaning of the title—this was a newspaper for a *nation*, a newly imagined community held together in part by the printed word.[3] "As it is his firm determination, that nothing shall be admitted into the National Intelligencer, which shall wound national, or calumniate private character, so it is his unalterable purpose freely to insert, and earnestly to invite, whatever shall promote the general welfare," Smith declared.[4] A printer on the side of the party that would become Thomas Jefferson's Democratic-Republicans, Smith stated that his paper's mission was nonetheless to support the "general welfare."[5] Over the next 160 years, the city of Washington and the character of newspapers would undergo multiple transformations. But that sense of responsibility for the general welfare, later called the public interest, would persist in the capital's newsmen. What was printed in the capital, they believed, mattered for the survival of a loosely bound country. They should not wound the national character.

The *Intelligencer*, its owner, and his "charming wife," Margaret Bayard Smith, who often entertained at their home, were among the first settlers to make Washington more attractive to newcomers and more livable for residents.[6] Newspapers were a sign that an intellectual crowd, or at least a handful of printers, had been willing to relocate from Boston, Philadelphia, or New York. During a period when congressmen usually remained in the capital for only five or six months of the year, living in boardinghouses along New Jersey Avenue, editors, writers, and printers made up an important part of the year-round society.[7] "Washington at work was the ruling group at work and Washington at leisure was the ruling group at leisure: for here the rulers not only worked together but also resided together, in a remote and isolated outpost with none but themselves for company," writes the historian James S. Young about the early nineteenth century.[8] From the beginning, Washington was a city whose society revolved around narrow professional networks, a trend that would help make it a town where everyone inside it could know something that outsiders did not.[9]

The content of newspapers also enabled further community growth, as they provided essential tools for development. "As vehicles of local advertising, purveyors of national news, and organs of political opinion, the papers contributed to Washington a more nearly urban air than the years of planning and building had contrived," notes Constance McLaughlin Green, a historian of the capital.[10] The air may have been urban, but there was little agriculture, little manufacturing, scant reason for free laborers to move there or immigrants to settle as they would other parts of the country over the next hundred years, and no tradition of arts or publishing.[11] Slaves would provide the labor, and the southern slaveholding aristocracy would establish the racial hierarchy. At the same time, the city was more attractive to free Black residents than most states to its south, since it allowed manumitted slaves to remain there and permitted education for free Blacks. This meant a vibrant Black community as well as a history of a Black Washington separate from the federal government's Washington.

The growth of the Black population in the capital coincided with the upending of the social order during the Civil War, and a white sense of loss of control over public space led to a proliferation of gentlemen's clubs.[12] Modeled after famous men's clubs in London, these spaces, established in many US cities in the nineteenth century, were explicitly built for exclusion. Their founders wanted no truck with immigrants, women, people of color, and the poor—all groups who were starting to multiply or become more visible in city streets.[13] Progressive organizations and clubs for Black and white women alike made enormous strides in the nineteenth century, opening up public space to them.[14] But as this was happening, men retreated to new sanctums that served as "buffers," limiting members' contact with people they regarded as the wrong sort.[15] The withdrawal into clubs, which were neither wholly public nor private, also helped direct the flow from one generation of white men to the next of social capital, which the historian Pamela Laird defines as "all those social assets that enable one to attract respect, generate confidence, evoke affection, and draw on loyalty in a specific setting."[16] Much like the self-reproducing professional circles of the business world, generations of journalists and policy makers pulled others like themselves into their orbits through these men's organizations. In Washington, clubs also served as important meeting spaces for the white-collar elite, who, whether by design or happenstance, met there to share information, ideas, and understandings.[17]

At both the Metropolitan Club and the Cosmos Club, founded respectively in 1863 and 1878, reporters circulated—acquiring knowledge and debts while cultivating loyalties and affections.[18] At the height of the Civil War, as Washington was dealing with an influx of newcomers, six men from the Treasury Department founded the Metropolitan Club, the city's first sustained gentlemen's club. In a hectic and crowded wartime capital teeming with temporary barracks, hospitals, and housing, these men were looking to found a literary and social organization that elevated them above the crowd. "No place in the country has more need than Washington of such an association, there being no resort in our city for gentlemen of literary or scientific tastes," the new *Daily National Intelligencer* proclaimed upon the club's founding.[19] A 1964 centennial history of the Metropolitan Club noted that the flight of Southern families from the capital during the war "had left [its] social life rudderless. Into this void poured swarms of newcomers, lured by the feverish purpose of organizing and conducting a major war, bringing with them a mood of restless transiency."[20] In other words, the genteel slaveholding sons and daughters of the Confederacy were no longer pillars of Washington society, and hordes of new arrivals had taken their places.[21] The Metropolitan's six founding gentlemen each contributed fifty dollars to rent a home near the White House on H Street, with four objectives: food, drink, socializing, and news.[22] Reading and discussing current events—bringing together a wide variety of opinions and coming to common understandings—was a club function from the outset, and 6 percent of its total budget went to newspaper and magazine subscriptions.

The Cosmos Club was another of the early gentlemen's clubs that remained important to the circulation of information and opinion into the twentieth century. It had the reputation of being the most highbrow of the capital's men's clubs, since its members needed to have distinguished themselves in the sciences, arts, or letters—to have demonstrated a public involvement in intellectual pursuits rather than merely an appreciation of them. According to a later joke, the Metropolitan Club had all the money, and the Cosmos Club had all the brains. (The Army and Navy Club, the punchline went, had neither.)[23] The brains initially gained the club notoriety for being boring. A 1906 satirical guidebook made by Washington newsmen poked fun at the Cosmos Club for its supposed intellectualism and scientific droning. "It Has an Insomnia Cure Annex," they wrote of the club, to which several of them nevertheless belonged.[24]

Clubs for Newsmen

In the late nineteenth century, the typically less wealthy men of the press founded organizations as well—specific to their line of work, during an era when workers in many fields were newly viewing themselves as professionals.[25] Much like lawyers and businessmen, reporters used private clubs to maintain control over their profession from practitioners they considered charlatans—those scribblers accepting bribes from sources, paying off sources, lobbying on the side, or simply not hewing to facts. The history of newspaper work in Washington is usually divided into two eras: the free-for-all of the pre-1870s and the respectability of the post-1870s. The Gridiron Club, a newsmen's dinner organization founded in 1885, was a product of the shift in respectability and in government-press relations. Until the late 1870s, journalists did not regulate themselves through qualifications or codes of ethics. Publications paid Washington reporters only while Congress was in session, so they often had second jobs lobbying or collected patronage from politicians whom they covered favorably. Ben Perley Poore, a correspondent who organized the Gridiron Club, complained that underpaid correspondents had to "prostitute their pens" as lobbyists.[26] So in 1879, the reporters covering Congress created the Standing Committee of Correspondents to set rules governing press accreditation. In trying to bar lobbyists, they ruled that only reporters who filed stories daily by telegraph could use the press gallery. Their rule consequently limited access by female and nonwhite members of the press, who most often worked for weeklies and monthlies.[27] In 1920, only six women reporters, out of hundreds, received accreditation. The Standing Committee refused to admit any Black reporter until 1947, and that was only after Congress intervened.

Before the 1870s, politicians had frequented Newspaper Row, a stretch of buildings on Fourteenth Street between F Street and Pennsylvania Avenue where most newspapers had their offices. It was near the White House and just down the horse-drawn trolley line from the Capitol.[28] However, during the 1870s the relationship between newsmen and senators, in particular, ruptured, partially over a leaked treaty. Then the already tense relations were exacerbated by the eruption of the Credit Mobilier scandal as journalists exposed congressional fraud. These were the days of the "press gang," the political journalists who shaped public policy and ideology.[29] At one point, in February 1883, a literal fight for control over the press gallery erupted in the House of Representatives when congressmen tried to fill its seats with friends, pushing reporters out of their "working seats" and causing newsmen to commandeer the gallery. "It may seem strange that these conditions should have led to the formation of a dining club which has achieved such high reputation as the Gridiron, but such is the fact," recounted an early member, Arthur Wallace Dunn. "In the first place, it brought the newspaper men together. They talked about a close organization; a union; press club; in fact, anything which would make them an organized force. They met at little dinners."[30] One dinner in 1885 was so agreeable that the men, all competitors, decided to form their own dinner club.

The Gridiron's first banquet consisted of eighteen members and twelve guests at Welcker's Hotel and Restaurant. It was modeled after the Clover Club in Philadelphia, a group of journalists and prominent citizens who met once a month for dinner at the Bellevue Hotel. Good fellowship was the stated reason for the founding of that club, and the Gridiron founders wrote that sentiment into their group's constitution as well: "The object of the Club shall be the promotion of good fellowship."[31] The idea of fraternity remained central to the conception of manly friendship into the twentieth century. The Clover Club would end in the 1920s, but the Gridiron Club continues to the present day. The Gridiron has always capped its membership—first at thirty-five, forty, then fifty, now sixty-five Washington reporters representing newspapers across the country. Gridironers considered their ranks to be composed of the best—longest serving, most influential, highest paid—reporters in Washington, as determined by themselves. The group was too small to have made a clubhouse worth maintaining, instead holding its meetings and banquet rehearsals in hotels. Plus, most of the Gridironers also belonged to the Metropolitan Club or Cosmos Club and had no need for another gentlemen's haunt. What they wanted was a professional journalism organization and dinner club, which they named for the grill on which chops were roasted.[32]

The club's banquets were punctuated by skits and song parodies, known in the early years as "burlesques," roasting the nation's "great

FIGURE 1.1. At the December 1939 Gridiron Club banquet, sheikhs asked the Sphinx, styled as Franklin Roosevelt, "is he or ain't he" running for a third term. The prop and the skit were huge hits with the audience, including the president, who requested the Sphinx for his home in Hyde Park. Box 31, Raymond Clapper Papers, Manuscripts Division, Library of Congress.

and near-great" in politics (fig. 1.1).[33] One banquet on February 29, 1896, in recognition of the leap year, included members' wives as guests. Apparently, the ladies did not appreciate the dinner as much as the men believed they should have. For instance, they did not laugh at the skit poking fun at women seeking suffrage—still twenty-three years away—as heartily as their husbands wished.[34] They were never invited back, and women would not be permitted as guests at the Gridiron Club dinner again until 1972. Membership would not be open to them until 1975.

Although the men publicly insisted that they were a social club (which during the 1950s allowed them to avoid integration), the Gridiron's professional importance was so well understood that many employers covered its membership dues as business expenses.[35] While the club's sole mandate was to host its formal dinners, members gathered on other occasions throughout the year, at meetings and rehearsals as well as additional social events, like the annual Gridiron golf tournament and dinner at Burning Tree Country Club hosted by a well-connected Washington banker. In a *Look* magazine piece from the late 1940s, the author, a Gridiron member, commented on the depth of friendship forged at the club. "Washington correspondents often hold their jobs for 30 or 40 years," he wrote. "They get to know each other, as well as the flow of history in their time, with startling intimacy. And so, much of both their friendship and their thrill of watching history unfold is linked to the Gridiron Club."[36] The overlapping of friendship and professional networks and the social obligation these men felt toward one another would be central to how they drew and observed certain boundaries in their reporting.

Regardless of a member's social origins or class, his inclusion in the Gridiron Club rendered him a part of the power elite. He had access to the highest ranks of businessmen and politicians, men eager to do favors for this concentrated mass of mouthpieces in exchange for invitations to the club dinners. Invitations were scarce, going each year to the most influential men in American politics, business, and publishing—or, as the leftist columnist Robert Allen referred to them in 1956, "the assembled throng of fat-cat publishers, millionaires, hucksters and what-have-you."[37] Even though the ballroom that the Hotel Statler had built especially for the Gridiron held five hundred guests, the invitations went quickly, with many of them spoken for by cabinet members, every Supreme Court justice, most of the ambassadors to the United States, congressional leaders, and the Gridiron members' publishers and editors from across the country. In 1892, Benjamin Harrison was the first president to speak at a banquet, setting a precedent for future presidents to attend, if not always speak, and making the dinner an event not to miss.

Invitations signified relevance. Lester Markel, the editor from 1923 to 1964 of the *New York Times Magazine*, was so sensitive about not being invited to the Gridiron for five years in a row that in 1958 he asked Scotty Reston why. Reston was sure to include him the following year. By 1964, it had been three more years with no invitation, despite assurances he would receive another, and Markel again asked why. He viewed the snub "as a symptom of something else"—namely, that he was about to be pushed out as Sunday editor, which he then was.[38] Thus, the Grid-iron was central not only to creating meaning out of events and infor-mation in news circles but also to delineating the circles themselves.

Intimacy and obligation, of course, did not mean that the Gridiron members agreed with one another all the time. To the contrary, bitter arguments arose over the content of some of the banquet skits. During the Truman administration, for instance, one club member, Marshall McNeil of the *Houston Press*, wrote a "song that was a particularly venomous attack" on the president. Many of the Gridironers wanted the song dropped, but only one man, Tom Stokes of United Features Syndicate, was willing to offend McNeil by calling for the skit to be cut, which it was. The others were reportedly relieved, but "McNeil was incensed, and ever since has been very cool toward Tom." A few years later, Stokes's wife, Hannah, related the story to Bob Allen's wife, Ruth Finney. "Hannah's story was a very interesting commentary on the Gridiron 'brethren' who are supposed to hold nothing but love and friendship for one another," Allen delighted in writing in his diary.[39]

Despite their differences, the powerful men at the center of the press establishment used stag dinners like the Gridiron Club's banquet to col-lectively make sense of the world while also defining themselves as the in group. In doing so, they frequently and ceremoniously reasserted the boundaries of their power. Time and again, the men of the Grid-iron and their hundreds of guests asserted their maleness, demonstra-ble in the drag performances in their skits, as well as their whiteness, performing in blackface to white audiences and being served by Black waiters.[40] The club's signature tune, "The Watermelon Song," was writ-ten in dialect: "Oh, de dew it am a fallin', dat 'million's gwineter cool / An' soon it will be very, very fine; / But bless yo' soul, my honey, dis dar-key ain' no fool / To leave it dar a hangin' on de vine."[41] As we will see, Gridiron Club minstrelsy and blackface skits continued into the 1950s and consistently normalized the exclusion of Black reporters from the annual dinners—and, for that matter, from any background meals with officials that became such important channels for information during World War II and beyond.

For the 1955 spring dinner, Scotty Reston wrote out a schedule for one of his guests, Arthur Hays Sulzberger, the publisher of the *New York Times*. It jokingly predicted that at a quarter past three in the morning, their managing editor, Turner Catledge, would bring the festivities to a close by delivering his impression of "Cotton Ed" Smith, the segregationist governor of South Carolina.[42] Catledge had introduced his Cotton Ed character in a skit in 1938 as a young Washington correspondent for the *Times*, and for the next thirty years he recreated it at cocktail parties. His impression was so beloved that in 1966, Richard Nixon joked to him that the main casualty of the Civil Rights Movement was the Cotton Ed routine.[43] Catledge responded congenially, "Poor old Cotton Ed's voice, even his echoes, had to be silenced someday, but it took a social revolution and a bushel of Federal laws to do it, didn't it?"[44] Even Nixon and Catledge, two men who intensely disliked each other, shared a private language based on fellowship.

Secret rituals have been a staple of homosocial spaces since the Victorian era and continued to underpin the elaborate orchestration of each Gridiron banquet.[45] At the outset of every dinner, the club president delivered the Speech in the Dark: standing in the unlit ballroom telling a few jokes, making a serious remark about the good fellowship of the evening, and assuring guests that "the Gridiron sears but never burns." Since the modern era, an electric light board with bulbs arranged in the shape of a gridiron then lit the darkened room. Next, the president always made a promise: that there were but "two rules— ladies are always present—reporters are never present."[46] Both maxims were rhetorical. He meant that the jokes would be in good taste, as if women were in attendance, and that everything said at the dinner, except information from the club's prewritten press release, was off the record. That made the dinner an important site of behind-the-scenes networking and consensus building not apparent in straight-news stories after the fact.

The Gridiron Club was for the elite of the white working newsmen, but the National Press Club was for all of them. During the early 1900s, the men who worked on Newspaper Row, especially those staffing local Washington newspapers that had daily deadlines and stringent budgets, could not rely on chance invitations to gentlemen's clubs or wait for an exclusive banquet to socialize. They required a permanent watering hole. Two nearby spots—Gerstenberg's, a German pub, and Shoomaker's, a cobwebbed bar—were popular with newsmen, but they often closed too early for those working late into the night on morning edition newspapers.[47] In March 1908, a group of thirty-two self-identified "newspaper writers" formed the National Press Club. From its inception, the Press Club considered itself a workingman's club, not an elite gentlemen's club. In fact, its founders expected members to be so pressed for cash that they feared the club would go bankrupt, as had earlier such attempts, from providing too much credit. They decided to operate on a cash basis.

After 1927, when the Press Club opened its own building at the corner of Fourteenth and F Streets, it would become the new hub of news work in the nation's capital. (President Calvin Coolidge himself had laid the cornerstone in 1926 [fig. 1.2].) News bureaus representing out-of-town papers rented office space there, and these everyday shared workspaces enabled reporters from across the country to interact, even if they belonged to no clubs at all. Many of them had lunch at the Press Club daily, but those who did not regularly go up to the bar still came into constant contact with other newsmen. By the 1940s, the *Chicago Daily News*, the *Chicago Sun-Times*, the *Philadelphia Bulletin*, the *New York Daily News*, the *Christian Science Monitor*, the *Buffalo News*, the *Hartford Times*, United Press, the North American Newspaper Alliance, the *Los Angeles Times*, the *New York Herald Tribune*, the *Nashville Tennessean*, and *Newsweek* were just some of the publications sharing offices on the twelfth floor.

During the early 1950s, the club had approximately 1,000 active working members of the press and over 4,500 total members (those in related fields). The men could pop up to the fourteenth-floor club to eat, drink, and play cards. "The food's not fancy, but it's cheap—the Press Club being, fortunately, a poor man's club—and nothing to despise," a foreign affairs reporter assured his working-class mother back in Urbana, Illinois, in 1946.[48] (He pointedly declined Gridiron invitations because he did not want to rent white tie and tails.) The Bar Commit-

FIGURE 1.2. The opening of the National Press Club building was so central to the functioning of official Washington that President Calvin Coolidge laid the cornerstone in 1926. The club's facilities included a dining room, members' bar, work spaces, and a large venue for banquets and speakers. Item 96512048, Library of Congress.

tee's report for 1953 estimated an average of 1,700 drinks served per day. ("Your committee knows the Club Members have manfully done their duty because one member at least was present at the Bar at all times," one member joked.)[49] The Press Club served a multitude of functions. In 1958, a reporter wrote of the club, "It's a hang-out, a drop-in, with overstuffed chairs for lazy bones. It's a restaurant, a bar. It's an auditorium where big shots make their speeches and lesser fry make their contacts. But, more than anything else, it is a place where men meet and talk, talk, talk. They talk mainly about the news of the day or the week. They roll it around, punch it and pat it, and sometimes twist it for a bit of shape."[50] They created their own sphere of consensus.

At the Press Club, reporters of all backgrounds could get affordable meals and fairly priced alcohol. But for all its supposed egalitarianism, it was tolerant of differences only in class and religion: no Black men were accepted until 1955 and no women until 1971 (fig. 1.3), with both these developments occurring under the social and legal pressure of

FIGURE 1.3. A reporter standing outside the National Press Club's bar, with its sign reading "Accompanied Male Guests Only." The club allowed women to become members only in 1971. Series 5, box 2, Courtesy of the National Press Club Archives.

changing norms outside the club's control. Like so many other club organizers, Press Club members desired a retreat for those who looked like themselves.[51] In January 1955, the club's board of governors voted six to four to present for a wider vote the application of Louis Lautier, the first Black reporter to integrate the congressional press galleries back in 1947. "Word of the action quickly spread throughout the Club and the city," a member recalled. "Local newspapers ran stories on it. To say that then 'all hell broke loose!' is to understate the case. Members quickly chose sides, applauding the Board's decision or condemning it in the strongest terms possible. Angry arguments raged through the day, and long into the night, in the bar, the dining room, the card room and elsewhere. There were even occasional fistfights."[52]

A group of ten members submitted a petition to the board listing reasons that Lautier was unacceptable for membership, as they deemed him a "presumptuous individual with no respect for the traditions nor rules of this Club." Even worse, in their eyes, "he has made clear that he intends to bring into the Club as many members of his own race as he chooses as guests, which would undoubtedly be the forerunner of an attempt to bring other Negroes into membership. This could not possibly contribute to the 'social enjoyment' for which the Club was created."[53] While racial exclusion had seemed a perfectly good rule for a club to have in 1927, by 1955 racist arguments had begun moving outside the mainstream discourse and into the uglier category of white resistance. Even eight years earlier, white reporters had relied on technical objections to Lautier's admission to the congressional gallery rather than racial ones.[54] Pro-segregation arguments had already begun losing acceptance in white Washington. Consequently, the Press Club's board of governors rejected the petition and scheduled a special election using written ballots, since "it is desirable to avoid discussion that might become acrimonious and unseemly."[55] (New members were usually approved by voice vote.)

Ultimately, the members voted 377 to 281 to admit Lautier, a man who was hardly radical. Ethel Payne, the *Chicago Defender* reporter in Washington from 1953 to 1973, called him a "water boy for the administration," whom other members of the press exploited to obtain accurate notes of press conferences, since Lautier had once been a court reporter.[56] The Black reporter Alice Dunnigan considered him "a staunch Republican, an ardent conservative, and an absolute male chauvinist," whom she believed actively undermined her professional standing at the White House.[57] In other words, Lautier was not a progressive who would advocate for further change from within.

With Lautier now a member, the executive committee of the Press Club felt it could no longer ban women entirely, especially from the frequent luncheons at which newsmakers from around the world spoke. The club announced in February 1955 that women would be allowed to report on these luncheons from the balcony that overlooked the ballroom.[58] But they could not eat lunch, and they could not ask questions; nor could they access the club's other facilities. These limitations created a more blatantly demeaning separation of the women while enabling the men to claim that female reporters had equal access. Their exclusion meant that editors remained reluctant to assign women to any beats that benefited from Press Club membership, leaving the highest-profile beats—foreign policy, economics, and politics—primarily to white men. The Press Club began accepting female members in 1971 and, perhaps as a result of this but also because of changing workplace norms, declined in importance to newsmen in the years since.

Although excluded from every newsmen's club that had a social purpose, women *were* allowed to be members of the White House Correspondents' Association, a professional group founded in 1914 by the reporters whose access to the White House had previously been subject to the whims of the president. These reporters wanted a way to negotiate with President Woodrow Wilson over the terms of press conferences, and the association stayed in place thereafter, accrediting reporters and representing their interests.[59] Even so, its women members did not share in all the benefits. Seven years after its founding, the men of the WHCA began hosting annual stag banquets. Allen Drury, the *New York Times* congressional reporter who wrote the best-selling novel *Advise and Consent* in 1959, described the dinner in his book: "For all practical purposes, the Government of the United States was concentrated on that evening in the Statler, for anyone who was anyone in that government, anyone who was anyone diplomatically assigned to that government, anyone who was anyone in the business of recording the events of that government, was present."[60] For Drury, it was self-evident that "anyone who was anyone" was male.

The WHCA dinner was a flagrant annual reminder to the women of the Washington press corps, Black and white, dues-paying members of the WHCA and not, of their second-class status. "The dinner may be 'off-the-record' for immediate news, but it is of considerable professional value for a newswoman to attend," wrote Ruth Gmeiner, a reporter for the United Press, to Martha Strayer of the *Washington Daily News* in 1954. "She observes news figures in action. Her prestige—

to her employer and in her working associations—is increased. If the woman reporter can bring a guest, or guests, so much the better. It never hurts a reporter to treat a news source, or boss, to a glamorous event—as the men well know."[61] The men, most of whom would not acknowledge the professional injustice publicly, did know this privately. They reaped professional benefits year-round by giving their bosses, many of whom lived outside Washington, access to influential men. In 1945, the president of the UP, Hugh Baillie, wrote his correspondent Merriman Smith, who had served that year as WHCA president: "One million thanks my friend for your hospitality on the occasion of the White House Correspondents Dinner, and for putting me in such a top priority seat, between General Marshall and Admiral Leahy. I enjoyed myself very much."[62] Even if Marshall and Leahy did not directly influence Baillie on that night, and even if Baillie said nothing noteworthy to the general and the admiral, lifetimes of accumulated stag banquet conversations did create norms and narratives among gentlemen, undisrupted by outsiders.

The members of the Women's National Press Club, founded in 1919, thought in 1954 as racial segregation was declining that they, too, could finally make an argument for their inclusion in the WHCA dinner—mistakenly, it turned out. The president of the WHCA responded to the president of the WNPC, "We had our first meeting on the 1955 dinner a few days ago and again the decision was to follow tradition and to hold a stag dinner." He explained, disingenuously, that it was an issue of space, because if women reporters were invited, the newsmen's wives would want to join. Perhaps when the new banquet hall at the Sheraton Plaza was finished they could establish a new precedent, he suggested, "by having the women in their rightful place."[63] The WHCA did not set a new precedent with a new hotel, though, and perhaps its president's notion of women's "rightful place" differed from that of the president of the WNPC. Meanwhile, the Gridiron dinner seemed untouchable. As the *New York Times'* reporter Bess Furman wrote Martha Strayer around the same time, "I didn't even take up the Gridiron Club—too fantastic."[64]

Men in the newspaper industry held fast to these professional benefits. As Gmeiner commented to Strayer, "It is an unfortunate truth that the chief discrimination against women reporters in Washington today is practiced by men reporters. Our male colleagues remain the most resistant to accepting us as equals."[65] Those male colleagues had no incentive to invite anyone who might challenge how they operated their clubs or conducted their reporting. In 1965, the political scientist and journalism professor William L. Rivers echoed Gmeiner's assertion that newsmen were the problem, not society at large. "The men of the press corps try to keep it a man's world even when it is not," Rivers wrote in *The Opinionmakers*. "Thus ABC correspondent John Scali's ultimate compliment for Frances Lewine of AP: She's such a good reporter everyone forgets she's a woman."[66] We cannot assume that Washington reporters were merely reflecting the broader society in their sexism; a majority actively worked to maintain the gender hierarchy.

For decades, occasions explicitly labeled *stag* were normalized at all levels of Washington society. Did this homogeneity result in groupthink that affected reporting?[67] The reporter Timothy Crouse noticed in 1972 that "some of the toughest pieces" on Richard Nixon were from the five women covering him during his campaign that year for a second term. "They had always been the outsiders. Having never been allowed to join the cozy, clubby world of the men, they had developed an uncompromising detachment and a bold independence of thought which often put the men to shame."[68] Women may or may not have introduced new perspectives to clubs, but their male colleagues certainly thought they might. During the 1940s, men could attribute their hostile attitude to what they saw as women's natural lack of objectivity, exactly the news value that by the time Crouse was writing had come under public attack. "Most of the working women in the Washington press corps are not as good as the men, because they are newer at the business, and because they do not have adequate training in objectivity," noted W. M. Kiplinger, publisher of the *Kiplinger Letter*, a newsletter, in 1942. He continued, "(There are a few exceptions.) The fault is temporary, and there is no basic reason why women eventually cannot become as good reporters as men."[69] At least Kiplinger thought there was hope for the women, while most of his colleagues would have been socialized believing in the irrationality of females, who had been voting at the national level for only twenty-two years at that point and had a long way to go before men would consider them equal as reporters.

Male exclusion of female voices at important social-professional events was total, and it usually went unremarked by the men policing the boundaries. A few examples capture the range of exclusion. In 1947, a few weeks after Secretary of State George C. Marshall announced the Marshall Plan, the *Washington Post* publisher Eugene Meyer held an informal stag dinner for him and the top four men at the paper.[70] In 1949, Overseas Writers, a group of male foreign policy journalists, hosted fifty visiting European journalists for a stag dinner at the National Press Club at which Senator Arthur Vandenberg spoke.[71] In 1952, the *New York Times* celebrated Arthur Krock's twenty-fifth work anniversary with a stag dinner at the Metropolitan Club.[72] And the Eisenhower White House held so many stag dinners that those occasions merited their own filing series in the presidential archives.[73] Even the Gridironers spoofed the number of Eisenhower's stag dinners (as well as his probusiness attitude and predilection for appointing millionaires to government positions) in their 1955 dinner—itself stag, of course—with a song set at the White House, "When the Stags Go Marching In." "They pray to Dun and Bradstreet / For the rating to get in / So they'll fit with those Dow-Jones boys / When the stags go marchin' in . . ."[74] The trend continued into the 1960s: Assistant Secretary of State for Public Affairs Andrew Berding gave a "farewell stag press reception" for Secretary of State Christian Herter in January 1961, writing on the invitation, "I am inviting members of the press who have been covering our foreign affairs during Secretary Herter's tenure, and also a few other officers of the Department of State. This is not a press conference or a backgrounder but an opportunity to say au revoir to a good friend."[75] Women, already excluded from reporting on diplomatic matters because of the stag system, apparently had no need to bid farewell.

While making plans, men might have had discussions about whether events should include wives, but they rarely if ever discussed whether women journalists should be invited. Female reporters were all but invisible to the men controlling the social-professional occasions of

Washington. The memos about these events typically read something like, "A stag affair would make for a better discussion"—as when the policy maker and politician Averell Harriman was planning a dinner at his home for newsmen to meet the German politician Ernst Reuter in 1951; or "I think it would be a mistake to have the wives, if you want to have a chance to do any talking to the staff"—as when the *New York Times'* publisher Arthur Hays Sulzberger planned to have a Monday night post–Gridiron weekend dinner with the members of the Washington bureau in 1955.[76] These men thought of women as wives, not as colleagues, although the Washington bureau of the *New York Times* did include women on staff. But the Sulzberger-hosted dinner, as well as other *New York Times* occasions through the 1960s, was held at the Metropolitan Club, where the women could not attend. Nan Robertson, one of the female members of the bureau at the time, remembered the exclusion with some bitterness thirty years later and attributed it to the bureau chief Scotty Reston's "blind spot about women as professionals."[77]

"The Capital of a World in the Making"

Despite the many attractive clubs a man might join, Washington by the early 1930s still was not an especially exciting city for the *Times*-man Arthur Krock, who resented his new assignment. World War I had brought influential men to the nation's capital, but many returned to their respective cities after hostilities ended, some deflated by the failure of the United States to join the League of Nations they had championed. These included the young Harvard University professor and future Supreme Court justice Felix Frankfurter, who returned to Cambridge, Massachusetts; and Walter Lippmann, a founder of the *New Republic* magazine, who returned to New York City, the country's capital of culture, media, and finance.[78] Influential magazines and journals of opinion, including the *New Republic*, were primarily based in New York, which even became the place to be for foreign policy deliberation. The Council on Foreign Relations opened its doors there in 1921 and began publishing the authoritative journal *Foreign Affairs* the following year.

Washington society during the 1920s had still revolved more around the debutante season than the publishing schedule of intellectuals.

Locals continued their attempts at city improvement, an effort begun in the 1870s, when the board of public works launched a program of paving streets, planting trees, and laying down sewer lines. In 1900, members of Congress ordered a commission to beautify Washington, establishing a plan for the parks and white neoclassical buildings that still grace the capital. Over the next twenty-two years, the commission remade the Mall—the stretch of land between the Potomac in the west and the Capitol in the east—into a landscaped area of lawns and reflecting pools. Near the Capitol, it constructed Union Station, which opened in 1907, and at the western end of the Mall it built and dedicated the Lincoln Memorial, which opened in 1922. During the reconstruction and continuing into the 1930s and 1940s, the city resegregated, with whites displacing Blacks in well-manicured historic neighborhoods like Georgetown, through development projects that forced out low-income residents; restrictive covenants were then used to reinforce segregation by location.[79] At the same time, city leaders obliterated poorer Black communities, like the West End, to make way for federal buildings and, later, war housing for whites.[80] Ongoing spatial segregation coincided with economic subjugation, as better-paying federal jobs were no longer available to Black workers after 1913, when Woodrow Wilson resegregated the federal government.[81]

City development and stratification continued into the Herbert Hoover administration, which developed plans to remake a "blighted" expanse along Pennsylvania Avenue, home to Washington's poorest residents. The new limestone and marble-columned buildings of the Federal Triangle would include the National Archives Building, homes for the Justice, Labor, and Commerce Departments, and new edifices for General Accounting and Internal Revenue. At the dawn of the 1930s, the city was just beginning to take its modern physical form.

Yet Washington could hardly compete for journalistic talent with New York, which had been the heart of the US news industry since the nineteenth century, with more newspapers than anywhere else in the nation. In contrast, Washington was relatively provincial and insular, a sleepy town, dull for a newsman, and jokingly characterized as a hardship posting for foreign diplomats because of its lack of culture and society. The government workday during the 1920s and early 1930s was from 9:00 a.m. to 4:30 p.m., and national reporters worked hardly more than that. Federal Washington closed for business on Friday nights and reopened Monday mornings, with news bureaus functioning with skeleton staffs during the slow news weekends. The federal government mattered, of course, and historians have demonstrated that the modern US administrative state has deep nineteenth-century roots.[82] But Washington did not hold nearly the place in the public's imagination—or in the newspapers it read—that it would start to during the New Deal era.

When Krock arrived in Washington in March 1932, his friend and rival Lippmann wrote from New York to congratulate him on the position but offer condolences on the location.[83] "I think it's the most influential and important single job in American journalism, and while I can well imagine that living in Washington has its drawbacks, I really think it's a fine thing that you should be doing it," Lippmann wrote.[84] He had, in fact, so vividly imagined the drawbacks of living in Washington that he had turned down the same position the previous year.[85]

Just one year later, though, on March 4, 1933, Franklin D. Roosevelt was inaugurated, and newspapermen in Washington felt a surge of excitement. "The New Deal had begun and you could feel its electricity wherever you went," one reporter recalled.[86] The unprecedented federal activity that New Deal programs created intensified the role of the press corps in the daily life of governance and expanded its ranks from the hundreds to the thousands. Often, the only way one bureaucratic agency knew what another was doing was by reading about it in the newspaper. Roosevelt understood the importance of newspapermen to his administration. As governor of New York, he had good relations with those in Albany and intended to continue that trend in Washington. To that end, the president created a climate of collusion with reporters, bringing them into his confidence to gain support for his legislation. This close relationship between reporters and the chief executive was particular to FDR, but he also set the precedent for regular White House press conferences that continues to this day.

Roosevelt also brought the wider world to Washington, seeming to relieve the city of its insularity. His New Deal programs and projects famously attracted people from around the country to join, advise, or report on the expanding federal government. In 1930, the population of the capital had been 488,000. By 1936, at the height of the New Deal, it had increased by more than 20 percent, to 600,000. Overall, from 1930 to 1940 the total population grew by 36 percent. The old families of Washington, known as the Cave Dwellers, had at first been pleased that Roosevelt was one of their own: an old-money patrician. But what they got from him was another upending of the social order. "The Cave Dwellers discovered that all these professors and thick-knuckled agronomists the Franklin Roosevelts had brought to Washington with them had not been similarly favored with these 'exceptional privileges,'" David Brinkley, the news anchor, put it.[87] President Roosevelt attracted workers from a variety of class backgrounds and, for the first time in federal government, appointed so many Jews to positions of prominence—foremost among them Treasury Secretary Henry Morgenthau—that critics like the radio broadcaster Father Charles Coughlin and burgeoning anti-Semitic hate groups referred to his plan as the Jew Deal.

A 1936 *Saturday Evening Post* article noted, "The effect upon the invasion of the capital by hordes of New Dealers had been to destroy, for the first time in the history of Washington, the incomparably delightful interrelation between official and social life. The two are now separate."[88] This was only partially true. The Cave Dwellers were perhaps separated forever from official life, which no longer revolved around "high society." But the official and social circles fused into a newspaperman's paradise. Entertainment continued apace. One society columnist, to demonstrate that entertainment in Washington was an industry unto itself, compared the dollar amount that Washingtonians spent on flowers in 1939 to that spent in New York City. "Washington, which is, in the main, a salaried town," she wrote—meaning it had comparatively little inherited wealth—"spent nearly twice as much for flowers in proportion to its population as the world's greatest metropolitan center."[89] Flowers signaled a lively social life, which had intensified for white-collar workers in the nation's capital because of Roosevelt's political agenda, and newsmen were foremost in reaping the benefits. The political scientist Leo Rosten observed in 1937 of Washington newsmen, "The better a correspondent 'mixes,' the more news he acquires. Lunches, dinners, cocktail parties, and formal receptions are fruitful sources of information for the socially active newspaperman and yield news of varying degrees of usability." Rosten noted that these men were not "social scavengers," though. The stereotypical capital correspondent had always been more gentlemanly than the stereotypical police or city hall reporter. "The newspaper correspondent is generally an acceptable person from the social point of view. He is married, a family man, moral, a good conversationalist, and, of course, a 'good fellow.'"[90]

As Washington correspondents became more influential by virtue of their position and their access to a powerful president, their editors and publishers at home worried about these reporters' pro-Roosevelt bias. The rapid social reforms of the New Deal especially concerned publishers, who were foremost businessmen: employers and profit makers. By contrast, the newspapermen in Washington—their employees—were more likely to champion Roosevelt and his New Deal.[91]

While the difference was largely one of class, location mattered as well, and the importance of living inside Washington to the formation of certain opinions was clear. We can see an echo chamber in action in this regard, and so could the men who operated within it. In June 1937, Raymond Clapper, a columnist for the Scripps-Howard newspaper chain, was admonished by his boss, Roy Howard, in New York: "I do not want to see [your column's] worth as reporting and interpretation diluted by having it degenerate into plain editorializing or a daily expression of your personal opinions."[92] Columnists were newly popular during the 1930s; newspaper owners were still determining what role they should play and whether they should provide analysis or opinion. For Howard, reporting and interpretation were all right; editorializing was not, especially if it did not reflect his opinion. Clapper conceded, "I am always conscious of the difficulty in keeping a sound perspective. You are living daily in the most bitter anti-Roosevelt community in the country"—Manhattan, where Howard's proximity to Wall Street placed him inside an anti–New Deal echo chamber of his own—"and I am living daily on the doorstep of the Roosevelt administration. That, as much as anything else, probably accounts for the fact which you suggest that I am probably a little more ready in my acceptance of Roosevelt's technique than you are. I suspect that if we were both able to escape the influence of our respective environments we probably would check almost straight down the line on these matters."[93]

But reporters in the nation's capital rarely escaped the influence of their environment. Reporters, editors, and publishers often discussed transferring Washington correspondents back home to give them a more realistic portrait of the country, which they presumed was different from the Washington perspective. But once these correspondents had achieved the pinnacle assignment of their careers—reporting on the federal government—and had joined the many clubs to which they needed to belong, not to mention enrolled their children in school and settled into their homes, few left voluntarily.

With the advent of the New Deal and the resultant population explosion of white-collar workers, a job in Washington seemed less of a sacrifice even to Arthur Krock and Walter Lippmann. The "drawbacks," as Lippmann had put it, became fewer. After all, there were constant events, conferences, and flower-filled dinner parties. Krock stopped looking for a successor; he remained bureau chief until 1953 and was a columnist until 1966. He never missed an opportunity to martyr himself with the home office, though, writing in 1937 to Arthur Sulzberger that since the only way he saw of getting out of Washington was "to commit suicide and leave feet foremost," he supposed he would be staying. And since it seemed like he would be staying, he continued, he also supposed he would need the funds to renew his Metropolitan Club membership.[94]

By 1938, Washington society had been tolerable enough for Lippmann himself to rent a house there with his new wife, Helen. This arrangement may indicate as much about his marital situation as it did about Washington: the couple were personae non grata in New York, since the new Mrs. Lippmann had previously been married to Hamilton Fish Armstrong, her husband's onetime best friend and the editor of *Foreign Affairs*. Nevertheless, with another war looming in Europe and Washington a major center of military and international consider- ations, Lippmann decided the capital was the place to be.

With the onset of World War II, men like Lippmann and Krock could live in Washington and still perform their work on a world stage. "Washington is called the capital of the nation, but it is really more than that—it is the capital of a World in the Making, for through it flow the forces which will help to make a new world when the forces of war are spent," W. M. Kiplinger wrote in 1942.[95] The town that had shaped opinions on politics and the economy would soon be creating opinions on the new international order.

The policies of the 1930s and 1940s that made Washington an eco- nomic center of the world did not change the basic structure of friend- ship, professional networks, and information gathering that had made official Washington so insular since its founding. Indeed, social capital was more important than ever, necessary to rise above the new hordes of government workers. Members of the press were some of the most active and stable participants in official society—in fact, among the *only* participants whose professional standing did not revolve around electoral politics at all. So while World War II would change much about the capital, some of its social peculiarity, as well as its priorities, remained untouched. On December 10, 1941, three days after the Jap- anese bombed Pearl Harbor, Jack Howard, son of Roy Howard, wrote Clapper what so many of his friends and colleagues must have felt upon hearing the news: "There may be some satisfaction in knowing that it took a war to keep us from meeting at the Gridiron Club dinner Sat- urday."[96]

2

THE NEWSMEN'S
WARTIME NETWORKS

World War II brought special and dire circumstances that helped personal relationships flourish quickly and intensely, shaping friendship networks and erasing professional boundaries. The result was a cohort of like-minded internationalist reporters. Within the military, the homosociality that typified life for male elites in boarding schools, universities, and clubs became a norm for men from all classes. The warm language of manly affection that was common in business mentoring seemed especially appropriate between men as they faced danger and death.[1] Language that would have seemed overwrought in peacetime became normal in a nation at war. For instance, when the young columnist Joe Alsop returned to Washington in 1942 after being a prisoner of war in China for several months, the older columnist Walter Lippmann wrote him, "I don't need to tell you with what affectionate anxiety and pride I have been thinking about you these long months."[2] War brought fear, and fear created lasting bonds.

The war was a life-defining event for the men who would report on the postwar world. Americans' experiences during World War II, the supposedly "total war," varied greatly by race, sex, gender, class, location, and other factors, usually making generalizations difficult.[3] But members of the postwar Washington press corps were a remarkably homogenous group; the variety of their wartime experiences was minimal. For these white men, World War II *was* the all-consuming total war of American mythology, affecting press coverage in the capital for a generation and normalizing journalism practices that lasted even longer. They formed bonds with one another and with their bosses as they shared in experiences that were often tedious or frustrating and sometimes harrowing. The spaces of Washington filled to capacity, and friendship networks and access to exclusive spaces became more important than ever. Newsmen had lunch at the Cosmos Club and drinks at the Press Club bar. They traveled to war zones in freezing airplanes, and they grew homesick in the bomb shelters of London. They expressed their patriotism by working for the federal government while on leaves of absence from newspaper work. They endured the frustrations of government bureaucracy, knowing they would be able to return to their news work once the war was over. Their ambivalence toward government officials who managed the news grew sharper, and their commitment to one another and to the idea that they were part of a professional band of brothers solidified.

The Boys in London

Socializing and chance run-ins in the spaces of Washington and its wartime counterpart, London, were more important than ever for maintaining social networks, especially for the newspapermen who had become part of the government apparatus. As one *Time* magazine editor joked to a colleague, "Although this is a global war encompassing the whole world, I find that one runs into everyone one ever knew at some point or other."[4] This was especially true in London, where American correspondents circulated among jobs in information, intelligence, and newspapers and built lasting friendships during the blackouts and air raids.[5]

As in Washington, American reporters in London knew where to find one another to socialize and gossip. In addition to a handful of hotels—especially Claridge's, the Connaught, and the Savoy—a few regular restaurants, like a Greek one in Soho that "feels to be quite a hangout for newspaper and radio characters," were magnets for journalists.[6] They also had the Association for American Correspondents in London, founded during World War I, to "serve the professional interest of members, to promote social co-operation among them and to maintain the ethical standards of their profession."[7] The club remained in operation during the 1920s and 1930s and again served American reporters' social-professional interests during World War II. Unlike the National Press Club in Washington, the London club included women. But during wartime, when the men in Washington and New York became the men in London, they heeded informally enforced male-only social rules. Prominent among them was Edward R. Murrow, CBS's chief European correspondent, and the men he recruited. Like most of his journalistic colleagues in the States, Murrow was not a member of an East Coast male elite; he had been born in poverty in North Carolina in 1908. In profiling him and his circle—the members of which tellingly referred to themselves as the Murrow Boys—the journalists Stanley Cloud and Lynne Olson noted, "Although the occasional female correspondent or researcher did manage to elbow her way into the circle, as a rule the male correspondents in London spent more time with each other than with their wives, girlfriends, or mistresses."[8] These men saw themselves both as a cohesive group and as a gang of impish boys. To them, a world of men seemed a natural state, both during the war and once they returned home.

Yet just as there were women reporters in Washington whom their male colleagues daily rendered invisible, there were women reporters covering the war in London and all over the globe. They were comparatively few, though, and their jobs were more difficult. Like the men, many went through the revolving door of wartime government service, such as Kay Halle, a *Cleveland Plain Dealer* reporter who served in the Office of Strategic Services (the predecessor of the CIA), and Bess Furman, a reporter who spent part of the war in the Magazine Division of the Office of War Information before going to the *New York Times*' Washington bureau. Two female columnists were especially prominent at this time, both covering foreign affairs: Marguerite Higgins, who wrote for the *New York Herald Tribune* and was based in New York or overseas until 1956, and Anne O'Hare McCormick, who wrote for the *New York Times* and was based mostly in Europe. Washington was conducive to the operations of a Walter but was a poor base for a Marguerite and an Anne. (When Higgins took over her newspaper's Washington bureau in 1956, she had excellent government sources and connections but was not welcome in the newsmen's fraternity. Typical of their attitude toward her was one that Joseph Harsch, who covered foreign affairs for the *Christian Science Monitor*, revealed in a 1956 letter to Walter Lippmann: "I don't know all the angles on the story of Walter Kerr's departure from the Trib, but the major conclusion appears to be in order that another male scalp dangles from the belt of Maggie Higgins.")[9]

As they excluded or derided women, the men meanwhile grew closer, as the fear and danger of wartime circumstances intensified their friendships. The Blitz—the German Luftwaffe's bombing of British cities—lasted from September 1940 to May 1941 and left an impression on everyone who lived through it. An estimated forty thousand civilians, three-quarters of whom were living in London, died during the bombing. As the CBS correspondent Larry LeSueur put it forty years later: "Murrow, [Charles] Collingwood, [Eric] Sevareid, Bill Downs, myself, we shared tremendously indelible experiences. We shared in the making of *history* in World War Two; we knew what it was like to be scared together."[10] Further, the shared experiences solidified their sense of being *responsible* for history—both the outcome of the war and the shape of the world to follow. They shared a certain cynicism bred in wartime as well. When the *Washington Post* publisher Eugene Meyer visited London in 1941, he met Murrow for lunch in a private room at the Savoy. Murrow brought "a group of newspaper men" with him. "The talk was quite frank and I find them a rather cynical group," Meyer noted in his diary.[11]

For fifty-seven nights bombs dropped on London, a city of nightly blackouts and constant air-raid sirens. "What can I possibly say to you about England?" Scotty Reston of the *New York Times* (fig. 2.1) wrote in October 1940 to Ferdinand Kuhn, who had hired him the previous year at the London office and was becoming a lifelong friend. "This terrifying siege has gone on now for a month, and there are a lot of things we cannot say, but it's a fact that things are going on remarkably well," he added, trying not to worry Kuhn.[12]

FIGURE 2.1. Scotty Reston spent much of the Blitz in London. When he returned in 1943 for a few months to fill in as the *New York Times'* London bureau chief, his wife, Sally, joined him. Box 137, James B. Reston Papers, Courtesy of the University of Illinois Archives.

Reston would be the diplomatic reporter in Washington for the *Times* after the war, its Washington bureau chief from 1953 to 1964, a columnist until 1989, and a shaper of the sphere of consensus. When he wrote that letter to Kuhn, he was thirty years old, with a round face that was often described as open or honest. His nickname derived from his Scottish birthplace, but he had grown up in Dayton, Ohio. His breeding was typical for his cohort: public college, followed by regional news-papering. Reston earned his journalism degree at the University of Illinois and worked for the *Ohio Daily News*. Then he moved to New York and later London with the Associated Press, primarily covering sports. Reston took pride in his immigrant heritage, and apart from a playful sense of humor, his leading characteristics were his Presbyterian sensibility, conscience, and work ethic. "Scotty used to vex me ever so slightly back in the days when he was constantly instructing me in my duties and responsibilities as a citizen and colleague," a fellow diplomatic reporter, Wallie Deuel, wrote his mother in 1960. (This was after

Deuel had left the news business for the CIA.) "But now that we never see them"—Scotty and his wife, Sally—"I can be a little more objective about him, and I must say I admire his skill, resourcefulness and energy. Nobody ever handed him anything on a silver platter; he's done it all by himself. And I am now so frequently exposed to Ivy League types that I find all my old prejudices in favor of men who make their own way are getting stronger and stronger all the time."[13]

During the Blitz, the bureau of the *New York Times* in Printing House Square was bombed into rubble, leading it to relocate to the Savoy Hotel—clearly not a hardship placement, but a decided interruption. The CBS offices, meanwhile, moved three times after bombings. The air-raid sirens seemed nonstop. "It has reached the point now where there are so many raids that you can't remember whether it was the warning or the all-clear that just sounded," Reston wrote his wife. "Down in the Southeast, especially, we ran through them everywhere we went. We saw several air battles and the guns were going all the time. . . . What we are doing now is that when the gunfire is heavy or we hear them right overhead, we get under. Otherwise, we don't."[14] If the bureau staff had to hide with each siren, they would have gotten nothing done.

As Reston's letters made clear, there was always a "we." Any romantic image of the lone-wolf war correspondent was fiction. In October 1940, he wrote Kuhn about three new friends, men whom he said "have been my intimates since the start of the war." There was Frank Kelley—"Frank Kelley and I have virtually been living together. He's a great fellow and just about the best young American reporter here. I wish we had him"; Edward Murrow—"He's working like a beaver and doing a great job, as you probably know better than I," since Murrow was broadcast so widely in the States; and Walton Butterworth—"I think he's a great guy. He's essentially our best American type, big, robust, intelligent, thoughtful, forthright. During the summer we used to get away down along the Thames and go swimming in the old hole there by the bridge."[15] Reston admitted that the planes overhead made the swimming less peaceful. In addition to being a swimmer, he had been a golfer in college and continued his game during the war, sometimes on a public course at Hampstead Heath with Ed Murrow and Larry LeSueur.[16] Reston's descriptions of his male friendships in wartime seem to have no self-consciousness about homosexual connotations. This homosocial world was a natural outgrowth of wartime circumstances—and prewar ones too. When they all got back to Washington, all-male luncheons at the Metropolitan Club and boozy receptions after the Gridiron Club dinners seemed the most natural state of affairs.

These individual friendships were ties in larger networks. Murrow's protégé Eric Sevareid became one of Reston's best friends in Washington—in fact, "my best friend," Reston said.[17] And Reston and Kuhn remained close. "What a debt I owe him!" he wrote of Kuhn in 1967. "It is not only that he brought me on to The Times—though that has now been my life for 28 years—but that he has taught me the ideal of friendship."[18] Meanwhile, Deuel and Reston already knew each other by reputation through the University of Illinois at Urbana-Champaign, where Reston had been in the same class as Deuel's younger sister. The two men then got better acquainted when they happened to sail on the same ship from England to America in December 1940.[19] After the war, they covered the same diplomatic beat. "As you well know, Scotty is one of the best friends I've got in the world, and I have an extremely high regard for him as a newspaperman," Deuel wrote his editor in 1947—as a preface to saying that he wanted a faster publication schedule than Scotty, since "God Almighty, he doesn't have a story in print more than once a week nowadays."[20]

Wallie Deuel and Joe Harsch got to know each other during the 1930s, when Deuel was one of the Berlin correspondents for the *Chicago Daily News* and Harsch spent a year and a half in Berlin for the *Christian Science Monitor*. When Harsch wrote about Germany in the spring of 1941 while based in the United States, he sent clips of his "Inside the War" series to Deuel. "I hesitate to send you a copy of the series in the Monitor because when you read it you are likely to find some of the ideas contained therein sounding very much like a few ideas expressed by one Wallis [*sic*] R. Deuel at the bar of the Adlon Hotel in Berlin."[21] Friendships, bars, and reporter hangouts all mattered to the circulation of ideas, though explicit documentation like Harsch's letter to Deuel is rare. Yet reporters did consciously work through ideas together over periods of years and then transmit them to their respective audiences all over the country. (Later, Harsch's son would be in Boy Scouts with Deuel's son, and though Deuel resented that Harsch did not carry his weight with the troop, he gladly filled in on Harsch's radio program when his friend was out of town.)[22]

Deuel was also connected to Ed Murrow from the 1930s, when they had both reported in Europe. He loaned Murrow the airfare from Berlin to Vienna in early 1938, when German troops invaded Austria—a crucial moment in Murrow's career that he never forgot.[23] As one of many examples of the favors and counterfavors these men did for each other over the years, Murrow helped Deuel in 1954 when Deuel was looking for work, inviting him for a three-hour "highly convivial lunch" at the Century Association in New York City. "Ed's one of the world's swellest people—even when tight, as he was down here, and one of the most charming and attractive," Deuel wrote his mother.[24] The genuine admiration these and other newsmen felt for one another was rooted in shared assumptions of loyalty, trust, and professionalism. They all worked for competing news organizations but were foremost allies—drunk or sober.

In wartime London, the men guessed at what the world would be like afterward. Of course, many of those who were attracted to assignments overseas were already internationalists. But in considering those war workers that the government sent, not necessarily voluntarily, who were then immersed in the world of newsmen, we can see how important the spaces of London were to the circulation of ideas about US internationalism. For instance, the information officer Thor Smith spent much of his time with the CBS boys, the gang at NBC, and the Associated Press gang, as he referred to the newsmen with whom he spent his working as well as his leisure hours. "As is probably no surprise to you, I have completely lost all my idea of a few years back re isolationism," Smith wrote his wife in October 1943. "It is a decadent political theory that won't work in a modern world that has shrunk to within a few hours plane trip from *any* place. And I find myself more and more annoyed with the press at home that continue to harp on it (mostly the Chicago Tribune, Daily News (N.Y.) and Wash. Times Herald, but also to a somewhat lesser extent, the Hearst papers)."[25] These were the newspapers considered irresponsible even by other newsmen for not advocating internationalism, which the men in London saw as the United States' only option for the future peace.

In his letters, Smith wrote about America's obligation to the world's future collective security, acknowledging, "I have just about swung around to the idea that the only salvation for the next few hundred years is to start in playing power politics to the utmost, have a modified form of imperialism ourselves (called by any other name), and preserve the peace of the world, just like we are fighting the war, by wielding a big stick."[26] This idea of fighting the peace militaristically— with "defense imperialism," as Smith called it—became a major foundation of the nation's permanent national security state.[27] Beyond the social interaction that allowed for the exchange of ideas, Smith was also influenced by the attorney and 1940 presidential candidate Wendell Willkie's book *One World*, then circulating widely among his group, which argued that after the war the United States must be internationalist but not imperialist.[28] The tension between those two approaches was never resolved. The idea that the United States would have to form some sort of empire, along with the notion that it should not be called an empire, was widely accepted by—and because of—the information network of London and Washington.

One of the activist journalists who endorsed internationalism was the tall and handsome CBS reporter Eric Sevareid—later a fixture of Washington radio and television journalism—who was just twenty-seven years old when the Blitz began. He had been born in Velva, North Dakota, and spent most of his childhood in Minnesota. After graduating from the University of Minnesota, he wrote for the *Minneapolis Journal* and while there joined the new Newspaper Guild. Like many of his peers, Sevareid was deeply disturbed by the rise of fascism during the 1930s. He considered his first experience with fascism to be close to home in 1934, when Minneapolis police shot at striking Teamsters. In a 1946 memoir, at age thirty-four, he wrote that this attack, which had left "the whole city divided in its sympathies," made him understand "deep in my bones and blood what fascism was."[29] That bone-deep fear was reinforced by the rise of the Silver Shirts, which had a Minneapolis chapter, and again when his bosses fired him just after the Newspaper Guild's contract had been approved and his pay would have increased. (The publisher's lawyer found a loophole in the contract: Sevareid could be fired for making a factual error, which he did when he mistakenly called the Veterans of Foreign Wars the American Legion.)[30] During and after the war, Sevareid would argue with CBS executives about journalists' responsibility for promoting intervention and internationalism. He lived in the world shaped by the fear of fascism—not, as some have seen it, in one retroactively shaped by anticommunism.[31]

After leaving Minneapolis, Sevareid and his wife went to Paris, where he worked briefly at the copy desk of the *Paris Herald* and in the United Press office, from which Murrow recruited him in August 1939 for CBS. When Nazi occupation forces approached Paris in June 1940, Sevareid fled along with thousands of others, under orders from CBS to follow the French government. When the collaborationist Vichy government in southern France then negotiated an agreement with the Nazi occupiers, Sevareid left for Great Britain, talking his way onto a Norwegian captain's Belgian-registered ship along with refugees.[32] The boat had to travel halfway to the United States before being able to circle safely back to Great Britain through the Irish Channel. Six years later, Sevareid wrote he had been both afraid for his life and ashamed by his fear. "And God! The terrifying violence of bombs near by, how they stunned the mind, ripped the nerves, and turned one's limbs into water!"[33]

Similar stories bonded men across Europe. Because he traveled to and from Moscow for seven weeks in 1943 with Arthur Hays Sulzberger, Scotty Reston became like a member of the Sulzberger family. By this time, Sulzberger was fifty-one years old and had been the *New York Times'* publisher almost ten years, succeeding the paper's modern "founder," Adolph S. Ochs, his father-in-law. Ochs, the son of German Jewish immigrants, had been a Tennessee entrepreneur until he purchased the *Times* in 1896 and built it into an institution, increasing the daily circulation from nine thousand to almost half a million by his death in 1935. Sulzberger had been born in New York to a family involved in cotton goods, and he attended Columbia University, where he would later serve on the board of trustees. At an officers' training corps in New York State during World War I, Sulzberger met Julius Ochs Adler, Ochs's nephew, who introduced him to his cousin, Iphigene, Ochs's only child. In 1917, Iphigene and Arthur married, with the understanding that Arthur would start training in the newspaper business. He eventually won the coveted titles of publisher and president, responsible for the editorial side of the paper, while Adler became general manager and vice president, running the business. Iphigene herself was never considered for a top position, and although she held influence behind the scenes, *Times*men remembered her inserting herself overtly into the newspaper only after her husband passed away in 1968 and her son was at the helm.[34]

During World War II, Reston was a relatively new hire at the *Times*, but he came to Sulzberger's attention after writing a book about the early war, *Prelude to Victory*. The two men then cemented their relationship during long hours in uncomfortable United States Army planes, taking eleven days to reach Moscow because of necessary stopovers in Miami, Puerto Rico, British Guiana, Brazil, Ascension Island, the African Gold Coast, Nigeria, Sudan, Egypt, Iraq, Iran, and two additional cities within the Soviet Union.[35] The sense that they were roughing it brought them together. They then faced the "mountains of food and gallons of vodka" their Muscovite hosts served them, and, importantly for Sulzberger, an avid card player, they played gin rummy.[36] Sulzberger was only disappointed that Reston did not drink as much as he did, a consideration the following year when he chose Turner Catledge to accompany him to the South Pacific. (Catledge was famous in Washington circles for his sense of humor and ability to hold his liquor. For one Gridiron Club dinner during the 1930s, another Gridironer recalled, "the ultimate hit song was synthesized by filling Turner Catledge with whisky and running his brain through a typewriter," which was just Sulzberger's sort.)[37] Even so, Sulzberger began loving the temperate Reston as a son. During their Russia trip, the pair acquired nicknames they would use in personal correspondence for the rest of their lives. Reston addressed Sulzberger as "Gus," short for

Guspadine, a play on "mister" in Russian, *gospodin*; Sulzberger, in turn, called Reston Pectoh, the Cyrillic rendering of his last name. In January 1953, Sulzberger assured Reston, "I couldn't have a more affectionate feeling for you than I do without having to go to a psychiatrist."[38] The joke, of course, was that if he loved him any more, he would be homosexual. While the willingness to joke about it might seem surprising, the sentiment does not. They loved each other with a genuine affection that the war made possible. Their postwar editorial struggles therefore played out on a more intimate level than those between publishers and employees of any other period.

Reston's secure position as an honorary Sulzberger was also clear in his relationship with Orvil Dryfoos, Sulzberger's son-in-law and successor. Dryfoos was just three years younger than Reston, and the two quickly became friends during the war. While Reston was away with Sulzberger, Dryfoos sent Reston's wife, Sally, flowers on Scotty's behalf every Sunday, with notes that Reston mailed from overseas in batches.[39] The many acts of friendship, favors, and manly intimacy that accrued in wartime created senses of personal and professional obligations. War meant that the usual rules did not apply: it seemed entirely appropriate, for instance, to impose on the boss's son-in-law to maintain one's marriage while out of town.

During the early 1940s, living in Washington with the couple's then two small boys, Sally herself occasionally wrote for the *New York Times*, mostly about issues of "womanpower" during the war. For instance, a 1941 Sunday magazine story, "Girls' Town—Washington," reported on the influx of female clerical workers.[40] She also accompanied her husband to London on one occasion and filed several stories from there. After 1945, Sally worked full time as a mother to their three sons, having no additional bylines until 1967 and 1971, when she filed stories respectively from Mexico and China while traveling with her husband. She was not a partner or research assistant in her husband's newspapering, as a faculty wife of the time might have been; journalists' tight deadlines and daily reporting routines did not promote those kinds of partnerships. Rather, like many wives, she ran the household and was in charge of the family's finances. Reston, having asked Sulzberger for a larger budget for entertaining, once closed a letter with a nod to that role: "Miss Sally, the chancellor of the exchequer in our house, joins me in thanking you once again."[41]

Reston was remembered by his colleagues, both male and female, for putting women on pedestals in a way that condescendingly diminished his expectations of their professional output. It also meant he always spoke glowingly of his wife.[42] "Sally, praise God, is in good health, and looks remarkably and wonderfully like the girl I first met 15 years ago last month," he wrote in his diary in January 1947. "I have been rewarded in my life with many loyal friends, but here is the dearest and truest of them all."[43]

Reston took a keen interest in the marriages of those loyal friends. By 1967, he believed that Ferdie Kuhn had "chosen his family rather than his work, and who is to say he was wrong?" while he, Reston, had made his wife the typical "newspaper widow."[44] Kuhn's wife, Delia, was his fully bylined writing partner, and their partnership was one of the reasons Kuhn quit the *Washington Post* in 1953, so that they could freelance together. Delia Kuhn had graduated from Vassar and during the 1920s had written and edited for the *New Yorker* and *Current History*. During World War II, she worked in the Office of War Information and over the next twelve years held various government posts before returning to writing full time with her husband. Meanwhile, Eric Sevareid spent much of the 1940s and 1950s taking care of and then, once his sons were grown, divorcing his mentally ill wife and remarrying a younger woman, something of which Reston disapproved. "It is not for me to judge, but to help where I can, which is the obligation of friendship, and yet this seems to me to be the ultimate forbidden act in life, to demand your personal happiness at the cost of your own wife's happiness," Reston wrote his son, conveying the seriousness with which he took marriage and accounting for much of his personal distrust of John F. Kennedy, known to be a philanderer.[45]

As in any group, the occupations of newsmen's wives depended on class as well as personal preference. For instance, Mary Deuel often undertook paid work outside the home—as a part-time accountant at the neighborhood bookstore at one point, and working for the District

Home Rule Committee at another—in part because she preferred it, and her income made up for the fact that she and her husband then needed to hire a housekeeper.[46]

During the 1950s, the Kuhns with their two sons and the Restons with their three would live within a three-minute walk of each other near the National Cathedral. Wallie and Mary Deuel were not too far away, in a small house in Georgetown with their two sons. Eric and Lois Sevareid lived with their two sons in the suburb of Alexandria, Virginia. And while these families obviously could not have coordinated their children's gender, they did share connections like their sons' schools, Boy Scout troops, and summer jobs as copyboys on Washington newspapers—all of which created yet further points of contact, fellowship, and solidarity for the fathers.[47] Loyalty and friendship were themes that often surfaced in the private writings of these men, who valued honor and reputation in their lives and work alike. Their bonds and obligations to one another as friends then strengthened the professional expectations they shared, especially in not betraying confidences, breaking dateline embargoes, or writing anything that they believed could endanger postwar peace.

Washington's Total War

When Eric Sevareid moved to Washington in the summer of 1941, it was an around-the-clock defense capital, though the nation was still a few months from declaring war. Washington's chief industry was defense preparedness, and the town was acting as though it was already at war. While the federal government never explicitly commandeered the capital's hotels, the Office of Price Administration in the summer of 1941 asked them not to book any conventions for the next twelve months.[48] Fearing an official government requisition, hotels complied. This meant that for four years, Washington's visitors were almost all working for the war effort. A city that was already an inwardly focused echo chamber became even more of a one-note town. For four years, throughout hotels and clubs, on sidewalks and crowded streetcars, the same conversations reverberated through a single-minded community.

Sevareid knew how important his environment was to his reporting. In July 1941, Paul White, his editor in New York City, criticized him for being too critical of American isolationists in his Fourth of July broadcast. Sevareid responded indignantly, "Perhaps you do not have the overwhelming feeling that this country is in a perfectly desperate position, the most desperate in our history. I do, 24 hours a day. I have an urgent sense of disastrous events rushing upon us. . . . To my mind, we are already in a state of war." In Sevareid's opinion, and the opinion of "a couple of the most responsible and thoughtful newspaper men I know," news outlets in the United States needed to "accept added responsibilities." "It goes to the heart of the function and responsibilities of a free press in a democracy," he wrote, using a high-minded and noble rhetoric that often appears in these men's private writings. "I think it cannot be reasonably argued that in a time of grave crisis, where the continued independence of a whole people is at stake, when all public institutions as well as private individuals are obliged to accept added responsibilities, the press has exclusive immunity."[49]

Sevareid was describing the foundation for the activism—during this period of objectivity, expressed as *responsibility*—of the wartime and postwar years. This sense of responsibility was central to Washington's advocacy journalism during those years. The men who felt responsible for conveying the urgency of the war also felt responsible for conveying the urgent need for peace in Europe. During this same period, the Hutchins Commission (formally known as the Commission on Freedom of the Press) was creating its report on US media, *A Free and Responsible Press*.[50] The language of responsibility was pervasive in the world of journalism. As mass communication studies matured during the 1940s and 1950s, principles of ethical reporting became theorized as social responsibility theory, which in a pluralistic democracy meant something different to every practitioner, scholar, and critic.[51] Even among the Washington press corps, *responsibility* could have different meanings. For Sevareid, it meant downplaying isolationism to prepare the country for inevitable war. We do not know exactly with which "responsible and thoughtful newspaper men" Sevareid had consulted, but we do know what Washington was like—how it brought men like

Sevareid into contact with the other men charged with making or writing about US foreign policy. We also know his close connections to the men of London, already experiencing war, and of his time in France. When he and his cohort spoke of US responsibility—and the responsibility of the US press—it was for winning the war, then securing peace.

Washington's population boom that had begun during the New Deal era peaked during wartime. In 1941, the city added at least five thousand new residents every month. In the six months before Pearl Harbor, more than one hundred new restaurants had opened to accommodate the influx of war workers.[52] The city reached its record high of nine hundred thousand in 1943.[53] When a young David Brinkley—later a Washington-based anchor on the NBC evening news—arrived, the city was so packed that he could not even find a laundry willing to take in his dirty clothes. One proprietor advised him to do what other newcomers were doing: mail his laundry home.[54] "Washington was like a city under siege," writes the Washington historian Constance McLaughlin Green. "Nowhere else on the continent, save perhaps in some of the mushrooming war production centers such as Willow Run, were living and working conditions more trying."[55] The city never quite kept up with the demand for office space and housing, despite issuing more than fifteen hundred building permits per month.[56] Public schools did not have enough chairs and desks for students. "Life in wartime Washington took on a nightmare quality," the reporter Bess Furman remembered in 1949.[57]

As Washington lost its small-town intimacy, men's social ties and friendship networks became more important than ever. The National Press Club grew so crowded that its board of governors instituted a wartime rule that no one could have more than three guests at any one time. "Like many other similar organizations, we must ask your cooperation in overcoming manpower shortages, dwindling liquor stocks, rationing troubles, and congestion in Club quarters," the club's secretary wrote the members in November 1943.[58] (His letter also demonstrated the limited extent to which the war ever really touched American soil.)

This restriction added another layer of club exclusivity and made it an even more valuable space in the minds of its members, still only male and white. The hordes of "government girls," or G-girls, as they were called, threatening to turn Washington into a "femmocracy" could be avoided at the Press Club.[59] The desire white men had felt to escape the teeming masses and their own wives had been the primary driver of the gentlemen's clubs of the nineteenth century. They had a similar reaction to the overcrowding caused by war workers, most of them women.

Hotel rooms and boardinghouses filled to capacity, making men's clubs with sleeping spaces all the more valued. In 1939, the Metropolitan Club had been on the verge of closing, with a total membership of less than one thousand. However, World War II increased demand for its facilities. The club's restaurant, which operated with an $8,059 deficit in 1941, enjoyed a $6,419 profit in 1943.[60] "Branded only a few years earlier as outmoded and decrepit, the Club had two principal amenities to offer a harried wartime capital—food and accommodations," its historian wrote in 1964. "It also afforded a place for concentrated discussion or negotiation in privacy, a well-stocked bar, a library in which to relax or look up needed information, a barber shop, regular taxicab, telephone and messenger services—all things that go into the conduct of a modern war."[61] The war revitalized the Metropolitan Club and ensured its survival.

By 1946, the club had almost fifteen hundred members, and a slight postwar dip was "soon offset by the march of international politics," as the club's centennial history proudly put it. By 1948, the membership waiting list would reach three and a half years, causing the board to amend the bylaws to increase overall membership, which reduced the wait to a mere two years. "Although this may have led to a slight congestion at 1:00 o'clock in the restaurants," the club reported, "the Officers and Board believe that this is more than offset by the financial and social advantages gained by the increased membership, which in every respect has been maintained at the highest standards."[62] In fact, during the 1950s, the dining room at lunchtime was so congested with men of high standards that the club added an additional dining room where previously there had been billiard tables. At the beginning of 1960, total membership approached two thousand.[63] Essentially, the United States' global postwar obligations kept the Metropolitan Club solvent, or, in the words of the club's historian, "The global military and economic commitments of the United States made Washington even more the hub of world-wide leadership, attracting to it a representative segment of the nation's talent."[64] The talent that arrived to direct all these global commitments were internationalists who believed in the rightness of US world leadership, making isolationism an almost taboo position in the capital.

The Metropolitan Club gave diplomatic reporters—even those who were not themselves members—access to relationships and conversations that shaped the postwar world but remained hidden to outsiders. One day in May 1950, Wallie Deuel, then the diplomatic reporter for the *St. Louis Post-Dispatch*, had lunch there with a source. He remarked in his diary on the profile of the crowd, a perfect model of Washington's social-professional information network. First, he ran into the syndicated columnist Walter Lippmann, who "asks if I am dated up and if not will I lunch with him. I tell him his last two or three columns on Germany have been magnificent. 'Have they really?' says he."[65]

Deuel then spotted two old friends from his days in Europe, with whom he had "an animated conversation about old times in Rome, etc." Next, he ran into State Department officer Walton Butterworth, who had been Reston's swimming companion in wartime London; the future ambassador to the Soviet Union, Llewellyn "Tommy" Thompson; and Dean Rusk, then an assistant secretary of state, "who thanks me for my sympathetic treatment in the profile I did of him recently." (Rusk would serve as secretary of state from 1961 to 1969.) Rusk was there with the assistant secretaries of state for United Nations affairs and for Latin America, also friends of Deuel's, "and the whole top command of the State Department, it almost seems."[66] These were the architects of US foreign policy, not just in 1950 but for twenty years to come. And even when their names were not yet commonly known, as many would be by the time of the escalation of the Vietnam War, in 1950 they were familiar to the club's dining room captain, and they were the often invisible sources for Deuel and his cohort.

The Cosmos Club also remained important in wartime. The Saturday before Christmas 1942, when Deuel was serving in the Office of Strategic Services and on leave from the *Chicago Daily News*, he had a leisurely lunch there as the guest of a member.[67] The slightly built, thirty-seven-year-old Deuel had a narrow face with angular features, a high forehead topped with hair parted neatly down the middle, and round-framed, dark-rimmed glasses. Though always uneasy with the ostentatious displays of wealth he encountered through his work, he had a bright intellect and sense of humor that made him fit easily into any surroundings. Also, race and gender were more important markers than class in Washington at the time, making Deuel, though of humble midwestern origins, a welcome guest at the elite Cosmos Club. He had earned his bachelor's degree at the University of Illinois in Chicago. After a few postgraduate years of teaching at the American University in Beirut, he worked for the *Chicago Daily News* in New York, Washington, Rome, and Berlin. Deuel was well known in Washington for his prewar Berlin dispatches, which his paper's wire service distributed nationally. With war in Europe imminent, he had requested a return to the States with his wife, Mary, and two small boys. In 1942, he published a book, *People Under Hitler*, which within Washington was widely read and well regarded. Soon after his homecoming, he asked his newspaper for a leave of absence to enter government service under General William J. "Wild Bill" Donovan, then directing the Office of the Coordinator of Information, which transitioned in June 1942 into the OSS, the wartime spy organization preceding the CIA. Deuel's wife and children lived in Connecticut until after the war, so he was on his own at a rooming house.

For that particular Cosmos Club lunch in December 1942, Deuel's host was an OSS colleague who ten years earlier had been an assistant secretary of state when Deuel had been a State Department reporter. The revolving door of war had blurred the line between sources and colleagues. That same night, Deuel had dinner at the home of a lawyer from Chicago, Adlai Stevenson, who had come to Washington as a special legal advisor to Secretary of the Navy Colonel Frank Knox, who owned the *Chicago Daily News* and was still technically Deuel's boss. Stevenson was already friends with "the gang" at the newspaper and was now becoming a friend of Deuel's. Reporters' relationships with men in policy positions, like Stevenson—who went on to be the governor of Illinois, a two-time Democratic nominee for president, and the US ambassador to the United Nations—was another important factor in their feeling of responsibility for the nation's well-being. Deuel and his wife remained close with Stevenson throughout their lives, one of countless friendships that were, of course, invisible to newspaper readers. Two months before the 1952 presidential election, in which Stevenson ran against Dwight Eisenhower, Deuel wrote one of his many encouraging notes to his old friend, typical for its affectionate tone, which the men in these circles used when privately addressing each other but obscured publicly. "You get wonderfuller all the time. You are really magnificent. . . . Keep it up. Our side's got to win."[68] Public men in policy circles, like Stevenson, were essential connectors among the information elite.

The next night, Sunday, December 20, Deuel had supper at the home of his good friend the reporter Ferdie Kuhn and then attended a special screening with him at the Treasury Department of the British war film *In Which We Serve*. Kuhn had most recently headed the *New York Times*' London bureau, where he had hired Scotty Reston. When war broke out in England, he returned home and became one of Treasury Secretary Henry Morgenthau's right-hand men. The thirty-five-year-old Kuhn had grown up in New York City, where he had attended Columbia University before joining the *Times*. After the war, he would be the *Washington Post*'s first full-time diplomatic reporter, a sign of the increasing importance that newspapers placed on foreign policy news. On the night he had supper with Deuel, he was transitioning from the Treasury Department to the Office of War Information, where many of his and Deuel's mutual friends already worked or had served temporary stints.

Deuel appreciated his fresh outlook, which was more sympathetic to the pressures on government workers and more skeptical of reckless, smart-alecky newsmen. "As a matter of fact, this leave of absence from newspaper and writing folk is proving to be a very amusing experience in that it is giving me a new perspective on them and their work," he wrote his parents in the fall of 1942. Continuing tongue in cheek, he noted, "I often long for the happy irresponsibility of a newspaperman, who only has to write articles telling how other people do things and how wrongly they are being done. This confession is only for your ears alone, though. I would probably be disbarred if some of my distinguished colleagues could hear me now."[69] Deuel was exaggerating; he was never so cavalier in his reporting. But prewar reporting hadn't been conditioned by the new and heavy burden of the survival of democracy that he and his fellow journalists felt obligated to assume.

On Monday night, December 21, Deuel returned to the Cosmos Club with the same OSS friend he had met there for lunch on Saturday. There they "bumped into," in Deuel's words, Elmer Davis, Robert Sherwood, Gardner Cowles Jr., and Archibald MacLeish—the OWI men— Kuhn's future coworkers and all fixtures or connectors in the news community. We know about this meeting because Deuel wrote such detailed letters home to his parents in Clinton, Illinois, but it was just one of countless accidental run-ins that make physical space so central to any community's functioning. Community-building endeavors happened in physical space, and the strictures on that space—limited to a fairly homogenous group of men—meant that a community was forming out of an already homogenous group.

In addition to providing physical space, clubs promoted loyalty among members, since men relied on one another for admission, a process revealing how news networks were also favor networks. One day in 1953, the radio commentator Elmer Davis was about to resign from the Cosmos Club, because he no longer used the facilities very often. He then received two letters in the same mail delivery that convinced him to remain a member. One was from his neighbor and bridge companion, Eugene Meyer, still serving as chairman of the *Washington Post*, asking Davis to support the *Post*'s managing editor, Russell Wiggins, for membership.[70] The publisher of the *Post* at that time, Meyer's son-in-law, Philip Graham, considered membership in the Cosmos Club so essential for his managing editor that he instructed the newspaper's accountant to pay the editor's dues.[71] In this way, professional standing in the news business became social capital for men who otherwise may not have been able to afford memberships in elite clubs.

The other letter that Davis received was from *Newsweek*'s Washington bureau chief, Ernest Lindley, asking him to write a letter for Cosmos Club membership on behalf of Paul Wooton, the Washington correspondent for the New Orleans *Times-Picayune*. Whether they worked in print or broadcast, whether they were progressives like Davis or conservatives like Meyer, regardless of the newspapers, magazines, or broadcast networks with which they were affiliated, these men all relied on one another to get their friends inside the orbits necessary to do their jobs. In Washington, this favor-swapping was accepted more than in the news world of New York, where the social-professional sphere was less circumscribed. For example, in 1958 some of the men of the *New York Times* were working on getting the publisher-to-be, Orvil Dryfoos, into one of New York City's top men's clubs, the Century Association. They wanted him to ask Nelson Rockefeller, soon-to-be governor of New York and someone whom the *Times* covered widely, for a recommendation. Dryfoos objected, citing a conflict of interest. Scotty Reston, then the *Times*' bureau chief in Washington, wrote another *Times*man about it: "I think Orv is perhaps being a little too careful on the Rockefeller business, but, of course, that is up to him."[72] Merely living in Washington constituted so much a conflict of interest that it was the proverbial water invisible to the fish swimming in it. After all, Reston had not thought that it was a conflict of interest to ask Senator Stuart Symington for a letter of support for Roscoe Drummond—the Washington bureau chief for the New York *Herald Tribune*, whom Reston was sponsoring for membership in the Metropolitan Club—any more than he would have thought of Drummond in this context as a competitor. (Incidentally, in working on Drummond's application in 1953, Reston and Symington also exchanged gossip about the relatively new Eisenhower administration, with Reston trying to answer the handwritten question at the bottom of Symington's letter, sent from Missouri: "What the h—— is going on down there?")[73]

The Revolving Door of War

Scotty Reston, Wallie Deuel, Ferdie Kuhn, and innumerable other reporters were in and out of government service throughout the war. By 1942, Deuel was already at the OSS, and Kuhn was at the Treasury Department. In July of that year, Elmer Davis at the OWI wrote the New York Times' publisher Arthur Sulzberger, asking to borrow Reston to help set up the organization's new London office. "I understand that Reston acquired undulant fever in London last year and would not propose to ask him to go back permanently to a place where the food supply is so uncertain in quality if not in quantity, but I do wish you could loan him to us for about four months," Davis wrote.[74] Undulant fever referred to an infectious disease most often caused by consuming unpasteurized dairy products, and Davis's knowledge of it is evidence of the gossip and information exchange constantly at work among these men. The letter was a formality at this point, putting in writing an understanding that Sulzberger and Davis had made in person recently in Washington. Despite the memories of the Blitz and the undulant fever, Reston heeded the call of duty and his boss's wishes and returned to London for the OWI.

One of the reasons that Reston was such an attractive recruit to Davis was that his first book, Prelude to Victory, on the importance of combating fascism, had just been released to acclaim in June. In the book's acknowledgments, Reston thanked his London and Washington colleagues for the conversations that helped shape the book, the first three of whom were, not surprisingly, Ed Murrow, Eric Sevareid, and Ferdie Kuhn.[75] Also not surprisingly, given the lack of social-professional boundaries, he owed the book's reception in part to Murrow and Sevareid, who praised it over the CBS airwaves. Sevareid told Murrow that Reston "was very much touched by your tribute to his book, which has made a considerable impression in government circles and in liberal intellectual circles."[76] Sevareid noted at the same time that the book probably would not be widely read among the public. These men understood that their most important audience was within three square miles in downtown Washington. They knew quite clearly that they were operating in certain "circles." Meanwhile, Wallie Deuel, still freelance writing while in the OSS, wrote the *New York Times*' book review of *Prelude to Victory*, which was a personal and professional conflict of interest he was careful not to disclose to readers. He called the book "brilliant and altogether admirable" and characterized Reston as an "exceedingly able young man, esteemed by his colleagues as one of the outstanding newspapermen of his generation."[77]

The *Washington Post* announced Reston's book in its society pages, cited it in editorials, and included it on its "Readers' Choice" list of the books most in demand in Washington.[78] Because of the book, Eugene Meyer, the *Post*'s publisher, began a correspondence with Reston about the praise he was receiving. "I am sorry that just about the time we are getting acquainted, my friend, Elmer Davis, is sending you to London," he wrote, assuring Reston they would continue the friendship when Reston returned.[79] (There would have been several ways for Meyer to have heard about Reston's assignment, but one was that Davis and Meyer were next-door neighbors on Crescent Place and regularly played bridge together.)

Prelude to Victory sought to drive home what America was fighting for, to avoid a return to complacency when the fighting was over. The high but necessary price of freedom was Reston's central theme. In his preface, written while in Washington, he wrote, "This is not a book so much as it is an outburst of bad temper against careless thinking; bureaucratic officials; selfish 'special groups'; irresponsible citizens, newspapers and politicians; people who think wars don't really settle anything; people who want to 'get back to normal'; people who think time and money are on our side; and people who are afraid to win because of postwar problems."[80] He emphasized that the idea of ensuring freedom in other parts of the world was not "highfalutin talk and propaganda" but the reason Americans needed to fight—that if freedom and a free press could be suppressed in Germany, then it could happen anywhere. Reston was separating himself and his friends from "irresponsible citizens, newspapers and politicians." Responsible news-papermen were not dispassionate bystanders, he believed, but support-ers of intervention, internationalism, and postwar collective security that ensured freedom for America's Allies. The book had a second printing in August 1942 and a third in January 1943.

Though the *Times* technically granted Reston a leave of absence for his OWI work in London during the summer of 1942, he still wrote Arthur Krock, his Washington bureau chief, upon arriving at Clar-idge's, the swanky hotel where he stayed. The revolving door of war-time service was so ubiquitous, and touched Washington newsmen so particularly, that Reston told him only half-jokingly, "I don't know how they'd run this war without the Washington bureau of the Times."[81] The circulation of US newspapermen in London was widespread, and the *Times'* Washington bureau was not unique in this regard. Military or government service was the normal experience for the newsmen of the immediate postwar era and gave them a shared understanding of their responsibility. In London, one of Reston's assistants was Chalmers Roberts, who in civilian life was a reporter for the *Washington Daily News*, then the *Washington Times Herald*, and the *Washington Star*. In 1949, he moved to the *Washington Post*, where in 1953 he took over from Ferdie Kuhn as the diplomatic reporter. Another of the men at the OWI's London office was Wallace Carroll, then directing psychological warfare, for which he became a government consultant after the war. Reston had met Carroll in London before the war, when Carroll was working for the United Press. Carroll, Kuhn, and Reston all remained friends after the war was over. The Kuhns' oldest son, Philip, even did a stint at Carroll's North Carolina newspaper in 1954, which Reston and Carroll also corresponded about, all of them keeping close eyes on one another's family affairs.[82] Then in 1955, Carroll left North Carolina for Washington to become Reston's right-hand man at the *New York Times*.

Meanwhile, two future managing editors of the *Washington Post*, Russell Wiggins and Alfred Friendly, were both in the Army Air Corps, as was their future publisher, Phil Graham. Wiggins, who turned forty while serving in the army, would be managing editor from 1947 to 1955 and a vice president of the company until his retirement in 1968. He had grown up in rural southern Minnesota and gone straight from high school to reporting for the *Rock County (Minnesota) Star*, a small paper he purchased two years later, becoming its editor and publisher. In 1930, at the height of the Depression and lacking a steady income, he sold the *Star* and became an editorial writer for the much larger *St. Paul Pioneer Press and Dispatch*, where he specialized in agricultural issues. By the fall of 1933, with the New Deal in full swing, agriculture had become a national story. As a result, Wiggins's newspaper sent him to be their man in Washington. "Close association with newspapermen of the gallery was one of the richest rewards of service in Washington," he wrote of that time, emphasizing the importance of masculine friendship. "The strenuous job of running a one-man bureau did not leave too much time for extracurricular activities but what time there was left over I certainly much enjoyed." He cited the two press clubs so central to newspapermen's homosocial life in the capital: "In 1937 I was a member of the Board of Governors of the National Press Club and served until I left the capitol [*sic*]. In March 1938 I was elected a member of the Gridiron Club."[83] Wiggins had remained in Washington for five years before becoming managing editor of the St. Paul paper, where he stayed until the war.

In December 1941, Wiggins, like so many of his colleagues who were too old for the draft, nevertheless "felt it to be my personal responsibility to get into military service somewhere," as he recalled it in his notes four years later.[84] He accepted a captain's commission in the United States Army, training as an Air Force intelligence officer in Harrisburg, Pennsylvania, where he became an instructor. At Harrisburg, one of his students was Al Friendly, the young *Washington Post* reporter who would succeed him as managing editor in 1955. When he arrived for training, Friendly recognized Wiggins as the former Washington bureau chief of the *St. Paul Pioneer Press*. "I thought his theological ardor about freedom of the press and its obligations, and his demeanor in general, very faintly ridiculous," Friendly wrote of his Air Corps teacher. "I was to mend my views, quickly and completely," he continued, a new admiration blossoming during a difficult period and forming the basis for a professional relationship at the *Post* after the war.[85]

Friendly had been born in Salt Lake City in 1911 as Alfred Friendly Rosenbaum, but by the age of eighteen he had taken his mother's maiden (and less Jewish-sounding) name as his own. He attended Amherst College, where he befriended Chalmers Roberts—the same Chal Roberts who worked with Scotty Reston in the OWI and would succeed Ferdie Kuhn at the *Washington Post*. Friendly and Roberts became best friends, and the two men spent a year after college, from 1935 to 1936, traveling the country together as migrant workers. Friendly had taken brief assignments in the Department of Commerce and the National Recovery Administration and wanted to experience migrant life for himself. Friendship and alumni networks have always been important in journalism, as in any business, but this wartime and postwar period was unique for the depth, breadth, and intensity of relationships, and ultimately the unity of purpose.

When members of the press corps enlisted in government service, they were most often sent to publicity and propaganda jobs. During the war, Friendly wrote a promotional book for the Army Air Corps titled *The Guys on the Ground*, giving what was thought to be much-needed publicity to the less glamorous nonflying men of his division. These positions did not shield those who held them from the horrors of war, though. Many witnessed suffering that left searing impressions and informed their sense of America's obligation to global postwar recovery. For Wiggins, assignments in Italy and Algeria in 1943 were especially poignant and horrific.[86]

The men who took leaves of absence from Washington newspaper work during the war were happy to return to journalism in the transition to peace. "You see me a fish back in water and loving it," Wallie Deuel wrote his parents in October 1945, from the Washington bureau of the *Chicago Daily News*. "The newspaper business is even sweller than I remembered."[87] Al Friendly, once again at the *Washington Post*, expressed a similar sentiment in his diary: "After a couple of days of work, or rather, of mooching around to see whom I still know and whom else I ought to I find I still like the business very much. More than ever, perhaps, now that I can set it off to more than three years of armying."[88] Their attitudes about government, reporting, and war could not possibly have remained the same after the ordeals they had experienced and witnessed.

Deuel, Friendly, and their fellow newsmen brought with them a new sense of duty for maintaining the peace they felt they had just worked so hard to achieve. Above all, they feared atomic destruction in a suddenly nuclear world. Before the war, foreign policy reporters had been writing about a nation at peace, with few life-and-death consequences to what they wrote. Afterward, the idea that the United States could still be in a "kind of war" dominated the nation's capital. The Washington newsmen's perceived responsibility for promoting national security and their emphasis on their roles as citizens as well as networked journalists would infuse their reporting during the new era.

3

RESPONSIBLE REPORTERS AND THE
EXCLUSIVE INFORMATION ECONOMY

The reporters who remained in Washington as practicing journalists during World War II developed a sense of responsibility equal to that of the men serving the federal government directly. "War imposes grave new responsibilities on all of us, but upon no public servant does the responsibility for truth and integrity rest more heavily than upon the press," a group of White House reporters wrote in a complaint to Franklin Roosevelt about censorship. "Theirs is the duty of keeping the people fully and truly informed."[1] Because of that responsibility to provide information, which coincided with a reporter's ability to remain employed, newsmen were in constant friction with the government, which brought them ever closer to one another against a common enemy.

Because of the sensitive nature of wartime news, the necessity for reporters to develop trust with their sources and among their fellow reporters was greater than ever. Out of this need, they established small dinner groups and seminars—occasions when influential men in government met with hand-selected reporters. Whether a newsman was included in these gatherings depended on his contacts, his reputation within Washington, and his being a trustworthy white man. The social capital of trust became more important to journalism during the war and remained critical afterward. How reporters spoke about being responsible newsmen shifted as well: a responsibility to inform the public became a responsibility to protect them, by limiting the dissemination of information they believed to be contrary to the Allied cause and the public interest. Indiscretion would also be contrary to their own interests, since violating norms could endanger their access and their jobs. The exclusive information economy they built during wartime then became a permanent one.

Private Smokers and Pipelines

Reporters' private dinners with important sources were not new, but they had often depended on the hospitality of individual publishers, like the *Washington Post*'s Eugene Meyer. Meyer was a wealthy financier who had moved from New York to Washington part time in 1928, at the age of fifty-three, to become chairman of the Federal Farm Loan Board. He stayed on when he became governor of the Federal Reserve Board in 1930. In 1933, when the failing *Washington Post* went up for auction, Meyer bought it and quickly shaped it into a paper that could compete with its more established rival, the *Washington Times Herald* (which the *Post* acquired in 1954, eliminating a conservative voice in the capital).

Meyer's purchase of the *Post* coincided with Roosevelt's arrival in Washington, and like many cosmopolitan men, he could for the first time imagine a permanent future in the newly vibrant capital. So in 1934, he and his wife, Agnes, bought the brick mansion they had been leasing on Crescent Place. The home had seventeen rooms, "not including bathrooms, servants' rooms, and storage rooms," and required fourteen servants to run it.[2] During the 1930s and 1940s, the house became as important to newsmen gathering and consolidating information as the bar at the National Press Club, but considerably more selective.

Meyer's presence in Washington society was titanic. He belonged to the three largest men's clubs—the Cosmos Club, the Metropolitan Club, and the Army and Navy Club—as well as the Alfalfa Club, a men's annual stag dinner organization; Burning Tree, a golf club in nearby Maryland; the University Club; the National Press Club; the Congressional Country Club; the Yale Club; and the 1925 F Street Club, a private dining group.[3]

In many towns, Meyer's Judaism would have prevented him from becoming a leading citizen and member of every elite club. But the subject of religion rarely comes up in his collected papers, except for one mention to Metropolitan Club members in 1954 that the Episcopal Church seemed to be overrepresented in their luncheon group. "And, while I have no rabbi or bishop or priest to recommend to be invited," he joked, "I want it understood that I am not going to surrender my religion in favor of the predominance of Episcopalians on the new list."[4] Meyer's religion seemed less of an issue both for him and for his newspaper than that of Adolph Ochs and Arthur Hays Sulzberger at the *New York Times*. There, religion was a constant concern for the paper's owners, who did not want it to become known as a Jewish paper.[5] The difference between the importance of religion in New York, which was ethnically and religiously diverse, and Washington, an environment that seemed to whiten all those who were not Black, may have contributed to Meyer's and Sulzberger's disparate attitudes.[6] Also, Meyer had married a woman who was not Jewish—and who set up a household in which Judaism was not observed, religiously or culturally—whereas Sulzberger had married into the Ochs family, one of the most prominent Jewish families in the country.

Still, Washington was an Episcopal town, even if church membership seemed to be a matter more of social status than of the status of one's soul. "When Methodists, Baptists, or Presbyterians come to Washington, they Always Rent Pews in [Episcopal] St. John's Church. It Helps Climbers Along," the Gridiron Club wrote in its 1906 dinner program, a tongue-in-cheek "Guide to Washington."[7] Gossip about why someone might join that church continued into the 1950s, when some people suspected that the reporter Doris Fleeson had joined only to improve her daughter's social standing.[8] (Fleeson apparently denied this, but it would have been a valid reason: she did not have the social capital that came with being male, but she could at least capitalize on being Protestant.) In 1907, an even grander Episcopal building was undertaken— the Cathedral of St. Peter and St. Paul, later known as the Washington National Cathedral, to this day one of the city's dominant landmarks.

In Washington, Meyer was simply a millionaire publisher, not a millionaire Jewish publisher. This is not to say that being Jewish was never a source of prejudice for Washingtonians, and like in other US cities, some neighborhoods had restrictive covenants based on ethnicity and religion as well as race.[9] But Meyer's wealth, standing, and non-Jewish wife meant his religion little affected his status. During the 1930s and 1940s, he hosted off-the-record "smokers" for reporters to meet top men in government. In invitation parlance, a smoker denoted a party at which dinner would not be served, but cigars and drinks would. Only men were included, since it was impolite to smoke a cigar in front of a lady. Occasions like these set precedents for determining which reporters should then be included in other meetings with sources, even those without cigars. Meyer invited not just those men who worked for his own paper but groups of correspondents he knew personally from papers across the country. This meant a variety of outlets would have similar frames for thinking about the issues discussed and the same hidden sources for their stories.

In a letter to Meyer after a particularly productive smoker with Assistant Secretary of State Sumner Welles in 1940, Raymond Clapper, the Scripps-Howard syndicated columnist, indicated how common and fruitful these gatherings were. "I have enjoyed all of the sessions which you have so thoughtfully arranged, and particularly I wanted to congratulate you upon the last meeting," he wrote. "I am sure it was an invaluable experience to everyone present, and all of those with whom I have talked are most enthusiastic. I want in this way to express my appreciation for being included. All of us are very much in your debt, and there is nothing more constructive being done to help those of us who have to write about these matters than this little series of meetings which you have arranged."[10] In writing so effusively, Clapper was partly performing expected deference to the powerful and older Meyer. But he was also expressing thanks from "all of us"—the whole newspaper fraternity. He and "all of those with whom" he'd talked—all of them discussing and interpreting sources after the fact, working through them together—were growing accustomed to the invaluable experience of being in these confidential meetings among gentlemen friends.

Private smokers allowed for private conversations, the substance of which never made it into the news. In January 1942, Alfred Friendly, then a thirty-one-year-old reporter for the *Washington Post*, described one of these sessions in his diary: "At night to Butch Meyer's, where were gathered some 15 newsmen and C. E. Wilson of General Motors. Such a night! I was in physical agony most of the time as the stupid bastard tried to show what a great patriotic outfit they were. . . . Paul Ward [of the *Baltimore Sun*], Blair Moody [of the *Detroit News*], Walter Lippmann [the syndicated columnist] and I gave the guy a good going over. Only Mark Sullivan [the syndicated columnist], a more objectionable subsidized stultified asskisser than which I have never seen, fed him leading questions."[11] Friendly's sarcastic assessment of General Motors was counter to the widespread public opinion of it as patriotically mobilizing for wartime production, an opinion Friendly and his cohort were not going to challenge in their articles quite as frankly as they did in their diaries. Most of these men were skeptical of Wilson that night and eager to challenge him. Only the elderly Sullivan—a famous columnist who had moved politically rightward under Roosevelt—was now an outsider.

Friendly continued in his diary entry, expressing apparent disdain for both Wilson and the United States Army: "No mention of the industry's bitter resistance to [wartime] conversion, all blame placed on Congress for not appropriating the wonderful Army more money. Ward didn't let him get away with it. . . . I asked Wilson how come he told us at press conference two weeks ago that his plans were of ultimate full capacity of 3.7 billion. Got no answer save the inference I was an s.o.b."[12] The next day, Friendly and his fellow smoker attendees bumped into one another on their fairly circumscribed reporting rounds, including at the National Press Club. As they debriefed and gossiped, they reinforced one another's beliefs: "Everyone I saw today who was at Butch's had the same reaction," Friendly wrote in his diary that day. "Dick Wilson [of the Cowles publications] said he never saw a case so badly presented."[13] Thus were established common perceptions of people and events, setting the boundaries of acceptable printed conversation. No immediate news stories arose from this smoker, as all the invited men understood. But they also learned to distrust C. E. Wilson; even after he became Secretary of Defense under Dwight Eisenhower in 1953, he remained unpopular with newsmen. The seeds of distrust between reporters and sources that grew like weeds during the 1950s were sown in wartime.

The frequency of Eugene Meyer's smokers prompted the *New York Times*' Washington bureau chief, Arthur Krock, to write one of his frequent missives to New York about his entertainment budget. He felt that the *Times* was at a disadvantage: "By virtue of being a local publisher, and a millionaire with a great house, Meyer has got himself into a very strong position to get the best facts and background from important persons," Krock wrote his managing editor in April 1940. "He gives these soirées often and has frequently been good enough to include me. But I have thought from time to time that I should, on behalf of The Times, attempt something of the same idea."[14] Sulzberger (whose mansion was in New York) was sympathetic, and while he did not immediately increase Krock's annual entertainment budget, he did reimburse him for at least one dinner within the next year, and probably more. In March 1941, Krock hosted an especially important off-the-record small dinner for Sulzberger to meet the top men in government who were respectively in charge of production, lend-lease, the war in Europe, and the overall financial picture: William Knudsen, James Forrestal, John J. McCloy, and Jesse Jones.[15]

That kind of single-paper dinner was not a new development, but it was falling out of favor with journalists as a "pipeline." Somewhat illogically but also understandably, Krock was in favor of dining with prestigious sources, but he was decidedly against pipelines and stories planted by sources. In the summer of 1943, Walter Lippmann joined Krock, despite their tense relationship, to complain to President Roosevelt about "pipe line journalism." They objected to government officials, of whom they believed the president was a prime offender, creating a direct pipeline of information to chosen writers—"giving 'background' to certain selected writers not available to all writers." Krock and Lippmann agreed that this development was an "insidious corruption of the press."[16] Krock, in fact, disliked off-the-record information entirely, believing that anything Roosevelt said in supposed confidence ought to be something that he, Krock, could find out from another source, on the record, and be able to print. Thus, he had long boycotted press conferences with FDR, who frequently gave information on background and off the record.[17]

After news stories in November 1943 emerged from a secret meeting at the White House about which Krock had not been informed but believed that Lippmann had, he reminded Lippmann of their conversation about pipeline journalism. "These White House meetings seem to me exactly in the same mold. One hardly can attend them, receive inside information or background, not given to others, and write critically or detachedly of the man who gives the background and who is the host," Krock wrote. "The whole business is repugnant to me, as I am sure it is to you. I think it is degrading to permit oneself to be so transparently used. The secrecy with which the visits seem to have been made make it particularly revolting. How do you feel about this? Is there anything we can do?" Perhaps defensively, Lippmann replied that he thought what had transpired at the White House was the "opposite of pipe line journalism," because all the press associations and radio networks had been present.[18] Krock disagreed that the size of the pipeline mattered; the problem was meeting secretly to hand-deliver information to some people at the exclusion of others.[19] He believed that the federal government was manipulating irresponsible reporters.

At first, the editorial board of the *Washington Post* took the same position as Krock. In March 1944, the paper ran an editorial on the subject of freedom of the press, which it tied to its criticism of the blue-ribbon Commission on Freedom of the Press, or the Hutchins Commission, which from 1944 to 1947 worked on a report released as *A Free and Responsible Press*. The problem, as the *Post* saw it, was this: the prestigious Hutchins Commission initially included no journalists. The *Post* editorial board, its members perhaps miffed at not being asked to participate, considered the commission's scholarly composition a mistake because, as it wrote, freedom of the press "is in as much danger from the inside as from the outside." Journalists on the inside should therefore have a role in the remedy. The board pointed to two new dangerous practices, one of which was "generally known as 'pipe-line journalism,' which we sometimes think, might more appropriately be called 'black market journalism.'" (The second threat was related, and nowhere more apparent than at its own publisher's smokers, which was that journalists "used to tell more than they knew" and that "the newer tendency is to tell less.")[20]

There was, in fact, general agreement that "pipe-line journalism" was undesirable, so the term, with its pejorative connotations, soon fell out of use. The practice, however, did not. Instead, the black market in journalism quickly became the official information economy, with wartime exigencies an easy justification. What was once called pipe-line journalism became institutionalized as background sessions, which included responsible men from multiple news organizations and meant that the pipeline spread throughout the country. Background information would become the norm for reporting on foreign affairs in particular because of wartime censorship and government officials' mounting sense that they needed something more systematic than Eugene Meyer's goodwill to get newsmen confidential information as a group.

Government-Press Tensions Rise

Tensions between newspapers and government officials ran high as they navigated their wartime relationship. The US government had a checkered history with censorship. Most recently, it had abused its power during World War I by pursuing cases under the Espionage and Sedition Acts, driving a wide range of dissenting, socialistic, or even merely German-language newspapers out of business.[21] The African American press was especially vulnerable to government recrimination.[22] It was largely thanks to the US attorney general Francis Biddle's protection of the Black press's First Amendment rights that the executive branch was kept from abusing its power again during World War II. Those precedents were still threats hanging over the newspapers of 1940 and had a chilling effect on what was reported.[23]

The 1920s were a crystallization period in the history of objective news coverage, as reporters grew more cynical about propaganda machines and lost faith in putative facts.[24] The newsmen of Walter Lippmann's generation and those younger men whom he mentored, like

Scotty Reston of the *New York Times* and Joe Harsch of the *Christian Science Monitor*, came to journalism in an age of skepticism of official sources. Lippmann even famously wrote about it. In 1920, and in the wake of their disappointment over the Senate's failure to ratify the Versailles Treaty, Lippmann, along with Charles Merz—who would serve as editorial page editor of the *New York Times* from 1938 to 1961—published a special section of the *New Republic* entitled "A Test of the News." They laid out how partial the *Times*, already considered the paper of record, had been in its coverage of the Russian Revolution. In their findings they wrote, "In the large, the news about Russia is a case of seeing not what was, but what men wished to see. The chief censor and the chief propagandist were hope and fear in the minds of reporters and editors. They wanted to win the war; they wanted to ward off bolshevism. For subjective reasons, they accepted and believed most of what they were told by the State Department, the so-called Russian Embassy in Washington, the Russian Information Bureau in New York, the Russian Committee in Paris, and the agents and adherents of the old regime all over Europe."[25] News professionals at midcentury certainly recognized their own subjectivity, as well as the government's efforts at propaganda and censorship, as dangers to fair reporting. The objectivity they tried to embody in this period never meant an unquestioning acceptance of official facts. Instead, it meant questioning all facts as well as one's own wishes and assumptions. While the pursuit of objectivity came in for special derision during the New Journalism of the 1960s and 1970s, the earlier generations had been no less clear-eyed about their own biases and the danger of relying on official sources.

World War II reporting, of course, would reveal the patriotic biases of reporters and editors, but it did not diminish the skepticism of government sources that had been baked into their version of objectivity. In fact, the history of twentieth-century journalism up to that point— which also included the muckrakers of the Progressive Era and battles with the especially corrupt Warren Harding administration—had been marked by mistrust between officials and reporters. World War II was not putting a new strain on the already tense relationship between the press and the US government, and reporters were not primed to trust their sources. By probing more deeply the problems that World War II created for journalists and the solutions they arrived at, we can understand why the period it ushered in seemed like a less skeptical time than it actually was.

On December 7, 1941, the Japanese military bombed Pearl Harbor, and the United States was officially at war. Roosevelt established the Office of Censorship on December 19 and appointed Byron Price, the executive news director of the Associated Press, as its head.[26] The following month, Price released the first iteration of the Code of Wartime Practices for the American Press, a voluntary censorship code. In an effort to head off negative reactions from the press, the government separated its censorship application from its propaganda dissemination. While Price handled censorship, information was first under the purview of the Office of Facts and Figures, which then became the Office of War Information under the radio commentator Elmer Davis.

The voluntary censorship code implied that the press corps would have access to information that it could not print—that it would *need* to exercise voluntary responsibility. Instead, frustration with the censorship process was common, especially early in the war when the information apparatus was new and untested. "Dissatisfaction with the government's handling of war news began right at the start, with Pearl Harbor; and various aspects of that episode repeated themselves in others that were to follow," Davis wrote in 1945 in a somewhat tragic, confidential postmortem.[27] The government had downplayed the damage to the naval base caused by the bombing. Once people learned that Japanese news accounts were closer to the truth than the US government's, it lost credibility, which Davis believed took months or more to restore. Reporters in Washington felt excluded from war news, or even misled. Meanwhile, reporters embedded overseas wrote their editors about feeling unwelcome by the armed forces, subject to inane censorship rules, and encumbered by poor communications facilities that led to severely delayed dispatches.[28]

The United States Navy repeatedly mishandled reports of ship losses, sowing confusion about what was general knowledge and what would aid the enemy. More than once, some newspapers would publish a story that other newspapers had agreed not to publish. Censors would then ban the story after the fact, so that any newspaper that had not yet published the story—now public—could still not print it. In his confidential history, Davis commented that the OWI should have been established by March of 1942, since in June, when Roosevelt put the order in, it had been too late. "By June the public had had three months more of mounting dissatisfaction with government information, and particularly with the handling of news of military and naval operations. Impressions created in those months took a long time to eradicate," he wrote.[29] The public expressed its dissatisfaction with government information as well as with the newspapers and radio news programs meant to convey it. Those outlets in turn resented the government for harming their relationships with their readers and listeners.

The day after Pearl Harbor, Arthur Krock assigned one of his men to cover the new restrictions on the news. The night before this story was going to run, it had gone out over the *New York Times'* syndicate wires to evening papers nationwide and come to the attention of Secretary of the Navy Frank Knox. Knox then called Arthur Sulzberger, asking him to kill the story and claiming that he was making the request on the authority of the president. He knew that Sulzberger would be sympathetic. As one *Times* editor had written another just three weeks earlier on another censorship matter, "As you know, the publisher is very scrupulous about observing all the rules, even those fixed by a crackpot Secretary of the Navy."[30] Krock was livid, and then he found out from the White House press secretary, Steve Early, that in reality, the president had had nothing to do with the kill order. Knox had lied. Sulzberger tried to assuage Krock's anger, reassuring him of the *Times'* commitment to reporting the news, but concluded, "If Frank Knox was mis-using the President's name when he spoke to me, it's too bad, but very frankly if a request is presented to me on the name of the President, and by the Secretary of the Navy, that sections of a story we are about to use [are] not in the best interests of the country, I do not feel I have any other choice than to comply with that request."[31] What was in the best interests of the country remained the standard of responsible journalism for years to come, even as disagreements continued behind the scenes in newsrooms about what those interests were.[32]

In his letter to Krock, Sulzberger then paid lip service to freedom of the press, an ideal that created resentment between publishers and their editors and reporters for its nebulousness. "I admit there are limits to this," he wrote. "A time may come when this newspaper will have to throw all such self-restraint to the winds and take the consequences, but I do not think that time has come yet." Despite that *yet*, which seemed to leave open the possibility of challenging the government publicly in the future, Sulzberger would never think that the time had come. That is, he always wanted the *Times* to err on the side of restraint and was frequently butting heads with his editors and reporters over what was in the interest of the *Times*, the government, or the nation. At the same time, he never felt quite right about taking orders from the government, and he and his successor, Orvil Dryfoos, did challenge the government privately. Sulzberger typically would write a follow-up letter to the complaining official, applying a little guilt and asserting some independence. In this instance, he wrote Knox, "I did what you asked the other night, although I am not at all certain that you were correct in asking it."[33] This was not an early move toward transforming newspapers like the *New York Times* into government stooges but rather an instance of friction between the press and the government, as well as among members of the press, over what could be printed and what could not. And of course, that friction was not part of the public debate, only that of the private records of men like Krock and Sulzberger.

Two weeks after Pearl Harbor, Krock got his chance to publish a critique of censorship policy that was not killed but that then raised the question of whether journalists should air their dirty laundry in public. He wrote on December 21, 1941, "The freedom of the press in the United States, guaranteed in time of peace by the first article of the Bill of Rights but clearly incompatible with national security in time of war, ended Thursday afternoon, when the President signed the revived War Powers Act of 1917, including censorship authority."[34]

For publicly stating what everyone in the newspaper business knew to be true, Krock received criticism, including an admonishing private letter from Walter Lippmann. "It seems to me a very serious matter that the Washington correspondent of the New York Times should make a statement of that kind at a time like this, casting doubt upon the whole press," Lippmann wrote.[35] He believed that people's faith in the press was central to the functioning of democracy. Krock continued to write critical stories, though, and Lippmann continued to criticize him privately. For his part, Krock was smug in his opinion that Lippmann was not a real newspaperman anyway. "He has appointed himself general disciplinarian of the press and me in particular, and I seriously doubt his qualifications," he wrote Sulzberger in April 1942, after four months of squabbles. He added a workingman's gut punch: "Lippmann came into the newspaper business by the skylight. He never was a reporter, and it shows."[36] Lippmann, he believed, was an intellectual, not a man who gathered facts. In one particularly sarcastic letter to Lippmann, Krock called him a "syndicated oracle."[37]

For Lippmann and so many others, not impugning journalism was far more central to democracy than not impugning the federal government. A similar conversation would play out again during the Vietnam War as reporters struggled to maintain the public's faith in their own institution while discrediting others. In February 1968, the United Press reporter Merriman Smith wrote to the ABC correspondent Howard K. Smith after the latter had written a column damaging to the press: "Objectivity, always a weak excuse but at least a striving of sorts, is now a cuss word. And subjectivity now equates with condemnation. . . . But is it any answer, does it help stop the killing, to smash public confidence in virtually every channel of information known to us?"[38]

Despite the public proclamations by government officials about the importance of a free press in wartime, newsmen in Washington were concerned that the government might use newsprint rationing as a way of diminishing that freedom without resorting to sedition charges. Newspapers had already been operating on reduced page counts because of wartime rationing; if the government chose to, it could limit newsprint rations to an extent that newspapers could not print any pages at all.

In May 1942, one *New York Times* Washington reporter drafted an article about censorship by newsprint rationing for the Sunday magazine; the magazine's New York–based editor rejected it as speculation. This prompted the reporter to send a memo explaining that the idea that the press was misbehaving and ought to be kept in line was common knowledge throughout the spaces of Washington. "Every party or place I go to, I hear this argument about the press," he wrote. He then gave a six-point list of all the places in Washington that he had heard it: a drink with Adolph Berle, the assistant secretary of state for Latin American Affairs, who said, "Cut newspapers to the bone through rationing of newsprint and make it impossible for them to criticize"; a private chat with Steve Early, the White House press secretary: "It might be a damned good thing if the newspapers were driven out of business"; a conversation with Robert Lovett, assistant secretary of war for air: "The newspapers are too big, particularly the Sunday newspapers"; a party at the house of the economist Kenneth Galbraith, chief aide to Leon Henderson at the Office of Price Administration: he "hinted strongly that action would be taken to force [newspapers] in line"; dinner at the home of Harold Ickes, the secretary of the interior, who was "perturbed about the possibility that the Government may take action on newsprint & etc. calculated to end the freedom of the press"; and finally, Harry Hopkins, the president's close advisor: "I know Hopkins has been for extreme control of the press for a long time."[39] But this story became just another that everyone within Washington knew as they hopped from one party to the next but that the public never did, leading to false impressions of harmony and cooperation between the government and the press during this period.

The government never did shut down any major newspapers during the war, but the tension around censorship remained. In October 1942, when Scotty Reston returned home from his London Office of War Information posting, he debriefed a group of reporters who were at the height of their dissatisfaction with the government's information and censorship policies. Reston himself had returned home jaded, disappointed with the OWI in particular and with government bureaucracy in general. Edward R. Murrow, who ran CBS News' London office, had seen how badly Reston was faring at the OWI and had written about it early on to their mutual friend Eric Sevareid, now back in Washington. "Scotty Reston, as you know, has arrived, and is, I think, baffled by the complexities of official procedure," he told Sevareid.[40] Reston did not have the stature to accomplish anything he set out to do, frustrating not just himself but his OWI boss, who called his cables "petulant" behind his back.[41] Neither Reston nor the OWI considered his posting a particular success, and when he returned to the United States he had little patience left for the government's information policies.

Ray Clapper, the influential columnist, was at Reston's October debriefing. The fifty-year-old, compact in body and square-faced with dark circles around his eyes, was originally from Kansas and had attended the state university. His reporting cohort liked him and considered him a fair and accurate columnist. In addition to being an active member of the Gridiron Club, Clapper and his wife, Olive, were popular guests in high-society Washington drawing rooms. His death two years later while reporting on combat in the South Pacific would leave a hole in his community. Clapper kept a detailed diary that tracked issues of censorship and information. "Reston convinced planning still woefully inadequate and that biggest job to be done is by press getting at operating levels below policy-making levels and digging out facts," he noted after the October meeting. "He leaving OWI in disgust to rejoin Sulzberger as adviser on New York Times. In general discussion point was made by me and others that we are behind eight ball since . . . beating on trip arrangements."[42] Clapper was referring to the fact that the previous month, President Roosevelt had made a "secret" cross-country train tour, holding public events throughout America. Washington newsmen were incensed that they would not only not be allowed to accompany the president but also would not learn his schedule in advance or be permitted to write about the trip until he had returned to Washington—supposedly for the president's safety, but in reality so he maintained control over his public image. At that point, Clapper and three other newsmen formed an ad hoc censorship committee and met at the National Press Club to draft a letter of protest.[43]

The committee members circulated the letter among their friends and colleagues in the Press Club, acquiring thirty-three signatures. Newsmen were banding together all the more in their fight against executive censorship. The signers represented thirty-two news organizations, from the *Cleveland Plain Dealer* and *St. Louis Post-Dispatch* to the *Los Angeles Times*, *Chicago Tribune*, and *Birmingham News and Age-Herald*. The fact that all these men (and they were all men) could gather at the club and agree on a single message to send the president is a significant demonstration of the easy cooperation that encouraged group thinking, sometimes in opposition to the federal government. It also demonstrates how the physical spaces in which they operated facilitated that consensus.

Clapper continued in his notes from the Reston meeting, "Dick Wilson [of the Cowles publications] said he had been threatened with espionage act for reporting on a controversy over policy. All were complaining of increasing restrictions."[44] The newsmen were determined to get in front of the eight ball. They felt they looked silly to their reading public when they had not printed stories about events that people could see with their own eyes, like Roosevelt's trip. They also took seriously the idea that they should practice responsible journalism when it came to matters of true national security—but that the government should not be able to abuse its power to cover up policy fracases, as it had tried to do with its threats to prosecute Dick Wilson.

Throughout this early wartime period, Washington reporters were in the difficult position of negotiating several thorny issues: self-censorship, tacit or sometimes blatant threats from the government to prosecute them under the Espionage Act, pressure from their home offices, and, for the most part, a desire to practice responsible journalism. Byron Price, the head of government censorship, succinctly summarized the strain they were under in a widely distributed speech given before the annual meeting of the American Society of Newspaper Editors in Washington in April 1942 and broadcast over the radio. "Irresponsible journalism is reprehensible anytime, anywhere; in wartime it may easily become a crime against national security," Price warned.[45] Reporters needed a way to practice responsible journalism without exposing themselves to accusations of treason.

Legitimating the Black Market in Journalism

A few months before the Reston debriefing, in May 1942, Clapper had had a meeting with Harry Hopkins, the president's confidant and troubleshooter, to discuss the friction that the war was creating between newsmen and their sources. Clapper wrote of Hopkins in his diary, "Said in England about a dozen editors and special writers are kept intimately informed of all war matters, including secret information. Wants to establish same situation here but uncertain how to proceed. Feels press is left at disadvantage under present system and needs more inside information for guidance and better service to war effort."[46] Between May and October, that conversation repeated itself around Washington, as at the Reston meeting. A clear information problem within the capital needed resolution, and perhaps widening the government's circle of secret-keepers to include reporters would be necessary.

Two weeks after Reston's talk, on October 30, General George C. Marshall, the United States Army chief of staff, held what Clapper called a "small conference hand-picked" in his office at the new Pentagon. Marshall was beginning to rely with more regularity on that English system of background information Hopkins had described.[47] *Background* meant information provided in confidence that could be used to inform one's writing but could not be directly quoted or attributed. On a practical level, the men running the war were too busy to provide confidential information to individuals; background conferences were more efficient. And unlike a press conference, which anyone accredited to the War Department could attend, private meetings included only the men that the other reporters trusted. They were practicing the same "pull" discrimination seen in the world of clubs, bringing into their circle only others like themselves. White male reporters did not have a sense of community obligation or fellowship toward women reporters and reporters of color, who were therefore deemed less trustworthy and excluded from the discourse. In November 1941, a US senator from Maine was so impressed with the ability of a female Washington correspondent to keep a conversation confidential—since, as he put it, "we sometimes think that women have trouble in keeping secrets"—that he wrote her publisher to commend her.[48] Men were presumed trustworthy until proved otherwise, as some men inevitably were; meanwhile, a woman keeping a confidence was so unexpected that it occasioned a letter of praise. Issues of trustworthiness that had seemed merely important before the war could now be justified as life-and-death matters of national security.

Marshall's hand-picked conference that day was filled with what he and his advisors considered to be trustworthy men. The sixty-one-year-old was the consummate soldier—tall, straight-backed, and formal—and a carefully spoken man who engendered respect. His agenda was clear. "Evident purpose . . . to clear up confusion over divided command in South Pacific," Clapper wrote in his notes.[49] In the South Pacific, the Allies' offensive Guadalcanal campaign had been ongoing since August and would last until February of the following year. While it was ultimately an Allied victory, news out of the South Pacific in 1942 was often bleak, and the competing strategies that Admiral Ernest J. King of the United States Navy and General Douglas MacArthur of the United States Army advocated sowed anxiety at home. Even when there was good news, as at the Battle of Midway in June 1942, there was rivalry. Clapper had heard of the enmity over a private lunch with Under Secretary of the Navy James Forrestal: "Navy men a little bitter at Army publicity over Midway."[50] Marshall, by holding *seminars*, as the men first called these innovative sessions, was trying to fix some of these public relations issues. He was successful. The next morning, the *New York Herald Tribune* ran a front-page story about the army's appreciation of the navy. The article quoted from Marshall's thank-you letter to King for safely convoying troops through enemy waters: "In this war, as in no other in our history, the Army and Navy are fighting together."[51] The feel-good story obscured the bitterness between the branches of the armed forces that was common knowledge within Washington and brought reporters into active complicity with the government.

The whiteness of the meetings was important to the men running them. One conversation at a secret Pentagon meeting with Marshall and reporters on August 25, 1943, demonstrates the kinds of conversations these men had among themselves and how an unacknowledged precedent was set during the war that no Black reporters would be included. At that meeting, according to the *Washington Post* newsman's private memo to the publisher, "[Marshall] was particularly forceful on the subject of negroes in the Army. He said that they were no good as combat troops, as the last war proved, and that it was getting to be a terrific problem as to what to do with this class of troops." The Black press itself also came under scrutiny as an "other" in the same conversation, as Marshall continued, "With this situation existing, the negro press was screaming about discrimination, while responsible army men know that these troops cannot be trusted in combat."[52] The Black press, this line of thinking promoted, comprised irresponsible screamers, the last sort of men who could be included in a hush-hush meeting of responsible men. (Publicly, of course, the army was promising to rectify discrimination.)

For the rest of the war, Marshall called certain newsmen to his office to provide information that could not be attributed to him, increasing their understanding of and patience for the government's war efforts. They also developed personal affection for the general. "Every time I see this man I am more deeply impressed by him," one of the reporters wrote in 1944 to his editor in New York. "There is no man in Washington in either party or in any office whom I respect more highly, and I believe that feeling is shared generally by those in the capital who know him."[53] As we will see, Marshall's reputation with reporters certainly helped a few years later when, as secretary of state, he needed to sell them on the Marshall Plan, a cornerstone of postwar US foreign policy.

The men grew accustomed to withholding information from the public. At one meeting with Marshall in June 1943—which the army had emphasized to reporters could itself not be disclosed—the general spoke of some of the stories being told about US bombing atrocities. The Vatican had protested that American forces were killing civilians in Italy. "I have never asked you Gentlemen, or the newspapers, to do anything for me before," Marshall said, according to the *New York Times* reporter's confidential notes on the meeting. "I am asking you now, however, to help us resist this sort of thing. I am asking you to help us convince everyone that this is tough business in which we are engaged and that we must pursue it with all the toughness we possess."[54] First, this was certainly not the first time the general had asked reporters for a favor, as their very attendance at a secret meeting was a favor in itself. But the ethics of responsible journalism mandated that the men all downplay collusion. They acquiesced. Second, while stories about atrocities committed by the enemy were common, abuse by the United States never made it into the public's conceptions of "the Greatest Generation" and "the Good War."[55] But spontaneous censorship by every white-owned newspaper in America was not the only reason Allied atrocities were downplayed, nor was unquestioning patriotism; group understandings reached at never-revealed meetings contributed, as well.

Marshall usually hosted these seminars in his office at the Pentagon. But Admiral King, chief of naval operations, soon contributed an innovation that gave them life well beyond the war: he added dinner.[56] Much like the smokers Eugene Meyer hosted, the shared meal made the occasion feel even less like a meeting and more like a social occasion. Social capital—the pillars of which were whiteness and maleness—became an even stronger part of the information economy. After the war, when women and reporters of color would more frequently be admitted to press conferences at the Pentagon, they were still usually excluded from putatively social gatherings.

On November 6, 1942, eight newsmen gathered at a home in Alexandria, Virginia, to meet with Admiral King. His reputation among newsmen was that he was "taciturn" and "difficult," and the navy as a whole had trouble with reporters.[57] King's good friend and personal lawyer, Cornelius Bull, had suggested inviting a small group of trustworthy newsmen who could all vouch for one another's responsibility. The admiral agreed to try this out—a background session, and most certainly not a pipeline, they all agreed to pretend—holding a four-hour conversation with a break for supper. Eventually, a group of about twenty-six men rotated throughout fourteen sessions that King held during the war, first at Bull's house and, after Bull's death in June 1944, at the home of Phelps Adams, the Washington bureau chief for the conservative New York *Sun*.

Since taking notes was typically prohibited at these gatherings, the men had to go home or back to the office to compose memos for their editors, with Strictly Confidential or Top Secret underlined at the top of each page. They ensured that their memos would be carefully read by increasing their editors' sense of being on the inside. Both reporters and sources quickly grasped the new rules, including the fact that confidential information would be shared with the home office—something Franklin Roosevelt had tried to forbid for off-the-record conversations in the Oval Office.

The officials who participated in the information sessions came to understand that *top secret* meant only "to be withheld from the public," not kept from other influential and trusted newsmen, who were essential to building policy consensus. For instance, in February 1945, when the future secretary of state James F. Byrnes returned from the Yalta Conference and briefed Turner Catledge, then a *New York Times* reporter, Catledge wrote his editors, "What he told me was, of course, in the strictest of confidence so far as he is concerned, but he knew I would pass the essential parts of the information along to my associates on The New York Times."[58] Those associates were all equally trustworthy and honorable.

Within a few years of the advent of background dinners, the guidelines governing them became known as the Lindley Rule after Ernest Lindley (fig. 3.1), *Newsweek*'s chief Washington correspondent, who was a frequent participant and organizer. Lindley was in his forties during World War II, and he was a World War I veteran, an Indiana native, and a graduate of the University of Idaho—the very model of a responsible Washington newsman. He was also one of the eight men at Bull's house that first night in 1942 as well as a member of the ad hoc censorship committee Ray Clapper had helped form at the Press Club bar in September of that year.

Reporters cited the Lindley Rule in their private memos for the next twenty-five years, whether or not Lindley had actually attended the background session in question. The ground rules nevertheless remained unwritten until Al Friendly of the *Washington Post* wrote a widely circulated memo for his staff in July 1958, defining rules for quoting sources. The memo was so famous in reporting circles that it was

FIGURE 3.1. Ernest Lindley (*left*) of *Newsweek* was so influential that the attribution rules for background dinners were named for him. In December 1951, he appeared on the panel of the television program *Meet the Press*—with May Craig, Scotty Reston, and Lawrence Spivak—to interview Rep. John Kennedy. The moderator, Martha Rountree, produced the show with Spivak, who bought out her shares in 1953, ending Rountree's tenure and making her the only female moderator of the program for at least seventy years. Box 137, James B. Reston Papers, Courtesy of the University of Illinois Archives.

remembered and reprinted forty years later in *Nieman Reports*, a journalism trade publication.[59] Under his definition of "For background only," Friendly wrote, "This convention, also known as 'Without attribution,' 'The Lindley Rule,' 'The Rule of Compulsory Plagiarism,' or simply as 'Don't quote me,' is a common one and is used—or should be—when a person of considerable importance or delicate position is discussing a matter in circumstances in which his name cannot be used for reasons of public policy or personal vulnerability." He then outlined the obvious problem with background information: "It is often abused by persons who want to sink a knife or do a job without risking their own position or facing the consequences to themselves." But the usefulness outweighed the risks, as Friendly went on to spell out: "In some cases, however, the 'background only' procedure is legitimate and provides an honest, worthwhile story which could not be obtained in any other way."[60] From the first background dinner, reporters were wary of sources who seemed to be settling personal scores or launching trial balloons—leaking a policy to determine its popularity before committing to it. Reporters traded in information, though, meaning that obtaining some worthwhile stories outweighed the risk of abuse.

The new information-sharing system clearly benefited officials. Admiral King achieved his goal of establishing rapport with the men who wrote about him. Glen Perry, a New York *Sun* reporter who had helped Bull arrange the first dinner, wrote his editor afterward that "King, reputed to be ice-cold, hard as steel, emotionless, disagreeable, turned out on closer inspection to be a man who loves to laugh, a man with a keen sense of humor and a quick wit, an extraordinary intellect, a clear, lucid gift for explanation, and the most amazing grasp of the world situation in its military, diplomatic and economic phases. He made a profound impression upon the correspondents. By the time we said goodbye they were for him 100 percent."[61] Their support quickly proved useful. When a week later a congressman from Minnesota, Melvin Maas, criticized the joint military command on the radio, Perry told King's aide that the men who had met with the admiral would "be delighted to do stories" refuting the charge that the high command was divided.[62] Perry drafted his story, sent it to King for correction, and then gave carbon copies to five men in the dinner group who were all working for other, supposedly competing, news organizations.

That practice of providing other newsmen with the black carbon copies of a story for them to reproduce—colloquially known as "blacksheeting"—was not new to World War II. This and other ways of sharing information had become more common during the New Deal era as the federal government expanded its provenance and any individual reporter had trouble assessing the whole picture.[63] Reporters had suddenly been expected to understand economics, agriculture, law, and more, and began relying more on one another to help educate themselves. In a 1942 speech at Kansas State College, Russ Wiggins, then of the *St. Paul Pioneer Press and Dispatch* and later managing editor of the *Washington Post*, touted information sharing as a useful development during the new era of big government, rather than as a practice that in hindsight could seem to have created a false sphere of consensus. "Exchange of information among correspondents tremendously amplifies the area which any individual reporter in Washington can cover," Wiggins said. "By informal discussion at luncheon tables or during the day, in the galleries, intelligence from many sources, filtered through many correspondents, is gathered together. . . . There is more and more of this cooperation in the gallery each year, and less of the highly competitive type of reporting in which the individual plays a lone hand."[64] Reporters most often cooperated with colleagues with whom they were not in direct competition. For example, the *New York Times* and the *New York Herald Tribune*, or the Associated Press and the United Press, typically would not have shared information. However, because there were no national newspapers—the *New York Times* did not have a national edition until 1980, and *USA Today* launched in 1981—competition was limited. From about 1935 to 1980, a distinct environment of routine cooperation, enabled by a lack of direct competition and an easy feeling of mutual trust, was the state of affairs.

On November 13, 1942, after circulating the blacksheet to his colleagues, Perry wrote his editor: "They wrote their own stories, based on the material in mine and we got a good play."[65] Play was so good, in fact, that Bert Andrews, the Washington bureau chief for the *New York Herald Tribune*, had his story on the front page, with the report that "some new facts about the functioning of the Army-Navy command were learned in high military circles."[66] Using the passive voice—*were learned*—and referring to euphemistic *high circles* were the commonly applied tactics that helped correspondents obscure the sources and scenes of their reporting to outsiders. Perry wrote triumphantly to his editor that "Senator Barbour is inserting my yarn in the Congressional Record. And that, coupled with today's news from the Solomons, puts Mr. Maas right behind the eight ball."[67] (The news from the Solomon Islands that day was that the United States had sunk twenty-three Japanese vessels while losing only eight.)[68]

Seminars, dinners, and hand-picked conferences with military officials continued throughout the war. They became so routine that Perry began referring to them as the Thursday Evening Supper and Study Club. No individual had the power to escape a practice entrenched in the group. In fact, by the fall of 1944, Arthur Krock, who had so stubbornly fought pipelines, participated in the sessions himself, writing up his own private memoranda. "Today I spent two hours with General Marshall, Chief of Staff of the Army, and three hours with Admiral King, his Navy opposite number," he noted. "General Marshall had a seminar in his office for about 25 special writers and radio reporters. Admiral King talked to a private group of eight at the house of Phelps Adams, of the New York Sun, in Arlington, from 8 p.m. until 11 p.m."[69] Krock even organized a background session personally in January 1945 when Senator Harry Byrd Sr., one of his oldest friends in Washington, asked him to "get a few newspaper men together for an off-the-record talk"—as the *Times'* Scotty Reston recounted it three days later—with the new secretary of state, Edward Stettinius, at Byrd's apartment in the Shoreham Hotel.[70] The language that Reston took for granted, including *newspaper men* and *off the record*, was by then entrenched in the discourse, which for years kept women out of foreign policy reporting and prevented reporters from sharing information with the public on the grounds of gentlemanly confidences.

The dinners cemented reporters' bonds among themselves and with policy makers. The men who met with Admiral King celebrated that bond at a dinner when the war was over. In October 1945, they held a small banquet to honor King in the Statler Hotel, enjoying shrimp cocktails, lamb chops with pineapple slices and béarnaise sauce, and French Burgundy (fig. 3.2).[71] The Statler had opened in January 1943 at the height of Washington's housing crunch and had a ballroom especially designed for the needs of the annual Gridiron Club dinner, including a designated entrance for the president of the United States and ample dressing rooms near the dining room.[72] The men who feted King puckishly called themselves the "Surviving Veterans of the Battle of Virginia." For the most part, they had stayed in Washington during the war, an older group of men who wanted to feel the importance of their own wartime experiences. Twenty-six journalists from newspaper

FIGURE 3.2. In October 1945, the "Surviving Veterans of the Battle of Virginia"—newsmen who had background sessions with Admiral Ernest J. King in the suburbs of Virginia during World War II—held a banquet in the admiral's honor at Washington's Statler Hotel. Box 2, Joseph C. Harsch Papers, Wisconsin Historical Society.

and radio were listed as these veterans—none of them from the *Chicago Tribune*, the isolationist paper whose newsmen did not contribute to, and therefore did not need to be represented in, the sphere of consensus.[73] Because their newspaper was so influential in the Midwest and had such a high circulation, the men of the *Tribune* would never be automatically excluded from all background dinners. But their peers believed they did not have the same sense of responsibility, and they were sometimes left out.

The reporters presented King with a tongue-in-cheek citation that solidified all their statuses as insiders, sharing a joke with the admiral: "For conspicuous bravery and intrepidity above and beyond the call of duty in performance of which he brilliantly rejected his best professional advice and daringly ignored his own natural instincts, and alone and single-handedly, at a moment when adverse winds of publicity were threatening to sink the whole fleet, exposed himself to a frontal assault by the picked shock troops of the journalistic enemy led by some of the most reprehensible and blood-thirsty Washington correspondents, and . . . conquered and captivated them completely."[74] Safe in postwar Washington, totalitarianism defeated, these newspapermen celebrated the end of the war, the relaxation of wartime food rationing, and the beginning of a new system of information sharing among responsible reporters.

4

THE GENTLEMEN OF THE
POSTWAR PRESS

Post–World War II Washington barely resembled the town it had been just fifteen years earlier, except in one important way: the men inside the social and professional clubs and banquet halls kept their doors closed to those they considered outsiders. Their experiences of the war made exclusion seem more essential than ever. The kind of information that during the war had seemed best kept among the trustworthy responsible reporters—the news of US foreign policy—continued to strike the men arranging background occasions as best suited for themselves alone. Women, "irresponsible" white men (too far to the right or left politically or prone to leaks), and reporters of color were not assigned foreign policy beats on mainstream newspapers in Washington from the 1940s through the 1960s. Between the foreign language press, the Black press, and the independent press, large events like presidential press conferences—now taking place in an auditorium across from the White House instead of informally around the president's desk, as Roosevelt had often done—could be quite diverse (fig. 4.1). However, background sessions continued to include only gentlemen and institutionalized a two-tier system of information. The privileged men of the top tier determined how foreign affairs would be reported in mainstream news outlets and what the dominant discourse would be.

FIGURE 4.1. Presidential press conferences, such as this 1950 conference at the Old State Department Building during the Truman administration, were open to all members of the press—including the many women reporters in Washington, easily spotted here by their hats. Because these forums were so large and inclusive, the white men of the press continued to hold smaller background dinners with public officials. Accession number: 96–151, Harry S. Truman Library.

Those Fit for "Fuller Disclosure of the Facts"

In December 1945, Secretary of State James F. Byrnes traveled to Moscow for a foreign ministers' conference. When he returned, critics said he had given away too much to the Soviets and should not have agreed to United Nations oversight of atomic energy without more safeguards in place for the United States.[1] With Byrnes's popularity at a low ebb, the columnist and Washington insider Joe Alsop sent "Jimmy," as he called the secretary, "some quite unsolicited and probably undesired advice" to help Byrnes overcome his "suffering from needlessly bad press."[2] His bad press had nothing to do with policy, Alsop argued, but came down to relationships with the men who wrote about foreign policy in Washington.

At that time, Alsop was a thirty-four-year-old syndicated columnist for the *New York Herald Tribune* who had arrived in Washington seven years earlier with decisive "connectability."[3] He came from an old Connecticut family and had attended the elite Groton preparatory school and then Harvard University, where he earned the blue bloods' ultimate seal of approval: membership in the Porcellian Club. He was gay, but his many class-based connections made him acceptable in Washington society. During a period of intense homophobia in America, Alsop was not out of the closet, though within Washington his homosexuality was an open secret.[4] The main justification for the Lavender Scare during the late 1940s and 1950s—the purge of homosexuals from the federal government amid the Second Red Scare—was that someone who was gay was, by definition, closeted and therefore could be blackmailed by communists.[5] But Alsop was barely closeted, and when the KGB did indeed try to blackmail him in 1957, he immediately told his friends in the CIA, who intervened on his behalf. Allen Dulles, the director of the CIA, personally signed a letter to the lavender- and red-hunting FBI director J. Edgar Hoover, enclosing a memo that stated, "Subject admits that since youth he has been a congenital homosexual."[6] Dulles strongly hinted to Hoover that the FBI better not make a federal case of it. This incident occurred a few years after the height of the Lavender Scare, so perhaps its timing was lucky for Alsop. However, another likely reason behind Dulles's intervention was that Alsop was protected, then and throughout his career, because of his connectedness among the East Coast elite and his special upper-class status. Those factors, combined with his power as a columnist, made him too influential to slight.

In his elite upbringing, Alsop was unlike most of his fellow reporters; the *Harvard Crimson* would not start minting Washington newspaper correspondents until the 1960s and 1970s. But like them, he did serve in the US armed forces in World War II. In June 1941, he enlisted in the United States Navy. Six months later, he was in Hong Kong when the Japanese captured it, and he spent the following six months in a prisoner of war camp before a prisoner exchange repatriated him with a group of diplomats and newspapermen. After recovering, Alsop took a commission in the United States Army Air Forces. When he returned to Washington in the late fall of 1945, he resumed his column with a new writing partner: his younger brother, Stewart, a Groton and Yale man who, as a straight man with an attractive British wife, was even more connectable than Joe. Stew was close friends with Scotty Reston of the *New York Times*, Eric Sevareid of CBS, and the rest of that cohort. He had spent the early war in the British army, then in the United States Army and as a parachutist for the Office of Strategic Services. The Alsop brothers were committed to internationalist ideals and to seeing the United States fulfill a leadership role in the postwar world—a viewpoint they made clear in their syndicated "Matter of Fact" column throughout the postwar period.

In his 1945 letter to Byrnes, Joe Alsop explained, "Your press is bad because very few American newspapermen understand the difficulties which confront you, and because none are given the opportunity to gain that understanding." The columnist wrote that there was resentment among newsmen that Byrnes had secluded himself. Everyone else in the State Department was so cautious about talking to the press that no one had friends there anymore. "A bad press for you, unfortunately, means diminished popular support for the policy which you are developing, and this is really grave in its consequences."[7] The world was only a few months past the end of the war. World War III would be the grave consequence of not pursuing an internationalist policy in which the United States took a strong role in postwar rebuilding, the dominant thinking went at the time.

Alsop told Byrnes that the difficulty lay with open press conferences and the misguided theory that information too sensitive to be given out at such gatherings was too sensitive to be shared at all. "Instead, the press conference should be regarded merely as a forum for formal statements; and a distinction should be made between those newspapermen who are, so to speak, only of press conference caliber, and those whose background, training and reliability fits them for fuller disclosure of the facts."[8] Women, African Americans, foreigners, and unconnectable white men would have been "only of press conference caliber," in Alsop's judgment. The true gentlemen of the press, however, could be trusted. As pretentious as he was, Alsop would not necessarily have discriminated by class background or breeding. Instead, within Washington's professionally based social circles, "synthetic social capital"—

of the kind that Reston and the diplomatic reporter Wallie Deuel had acquired through their work connections—was a suitable substitute for an expensive upbringing.[9] As white men working for influential news organizations, Reston and Deuel had the proper "background, training and reliability" to be trusted.

Alsop continued to Byrnes, "You can be confident that if you take the trouble to inform them, they will play the game square with you. If you win over the small number of newspapermen who dominate opinion—who give the lead, so to speak, to the rest—you can then be confident of a good press." This trickle-down theory of information sharing was widely held in Washington, forming the backbone of the background system and explaining the echo chamber, but rarely so baldly committed to paper. In concluding, Alsop listed the steps that Byrnes needed to take, with the final one being "adoption of some such informal system as I have outlined, by which these men will be admitted to your confidence, and thus made to serve as channels through which explanations of American policy may be conveyed to the public."[10] Members of the press resented being used as conveyors of official positions and worked hard to assert their theoretical independence from the government. But reporters needed access to information above all; their jobs depended on it. If a newsman was fortunate enough to be considered a gentleman, he would be foolish to protest his inclusion in small, off-the-record discussions with officials.

James Byrnes's press relations did improve over the next few months, especially with columnists, including Roscoe Drummond, the bureau chief of the influential *Christian Science Monitor*, and Arthur Krock, the bureau chief of the *New York Times*. Drummond and Krock were both Veterans of the Battle of Virginia—Admiral Ernest J. King's group of trusted newsmen from World War II—and would have been men Alsop considered able to "give the lead." When the United Nations met in March and April of 1946, one of Drummond's front-page "State of the Nation" columns began with the line, "It is the consensus of the American press corps reporting the United Nations—a group not casually impressed—that Secretary of State James F. Byrnes has handled his share of the Security Council deliberations with skill and force and persuasiveness."[11] Here Drummond claimed he was giving not his own opinion but one at which all the working press covering the UN had arrived. He praised Byrnes especially for his handling of a successful resolution to accept the Soviet Union's pledge to remove troops from Iran and to delay revisiting the issue. On the Sunday after the resolution had been passed, the Alsop brothers' column, which ran in the *New York Herald Tribune*, the *Washington Post*, and around two hundred other newspapers, began, "There is no longer any question of the success of Secretary of State James F. Byrnes' approach to the Iranian problem in the United Nations Security Council."[12] They noted that Byrnes had avoided an irreparable break with the Soviets and that another foreign ministers' meeting, taken as a sign of cooperation in peace negotiations, would be the result. Joe Alsop would later be remembered as a "cold warrior," and although he would come to believe that the United States was in a war of ideas with the Soviet Union, in the spring of 1946 he was advocating that the United States keep the alliance from World War II intact. Communism was not yet the most important issue of the postwar world, nor, as we will see, would it ever become central to most of the newsmen reporting on foreign affairs.

Krock's column of the same Sunday, in an edition with twice the circulation as the weekday newspaper, directly referred to a positive shift in opinion about Byrnes in the previous few months. "One round of acclaim after a season of sporadic criticism does not assure that a Secretary of State will in history be adjudged great or even successful," the article cautiously began. "But it does provide a foundation on which these judgments can be built. And this opportunity has now come to James F. Byrnes of South Carolina, in consequence of a personal achievement," it continued, referring to the Iran resolution.[13] Byrnes dashed off a typical note of appreciation: "Thanks very much for your complimentary article which appeared in Sunday's Times. You were very generous to me."[14] Krock wrote back tellingly, "It was no more than you deserve. If my feeling toward you personally were not so friendly, I should perhaps have gone further. But I have learned to distrust my judgment where friendship is involved."[15] Krock would not have wanted to appear to his readers as someone propping up the secretary of state. But he had no similar scruples about appearing that way to Byrnes.

Ongoing discussions over whether war with the Soviet Union was inevitable became an easy excuse for differentiating those reporters who were merely press conference caliber from those who could be trusted with more information. After all, Soviet spies working at *Pravda* could slip into large press conferences.[16] The private sessions that supplemented the press conferences and replaced them in importance then helped bind reporters to their sources and to one another with the easy camaraderie of men sharing confidences over bourbon.

Byrnes was cultivating not just the columnists but also the news reporters. At a typical April 1946 background session, Wallie Deuel of the *Chicago Daily News* entered Byrnes's office around 5:15 p.m. and noticed that Bert Andrews, the *Herald Tribune* man, had "disappeared into the little boys' room to the left of the door entering from the press conference room, where we had assembled, and that he and the Sec were pouring drinks out of an Old Grand Dad bottle." Byrnes good-naturedly called out that there was nothing exclusive about the gathering at the makeshift bar, and he waved Deuel and a few others in. The men poured themselves bourbon and water into plain water glasses and gathered around the secretary's desk. "We talk for an hour and a half. On the way out, we have another snort. It is all utterly informal and friendly, as JFB almost always seems to be."[17]

Even Byrnes's new friends in the press could not save him from President Harry S. Truman, who was finding him to be a political liability as Truman became increasingly anti-Soviet.[18] At the same time, Truman allowed Byrnes to stay on for more than seven months after asking for a private submission of his letter of resignation. Byrnes's friendly relationship with the Washington press corps would have played no small part in securing that lengthy period of protection. That relationship also set newsmen's expectations for informal sessions and bourbon with the future secretaries of state, many of whom—though not as personally popular as Byrnes—benefited from the reporters' having already built their own network of trustworthy men of higher caliber.

Other government officials began adopting informal background sessions as their efficacy became more widely accepted in the State Department. (State was always a step behind the War Department, which had adopted these sessions during the war.) In 1948, when the diplomat Averell Harriman was based in Paris for the Economic Cooperation Administration, the organization that administered the Marshall Plan, his top press relations man—himself a Washington reporter on leave—imported the custom of background dinners for him. Like James Byrnes and other elite policy makers, Harriman mistrusted reporters at press conferences. However, getting to know them socially and individually helped him stop regarding them as the enemy. The trustworthiness of *gentlemen* in particular was so inherent to the larger concept of journalistic responsibility that a press aide recalled nearly twenty years later, "Somehow, psychologically, Mr. Harriman must have thought that if the fellow was in his house drinking his whiskey, he obviously was a gentleman or he wouldn't have gotten there in the first place, and therefore one could trust him. Relations were much improved."[19]

Reporters of this period were often more informed than congressmen, who were not always gentlemen but, more important, had no punishment mechanism for peers who betrayed confidences. At one completely off-the-record talk with reporters in the summer of 1947, George C. Marshall, Byrnes's successor as secretary of state, ended with a "bitter complaint" that he had spoken to sixteen congressmen who had "persuaded him to talk frankly under a pledge of absolute confidence." One, whom Marshall called an "SOB" to the reporters, had then told the columnist Drew Pearson what had been said. "That little anecdote was by way of an obvious warning," Tom Reynolds of the *Chicago Sun* wrote at the end of his notes. Reynolds then provided his notes to Wallie Deuel of the *Chicago Daily News*, who could not attend the conference. The two men were both trustworthy insiders, which mattered more than the fact that they were ostensibly competitors.[20] A congressman telling Pearson, with a reputation for publishing leaks, made him an SOB, but Reynolds telling Deuel in confidence would have been considered responsible.

It is not clear which of Pearson's many scoops came from that partic-

ular leak. However, an especially striking example of the kind of information that Marshall shared with reporters that reporters then did not
share with their readers concerns China, where communists were near-
ing victory in a lengthy civil war. "We need to clear up the problem [of
China] for the US people, but to tell the full truth would pull the rug
from Chiang and destroy him," Marshall had said in confidence one
Friday afternoon at the Statler Hotel.[21] He was referring to Chiang Kai-
shek, head of the anticommunist Kuomintang government, which had
retreated to Taiwan. The "truth" he referenced was that the US government believed that Chiang was incompetent and unreliable. Marshall
"cite[d] figures on losses of ammunition and equipment by the KMT
forces in recent weeks that are absolutely appalling. They have been
surrendering them to the CP faster than we could supply them even if
we didn't have any other troubles."[22] The State Department's internal
notes from the meeting were labeled *Extremely Confidential*, despite
the fact that twenty-six newsmen had been present.[23] Of these, six were
from wire services, four from broadcasting networks, three from magazines, and thirteen covering every important outlet with the notable
exception of the right-leaning *Chicago Tribune*. All were trustworthy;
and while coverage of Chiang was more neutral than actually favorable
in the coming years, little of it was as negative as it seems to have been
in the private discussions.[24]

The off-the-record culture standardized during the war quickly became
so ingrained that reporters often took it for granted, no longer thinking
of it suspiciously in terms of pipelines. But inherent problems with the
system remained. Raymond P. "Peter" Brandt, the chief Washington
correspondent for the *St. Louis Post-Dispatch*, unintentionally reflected
the tensions in the new culture in a 1947 memo to his editor in Missouri. In response to a query about W. M. Kiplinger, who published a
small, subscription-based Washington newsletter, Brandt wrote, "I do
not know what Kiplinger meant in his Feb. 1 letter when he said that
our political leaders should say publicly what they say privately. I suspect that it was put in to indicate to his subscribers that he has sources
of information denied reporters. This I doubt." Yet having just denied a

difference between public and private information, he continued, without apparent irony, "At an off-the-record session with Admiral [Ernest] King last night I put this question to him in so many words. He had no idea what it meant." Brandt then mentioned yet another off-the-record dinner: "Virtually everything the politicos and military leaders have been saying about our diminishing military prestige has been said on the record, such as Marshall's press conference in which he came out strong for universal military training. I was at an off-the-record dinner with him Friday night. He said nothing on topics mentioned by Kiplinger that had not been on the record."[25]

A few weeks later, as Brandt tried to write his own story on US foreign policy, he was less sanguine and contradicted his earlier characterization of openness. "The attached is based on off-the-record sessions with Marshall, [Robert] Patterson, [James] Forrestal, [Dwight] Eisenhower, and King," he wrote his editor. "The confidential nature of these talks made the article difficult to organize and write. I firmly believe the President or some competent spokesman should officially tell the American people and the rest of the world what we are trying to do," he said, unself-consciously echoing Kiplinger's criticism. "In the meanwhile, this is the best I can do to try to inform the readers of the Post-Dispatch."[26] Responsible reporters like Brandt were resigned to the reality that they could get only some information on the record. Their spoken pledges to officials to keep something confidential outweighed unspoken pledges to readers to inform them.

Background dinners always had their critics, and whenever information about such a dinner leaked into the public record, the critics went public too. An infamous example of this—"the first really serious break by our group," as Brandt assured his nervous editor—was the so-called Carney incident, long forgotten now but almost all anyone in the capital talked about for a month in the spring of 1955.[27] On March 24, Admiral Robert Carney, the chief of naval operations, told a dinner table full of reporters that Communist China would likely attack the islands of Quemoy and Matsu off the Chinese mainland on or soon after April 15, leading to all-out war (in which the United States would join). Members of the Eisenhower administration were divided on the desirability of a war in Asia. According to the Lindley Rule, the reporters could use this information only on their own authority. Yet the front page of the *New York Herald Tribune* the next day ascribed the news to "Top American military officials."[28] The *New York Times* felt comfortable running the story as well, because Secretary of State John Foster Dulles had been in the paper's New York office for a private meeting the week before, also predicting war.[29] The *Times*man who wrote the story maintained the passive voice throughout his piece, which contained no attributions.[30] However, Carney's name quickly leaked, leading President Eisenhower, part of the antiwar faction, to rebuke him publicly and assure an angry Congress that the administration had no secret plan to go to war in three weeks' time. The dean of the Washington columnists and founder of *U.S. News and World Report*, David Lawrence, tried to come to Carney's aid, writing in the *New York Herald Tribune* that newsmen had "distorted" secondhand facts and that Carney had not said war was imminent.[31] In a note to Lawrence, Carney wrote, "My dear Dave . . . On a man-to-man basis, I admire your courageous stand; and, personally, I am most appreciative of your efforts toward putting the thing in perspective."[32]

Man-to-man bases—entailing loyalty, trust, and fellowship—were crucial. Richard Harkness of NBC, who had co-organized the dinner with the syndicated columnist Mark Childs, wrote President Eisenhower defending Admiral Carney and, implicitly, himself as host: "I feel called upon to write out of a sense of loyalty to you, my appreciation of Admiral Carney as an officer and a man, and out of my own conscience." He told Eisenhower that Carney had clearly prefaced his statements with "in my personal opinion as a military man." "I must say, also in frankness, that I feel that two reporters wrote somewhat irresponsible dispatches from the dinner."[33] Responsibility remained paramount in the minds of those reporters who freely admitted, albeit in private correspondence, that their "loyalty" lay with their commander-in-chief. Within Washington, being seen as irresponsible meant professional suicide. In a letter to his mother, Wallie Deuel called the keeping of confidences "a matter of professional life and death." Losing access to the in group would lead to being fired. "Such are some of the tightropes you walk in this business of mine every day—and the better informed you are, the tighter the ropes, because the more things you know that you have to be careful in using if you can use them at all," Deuel lamented.[34]

At the *New York Times*, the Carney incident loomed large over the newsroom. The publisher, Arthur Hays Sulzberger, was "very security minded" to a fault, as one of his reporters expressed it in a private memo to an editor.[35] A chiding letter about Carney from Sulzberger's Wall Street friend John J. McCloy—who would later return to Washington and become one of the "wise men" responsible for Vietnam policy— worried the publisher that the *Times* had acted improperly.[36] Reporters, editors, and executives on the *Times* exchanged several memoranda on what had happened, what the paper could have done differently, and who was at fault for the "doubtful ethics" of some members of the press, in the words of their chief military writer, Hanson Baldwin, who was based in New York.[37] Scotty Reston, the Washington bureau chief, told Baldwin that he agreed with his summary of the situation, with one telling exception: "I do not, however, think it is a question of doubtful ethics—it is a question of a plain breach of ethics. There was also a breach of ordinary manners," he wrote, his Presbyterian indignation leaping off the page. "After all, whatever his motives, Carney was a guest and the reporters were the hosts. Aside from our professional responsibilities, a host does not pass on, let alone publish, the remarks of a guest."[38] The system meant that sources were guests first, sources second; and what did Baldwin know about the social regulations of Washington's information economy? After all, he lived in New York. Washington was still an insular, one-industry town, where the keeping of confidences was of tantamount importance, and the ethics of man-to-man bases outweighed newspaper ethics.

Reston was not alone in his perception of proper newspaper ethics among the gentlemen of Washington. Moral indignation was also the *Washington Post* reporter Chal Roberts's reaction to a leak from a background dinner he hosted in December 1956 with the British Ambassador to Washington, Harold Caccia. *Time* magazine, which consistently ranked low in polls of periodicals that Washington reporters trusted, ran a story about the dinner. Roberts was outraged that Jim Shepley, *Time*'s bureau chief, had accepted the initial invitation, had not shown up, and then had allowed someone else from his office to file a story about the event. Roberts already resented both *Time* and Shepley, evident in his note to his publisher, Phil Graham: "If any further proof was needed that Shepley is a shit, this is it."[39] Graham tried to defend Shepley and placate Roberts, who said the explanation was not sufficient, because "(a) it does not explain the incorrect reporting which, of course, one assumes from Time," and "(b) the lapse of morality—to be charitable by using 'lapse,' which I am really not inclined to be—in reporting on a dinner to which he had been invited confidentially."[40] The incident did not sour Caccia on background dinners, which he continued to attend, but it did sour the dinner group on Shepley.

Because of the Carney incident, Reston attempted to restate the editing "ground rules on background dinners, or so-called off-the-record sessions with prominent officials." He did so mostly for the benefit of the New York editing desk of the *Times*, which never seemed to grasp the rules that obtained in Washington. "I am urging everybody in New York not to chisel on the question of attribution of these stories and not to change the Washington Bureau's attribution without checking back here," Reston wrote. He also wanted the men in New York who composed the paper not to "lead the paper with"—meaning place on the front page—stories that lacked direct attribution. "This greatly adds to The Times' responsibility for the accuracy of information, the source of which we cannot identify," he admitted.[41] Apparently, the staff of the newspaper of record was only *somewhat* certain of anything printed on its inside pages.

Like other newspapers, the St. Louis *Post-Dispatch* ran an editorial after the Carney incident saying that background dinners should cease. News writers within the capital disagreed, including those within the *Post-Dispatch*. Pete Brandt, the bureau chief, wrote a personal letter to the editorial page editor to tell him how misguided his opinion was. "By sitting down together in a congenial atmosphere for three or four hours, reporters have a chance to judge an official's philosophy, his mental processes and his judgment," Brandt maintained. "I know that our wartime sessions had a salutary effect on Admiral [Ernest] King, who had a naval reputation of stern aloofness. A dividend was that I was able to see King during working hours on urgent, important news questions more easily than I could talk to his press officer." In the end, however, it did not matter what an editorial director in St. Louis or even a publisher in New York thought: "The sessions will continue because many officials and reporters think them highly desirable," Brandt concluded.[42] Besides, most of the newspapermen entrusted with background information respected the rules governing it. As Robert Riggs, the Washington reporter for the *Louisville Courier-Journal*, concluded in an April 1955 *New Republic* article, "Despite the fate that overtook Admiral Carney, nothing so mutually advantageous as the Washington 'private briefing' will be allowed to die."[43]

Evidently, the memories of the early wartime skirmishes between reporters and officials and the difficulty newsmen had in getting information remained fresh. Twelve years after the fact, Brandt was still thinking about the King dinner. Reporters could justify the background practice on the noble grounds of serving their readers by having access to better information, as in World War II. Once a reporter was on the inside, he then had to remain liked and respected. A combination of peer pressure and the threat of losing access prevailed in limiting circulation of information. "The regular Washington reporters, specials and press association men exercise their own self restraint in not writing about confidential information," Brandt reassured his editor in 1951. He had inquired about the wisdom of voluntary censorship—what background dinners amounted to, in his eyes—of military information that should, he thought, actually be *more* closely guarded. "In our own little group which has off-the-record sessions with top officials we drop from the list any person who approaches the breaking of a confidence."[44]

Insiders, Outsiders, and Overseas Writers

In addition to the small gatherings of reporters, one particular institution formalized exclusion on the foreign affairs beat—creating insiders and outsiders—but was seldom written about publicly: Overseas

Writers. Overseas Writers was a private Washington newspapermen's club that hosted foreign policy sources for lunches and off-the-record or background questioning. The club had been founded in 1921, when a group of about ten reporters at the Cosmos Club were discussing their experiences reporting on the Versailles Treaty following World War I.[45] They believed that the public had not been adequately informed about international relations and that this had contributed to the failure of the US Senate to ratify the treaty. They also wanted to position themselves better to reciprocate the hospitality of those visiting officials who had hosted them in Europe. The group that these men founded grew into an essential but hidden tool for reporting in Washington, which had become more of a hub of global foreign policy after World War I. Within two years of its founding, the group had 70 members. By the late 1940s, it had 169.[46] In February 1947, even Joe Alsop, who snobbishly viewed press conferences as plebeian, agreed to join the group, "which I have long thought was one of the very few sensible and fruitful organizations of the kind I have ever heard of," as he wrote Roscoe Drummond, then its president.[47]

In inviting Alsop, Drummond had written, "I hope you will be able to attend our luncheons and other gatherings, and to participate in the exchange of ideas. We want to make the group representative of informed American opinion on foreign problems, which means that no one set of ideas should dominate, and your contribution to this goal will be valued."[48] At such meetings, newsmen gave themselves a sense of open-minded exchange of ideas but were also then able to smooth out dissent. The Overseas Writers luncheons were restricted to discreet white newsmen. Typical of a member's desired qualities were those described in a nominating letter of 1943: "His political views and his social manners are impeccable, and constitute an asset in any gathering."[49] The fact that a gentleman needed to have both the social manners and the political views to mix well meant that reporters considered on the fringe of either society or politics were unwelcome. They also mistrusted women and remained male-only until 1962. This exclusion held even during World War II, when so many women reporters in the capital had reported from abroad and therefore would have been eligible for membership based on the only stated criteria apart from maleness—that journalists had "been on overseas assignments and were actively practicing their profession in Washington."[50] In 1940, when the group invited as its guest lunch speaker the reporter Doris Fleeson, who had recently returned from Europe, the club president reminded members that they could bring only male guests to hear her.[51]

After World War II, Overseas Writers became even more exclusionary: only American reporters writing for American news outlets could be trusted. In January 1947, the group formally instituted a rule that some of its discussions would be for "active members only"— "to increase the usefulness of Overseas Writers by making it possible for us to provide occasionally an audience of only representatives of American-owned newspapers, magazines, press associations, and radio stations when such an audience would enable us to get the most out of our speakers."[52] In addition to reporters who worked for foreign-owned media, members at the associate level—as opposed to active members—included American men based outside Washington and therefore not steeped in the capital's off-the-record culture. In restricting these luncheons to active members, Overseas Writers controlled who had access to valuable knowledge and ensured that its speakers would never be embarrassed by journalistic impertinence. The men who gathered to talk before and after the luncheons could arrive at interpretations, compare notes, and decide what should be printed or withheld.

Overseas Writers could also control major foreign policy narratives. On May 16, 1948, the body of George Polk, a member of the group and a correspondent for CBS, was discovered in Salonika Bay in Greece. This was during the Greek Civil War and a period when the United States was pumping dollars into that country's corrupt, rightist government under the aid effort known as the Truman Doctrine. At the same time, the United States was taking over the role on the ground in Greece that the United Kingdom had previously played, with a heavy hand in the sprawling bureaucracy and a mandate to protect the status quo. In his radio broadcasts, Polk had been critical of the ruling government, making realistic appraisals of both the reigning Populists (the name for the royalists) and the insurgent Communists. In the December 1947 issue of *Harper's* magazine, he had written a lengthy piece on the status of the Greek army, the various government factions, and the US aid mission, sounding notes of doom about corruption and structural economic weaknesses. *Harper's* was a popular freelancing outlet for the men who, in their daily reporting jobs, felt constricted in what they could say. Nevertheless, Polk ended that piece in a hopeful vein, implicitly endorsing the Truman Doctrine while still questioning its feasibility by putting its main goal within quotation marks: "In 'saving democracy' we must quench the fires of both the extreme right and the extreme left to give the great majority of the democratic-minded Greek population some faith in their future. To argue that the United States should not 'interfere' in Greece is foolish—something like a fireman refusing to enter a burning house because he has no formal invitation."[53] Polk was both cynical and optimistic—the enigmatic combination so commonly found in the foreign affairs reporters of this period.

The article still enraged the Greek ruling party as well as the American Embassy in Greece. After its publication, Polk gathered more incriminating evidence on Greek government corruption. A few days after a particularly heated meeting at which he confronted a Greek official with evidence that this official had transferred money out of the country illegally, Polk was drugged at a dinner by men posing as Communist contacts, who later dragged him from his hotel in his pajamas, shot him in the head, dressed him in his suit, bound him with rope, and set him out into the bay, to give the appearance of a crime committed by the Communists whom Polk had sought to interview.[54] There is still no certainty about who killed Polk, but there is certainty that it was not the Communists and certainly not the men convicted.[55] And there is consensus that the royalist Greek police, the British Police Mission, the CIA, and the American press conspired to frame them for the murder.

The Greek government officials who investigated the murder unsurprisingly blamed the Communist guerrillas. But the *Washington Post*'s front-page version of an Associated Press story questioned that initial conclusion and included information that other newspapers using the same AP copy—like the more conservative *Chicago Daily Tribune* and

Los Angeles Times—did not. The AP/*Post* version concluded with the information that Polk had told a fellow correspondent he had received threatening phone calls from anti-Communists, which "indicated that anti-Communists might have desired his death."[56] (The editing of AP news stories in different parts of the country is one of many ways conversations inside and outside the capital could differ.)

Two Washington columnists warned that the charge that the Communists had killed Polk "must not be taken at face value," as Mark Childs put it in his nationally syndicated column, "Washington Calling." "This comes at a time when rumors persist of a new build-up to be launched from Athens and Washington—a build-up of the need for American troops in Greece. What George Polk might have said and written when he returned to the United States—as he planned to do—could have interfered with that build-up," Childs wrote, implicating the Greek ruling party and, by extension, the United States, in Polk's murder.[57] Three days later, Drew Pearson, who wrote the syndicated "Washington Merry-Go-Round" column and was known for rooting out corruption, stated the case more bluntly: "Evidence points to the probability that rightest [*sic*] forces within the government were responsible for Polk's murder."[58]

Childs and Pearson represented common views in those early weeks after the murder. Tracing the shift in the mainstream viewpoint demonstrates how homogeneity, collaboration, and contact among reporters created consensus about their duty as American citizens to protect national security and not to challenge their readers' faith in "American folklore," as the correspondent Joe Harsch put it on another occasion.[59] Originally, the dominant opinion within Washington was that the ruling royalist party had wanted to dispose of Polk and had framed the Communists. In fact, when Dwight Griswold, the US aid commissioner to Greece, spoke on background at an Overseas Writers lunch at the Statler on May 26, 1948, ten days after Polk's body had surfaced, he was trying to overcome that interpretation. "Griswold is doubtful of the validity of the assumption that Polk was murdered by Rightists," Wallie Deuel noted. (Griswold, incidentally, was someone whom Polk had called an "unmitigated jerk" in a 1947 letter to his family.)[60] "He thinks it extremely doubtful that it will ever be ascertained how Polk was killed and by whom. . . . Rightists had nothing to gain by alienating US public opinion; Leftists have much to gain by doing so."[61] The tide began turning. Two days later, the *Washington Post* ran an editorial cautioning that the right wing of the Greek government had little incentive to murder Polk and that "it may well be, therefore, that George Polk was killed by the Communists themselves."[62]

Polk was thirty-four years old when he was killed and had served in the United States Navy during World War II. Handsome, affable, and respected by his peers, he naturally had many friends among the members of Overseas Writers, and they did not trust the Greek government to investigate the murder. They voted on May 21, 1948, to form a committee "to determine whether a full and complete inquiry into all the circumstances of the crime is being conducted."[63] But they also wanted to conduct an investigation that their own government would tacitly endorse and aid, not paint as communistic. They invited the veteran columnist Walter Lippmann to head the committee, since he seemed perfectly to balance the interests of the newsmen pursuing the truth with the interests of the nation pursuing peace in Europe. Lippmann had credibility with the newsmen, since he had lately been so critical of the Truman Doctrine. And while not in the federal government's pocket, he was already an éminence grise of Washington and an unlikely target for a House Un-American Activities Committee investigation or other retribution.[64] The Polk committee comprised sixteen members, all working for different newspapers or syndicated services and representing a cross section of the Washington press, giving an expectation of independence and nonconformity.

Overseas Writers was not the only journalists' group investigating the Polk murder, but it wanted to be. Its members sought total control over the report's conclusion and, in fact, promised Secretary of State George Marshall that this would be so, in return for access to State Department information. So Overseas Writers men served as liaisons to other groups in which they also held membership, tightening the circle rather than opening it up to outsiders. For instance, the American Society of Newspaper Editors designated Lippmann and the *Wash-*

ington Evening Star's Benjamin McKelway, already on the committee, as its two affiliated representatives; the State Department Correspondents' Association appointed John Reichmann of International News Service, also one of the sixteen; the United Nations Correspondents' Association made Scotty Reston its man on the ground, despite the fact that Thomas J. Hamilton, a New Yorker, was the *New York Times*' UN correspondent. The iconoclastic reporter I. F. "Izzy" Stone, then in New York, tried to investigate with other members of the New York Newspaper Guild but got no government cooperation. He was left a single dissenting voice, writing critically about the Polk investigations for the *Daily Compass*, a short-lived leftist newspaper in New York City.

There is no evidence of a blatant press-assisted cover-up on behalf of the Greek government and the British intelligence service, which had taken a suspiciously active interest in the Polk case. At the same time, Overseas Writers members never put themselves in a position where they might need to be part of a cover-up. Instead, they selected as their "independent" investigator General William J. "Wild Bill" Donovan, who during the war had been founder and director of the Office of Strategic Services. As the committee's chief counsel, Donovan ran the investigation, traveling to Greece and making sure all evidence and documents flowed through him (or, more frequently, stopped with him, as a reporter discovered during the 1980s).[65] Donovan had personal relationships with several Overseas Writers members, some of whom, like Wallie Deuel, had worked for him during the war and knew his modus operandi well. In fact, just one month before the investigation began, Deuel had written his boss at the *Chicago Daily News* with insight into Donovan. Responding to a query about a piece on intelligence operations, he noted, "The anonymous article in last month's Atlantic was written by Bill Donovan, and was one of the most disingenuous—and ingenious—jobs of special pleading I've ever seen him do, which is saying a lot."[66] In other words, these men were under no illusion about how truly independent of the US government Donovan would be, nor did they have faith in his transparency, despite their public rhetoric that they would follow the investigation no matter where it led.

In 1951, after a trial during which the Greek government blamed the

Communists—and one in particular—for Polk's murder, the Overseas Writers committee published a seventy-six-page pamphlet of Donovan's findings, supporting documents, and trial transcripts. Within its lengthy report, it printed evidence pointing to its own uncertainty about the verdict, including a letter from a Harvard professor indicating that the convicted man could not possibly have committed the crime. However, the committee concluded that the defendant had received a fair trial and was responsible for the murder. Izzy Stone wrote a devastating indictment of the committee in a five-part series in the *Daily Compass*: "Some day perhaps the truth will be known and these men will blush for their role in its unfolding."[67]

The scholarly and journalistic investigations into the trial during the 1980s and 1990s, which relied on newly declassified documents, contain no smoking gun that proved reporters' complicity. Yet all three accounts conclude that the trial was a sham and that there was some collusion between officials and reporters to deny that fact. The Deuel papers do contain evidence that the men of Overseas Writers knew more of the truth or had greater doubts than they admitted in print. A State Department source told Deuel in January 1949 that the British intelligence services had been involved in the Polk murder—a revelation that, if leaked, would have harmed the US position in Greece as well as the CIA's relationship with British intelligence. In a letter to his editor that Deuel seems not to have completed or mailed, he wrote that he had bumped into a source on whom the left-leaning Robert Allen had based a column. Deuel wanted to let the source know that the *Chicago Daily News* had run the syndicated piece. "He was much gratified, and in the resulting glow, told me the real, inside story of the killing of George Polk," Deuel wrote. "I thought you ought to know it. It seems that it was the British Secret Service that did the job. They did it because Polk was about to see [Communist leader] Markos and Markos was about to ask Polk to act as intermediary between the rebels and the Athens government in working out peace terms. H M Government didn't want there to be peace, so they liquidated George. It's perfectly obvious, once you stop and think a little."[68] Deuel was active in Overseas Writers, serving on its executive committee from 1948 to 1951, the years of the Polk committee. Of the six men who served on the executive committee with Deuel, five were also on the Polk committee: Ernest Lindley (of the Lindley Rule), Scotty Reston, Joe Harsch of CBS and the *Monitor*, Paul Wooton of the New Orleans *Times-Picayune*, and Peter Edson, a syndicated columnist for the Newspaper Enterprise Association. (Edson lived one block away from the Deuels, was from Wabash, Indiana, was a frequent background session participant, and was, in Deuel's assessment to his mother, "a very good guy."[69] Pete Edson was one of the boys.) Although it makes sense that Deuel did not ultimately mail information about British intelligence to an outsider—his editor in Chicago—it is inconceivable that he would not have verbally discussed it with one or more of the men on the Overseas Writers Polk committee, or that his State Department source would not have told anyone else in their circle.

At the time, the men did "think a little," as Deuel put it, about the role of Her Majesty's government and their own government in Polk's murder, but none ever admitted to the doubts. Lippmann's biographer, the historian Ronald Steel, repudiates the idea that Lippmann would have actively engaged in a cover-up. But he still acknowledged that he would have known the truth. "When, for example, he was appointed by a newsmen's committee to head the investigation of the murder of George Polk . . . he did not seriously question the State Department's contention that communist guerrillas were responsible—even though he privately recognized that discrepancies in the evidence pointed damningly toward the Greek government and the CIA," Steel wrote. "Lippmann would never have gone along with a State Department cover-up, but neither could he believe that the honorable men he knew would be capable of such an infamous action."[70] But if Lippmann did not "seriously question" the results of the investigation, it would have been because he did not want to know the answers. Gentlemen kept their doubts private and discussed them verbally among themselves at the Statler. They did not announce them to the world in print. Selecting William Donovan, head of America's first intelligence agency, to run the Overseas Writers investigation meant that no journalist on the committee would need to engage in a cover-up. Donovan would handle everything for them, and they could feel like responsible newsmen as well as responsible citizens.

Joe Harsch's memoirs came out in 1993, shortly after two books investigating the Polk murder were released, and he absolved himself about as poorly as Steel absolves Walter Lippmann. Of the two living members of the Overseas Writers committee investigating the murder, he and Reston, Harsch wrote, "Both of us believe that the Greek government produced a flawed and improbable version of what happened, but we cannot accept that any member of the committee, and certainly not our chairman, Walter Lippmann, ever consciously participated in a whitewash or cover-up."[71] They knew that Donovan would likely have taken care of any cover-up on his own, though, without needing to involve any journalists "consciously." In fact, when one of Izzy Stone's biographers, Myra MacPherson, interviewed Reston in 1990, he remembered nothing about the committee at all, only that as a general matter, he would not have trusted Donovan's judgment. "If we did, we were stupid," he told MacPherson.[72] Committee members did not trust the devious Donovan, and they were not stupid. They simply could not act or write independently when they had agreed to be part of a group.

Other reporters pointedly stationed themselves outside the group. Stone and the columnist Drew Pearson were kept outside or at arm's length in places like Overseas Writers. Both men were exceptions to the rule of white reportorial privilege. Neither held great influence within Washington reporting circles, and neither was a diplomatic reporter covering daily foreign policy decisions. They were significant exceptions to the sphere of consensus, but they were not typical of the cohort of men who provided the majority of Americans with their foreign policy news.

Stone had been involved in the Popular Front and the League of American Writers during the 1930s and 1940s, and official Washington considered him to be a "fellow traveler" of the Communist Party.[73] During the 1940s, he had written mainly for *PM* and the *Nation* magazine, living in Washington and New York before settling in Washington in 1953 to begin his own newsletter, *I. F. Stone's Weekly*. In his reporting,

Stone relied on public documents, especially underreported congressional hearings, rather than interviews or any method requiring access to certain sources or private spaces.[74] He published the newsletter himself so he had no newsroom bosses to please, making him one of the only truly independent voices of the period. His views often aligned with those of the mostly liberal foreign policy reporters at other newspapers, but the difference was that he wrote straightforwardly to his readers about what was going on in Washington. Instead of writing anguished memos to editors about what to withhold from the public and couching stories in veiled language clear only to other insiders, he simply told the public what was happening.

Overseas Writers considered Stone too radical to be a member. When a friend finally put his name up for membership during the late 1960s, Stone ended up withdrawing from consideration after members questioned his fitness to join and he decided he did not need the trouble.[75] Stone was not even a member of the larger National Press Club. He had resigned in 1941, after the club would not permit him to bring a Black guest to dine there. When Stone reapplied for admission after the club integrated during the 1950s—allowing in a single Black member in 1955—he was blackballed. (The club readmitted him in 1981 at the age of seventy-three, when iconoclasm was back in fashion and Stone was too old to be considered a threat.)

The muckraking syndicated columnist and radio commentator Drew Pearson occupied a liminal space in the newsmen's sphere. He had a huge reader- and listenership nationwide and more friends in Washington than Stone.[76] He was a frequent dining companion and party guest, as long as the Lindley Rule was not in effect. With his reputation for leaking, he was rarely included in off-the-record gatherings. In thirty-eight years as a columnist, he was sued for libel 275 times. Pearson especially targeted corruption, and while his stories could be damaging to corrupt public officials, he had a reputation for never letting the truth get in the way of a good story. Other Washington reporters did not take him seriously, no matter how well known he was in American households. So while he was influential outside the capital, his peers often dismissed his work as irresponsible. In 1946, for instance, Roy Howard, the Scripps-Howard newspaper executive based in New York, wrote Deac Parker, the managing editor at his Washington paper, to ask what he thought of one of Pearson's allegations. Parker assured Howard that even if there were some truth to it, they need not follow up on Pearson, since his "sensations never seem to pan out." If the editor had any faith in Pearson, he wrote, he and every other newspaper and press association would hire an investigator to do nothing but follow up on his leads. But they didn't. "I must say—or confess—that I read him regularly and listen to him on his Sunday night radio program. But, despite the fact that he is interesting, he nets out phony. He carries a lot of reader and listening interest but very little weight."[77] Parker made Pearson seem benign; some reporters disliked him more actively. One *St. Louis Post-Dispatch* political reporter believed that one of Pearson's "legmen"—someone who helped with reporting—had called up a source at the White House pretending to be him. "My name may have been selected for use in this duplicity because it may be known that I personally consider Pearson's methods ruthless and vindictive, an opinion shared by the majority of the Washington press," the reporter wrote in an internal memo, hoping to absolve himself of a leak perpetrated in his name.[78]

Within Washington, Pearson's syndicated column, "The Washington Merry-Go-Round," ran in the mainstream *Washington Post*, so his tactics sometimes also put him at odds with the paper's more conservative editors. In September and October 1944, the *Post* refused to publish a series of Pearson's columns criticizing John Foster Dulles, then under consideration as a potential secretary of state by the Republican presidential candidate Thomas Dewey. The *Post*'s managing editor, Alexander F. "Casey" Jones, who also had a personal vendetta against Pearson for something Pearson had written about his son, wrote him an explanation: "You have a formula that is very effective in the hinterland, as evidenced by the vote in the recent Saturday Review of Literature poll. In the same poll, on the basis of influence in Washington from the standpoint of reliability, you probably noticed that you got two votes."[79]

The attitude within Washington that there was a "hinterland"—believed to be narrow-minded and uninformed—was one of the reasons the echo chamber could exist in the capital. Then, in a new paragraph that consisted of one imperious sentence, the *Post* editor declared, "The Washington Post is not published for the benefit of the hinterland." Although few journalists were as blatantly condescending as Jones, they did believe that living in Washington meant that they knew better and needed to educate the rest of the country on its worldwide responsibilities. The public also sometimes needed to be protected from the truth.

Pearson's formula, as the managing editor accurately described it, was leftist and critical and probably led to Pearson's having more accurately characterized Dulles early on than any other reporter did in public besides perhaps Izzy Stone. (Stone repeatedly pointed out that both Dulles brothers had happily done business with Nazis during the 1930s.)[80] The article that the *Post* killed, which still ran in outlets outside Washington, stated, "Almost any lawyer, especially one connected with so large a firm, has to take all kinds of cases, representing all views and walks of life. However . . . many international cases, some connected with the dictator countries, seemed to gravitate toward John Dulles."[81] He was thus identifying in 1944 the criticisms of the Dulles brothers—especially their close ties to rightist dictators—that would become standard reporting during the 1950s and 1960s.

Though he was not welcome in professional reporting circles, Pearson nonetheless remained socially connected, including to the owners of the *Post*, Eugene and Agnes Meyer, and their daughter and son-in-law, Kay and Phil Graham. The fact that Pearson and Meyer's friendship survived the 1944 Dulles incident was largely due to Pearson's wife, Luvie, a popular and well-connected woman. During the disagreement, she went by herself to see Eugene Meyer at home and apologized on behalf of her husband.[82] She then persuaded Drew to hand-write Meyer a letter of apology, and Meyer and Pearson met the following day to clear the air. Pearson did have connectability, but he was still not part of the consensus-making group of reporters who attended Overseas Writers and background conferences. His willingness to criticize public figures so harshly in print, rather than only privately, put him outside the mainstream.

That responsible reporters also needed to be gentlemen was gospel in Washington at midcentury. Their trust among themselves was central to their operations. They recognized at the time that the professionally helpful systems they had established were also ethically dubious. Still, reporters understandably withheld information and tolerated hypocrisy because their own livelihoods and reputations were at stake. In 1966, Chal Roberts, still at the *Washington Post*, recalled an early background meeting that his predecessor as the *Post*'s diplomatic reporter, Ferdie Kuhn, had skipped, "on the grounds that the Secretary of State had no business operating this way. If he wanted to say what he wanted to say, he should say it on the public record. A lot of people felt that way." But Roberts admitted, "This was then really a new technique, but naturally we bent to it because we couldn't escape it. It went on and on and on, and it's been carried on by all of his successors—even the present Secretary," referring at the time to Dean Rusk.[83] Once background dinners had become part of routine reporting in Washington, there was no escape for anyone who wanted to remain on the inside.

5

BATTLING THE
"RESIDUE OF ISOLATION"

Beginning during the 1930s, Arthur Hays Sulzberger, the publisher of the *New York Times*, believed that his newspaper should play an important role in promoting "collective security"—a key phrase for internationalists who had been advocating for US participation in a supranational peace organization since World War I.[1] In October 1939, a month after Hitler invaded Poland, Sulzberger laid out his thoughts on the world situation in a memo he labeled *Strictly Personal*. "Out of all this strain and effort and bloodshed there must come a Bill of Rights for the peoples of Europe and the world, with some type of collective security for guaranteeing it," he wrote. He argued that the type of union was "immaterial" and continued, "The task before The New York Times is to prepare the country to the best of its ability to be ready for such an effort at the proper time. It will not be easy. Our isolation shell seems to be hardening, and yet I am certain it can and must be done."[2] He believed that the *Times* could help permanently move the country from isolationism to internationalism—as indeed it and other news media, chief among them radio, had started to do.[3] Central to achieving collective security was the idea of never again returning to peacetime, as it was previously understood, or at least of waging peace as war. "Peace, if we are to maintain it, cannot be static and opposed to the dynamic quality of war. We must wage peace and sacrifice for peace and work for peace, only then can we enjoy it," Sulzberger said in speeches during World War II.[4]

Sulzberger privately expressed a willingness for the Great Powers to be "ruthless" in their postwar planning. His daughter, Ruth, who spent part of the war as a Red Cross nurse in England, wrote him from there in the spring of 1945, concerned about how much power the Allies would have over the postwar world. That correspondence illustrates how an internationalist's anxiety about isolationism translated so seamlessly into what would become support for US interference in other nations for the next eighty years at least. Sulzberger wrote, "I agree with you that the Dumbarton Oaks plan places extraordinary power in the hands of the great nations; but if we can preserve peace, we will have accomplished our purpose, for democracy flourishes only in peace, and, I am confident, is a way of life that all will seek sooner or later if the peace is lasting." He worried that democracy might not last in the United States, though, let alone find its way around the world. "In order, however, to attain the end that I am seeking, I think you need world peace, and that is why I am in favor of being a bit ruthless if need be in order to attain it."[5] Men like Sulzberger, who wielded power in the postwar world, took for granted that the ends (peace) justified the means, even if they were "a bit ruthless."

Like many internationalists who had lamented the failure of the United States to join the League of Nations, Sulzberger wanted the Allies to establish a permanent United Nations Organization. He was just one of many influential men and women trying to shape the terms of peace. Henry Luce—the founder of *Time* magazine as well as *Life*, *Fortune*, and other Time Inc. properties—is perhaps the best remembered of the internationalist publishers. He authored an often cited 1941 *Life* magazine article, "The American Century," which argued for US intervention and preeminence around the globe. Luce's reach with the American public was wide, but within Washington policy circles, *Time* was not respected for its journalism and had a poor reputation among reporters and officials. By contrast, the *New York Times* and the *Washington Post*—along with the *New York Herald Tribune*, the *Christian Science Monitor*, and one or two other newspapers—influenced the foreign policy discourse in the capital and set the tone for many smaller newspapers nationwide. At the time, the *New York Times* had the largest Washington bureau of all newspapers: twelve correspondents in 1932, twenty in 1940, and twenty-nine in 1946. A longtime reporter for the *Times* recalled in 1983 that when he had worked for the *Washington Post* during the 1930s, the editors received a nightly dispatch telling them what was on the front page of the first edition of the *Times* so that their own second edition could reflect that content.[6] A 1950 *Time* magazine cover story about the paper—with a portrait of Sulzberger under an all-seeing eye and all-hearing ears—declared that "the *Times* has long since become the most influential paper in the nation, and since the U.S. became the No. 1 democratic power it has become the most influential in the world."[7]

The language of a "fight for peace" that Sulzberger favored was widespread during this period. The editor of the St. Paul *Dispatch and Pioneer Press* was one of the many newsmen who visited England as the war was ending. There he gained a sense of America's great responsibility for the work ahead and returned with fighting words to print. Back in Minnesota in November 1944, he wrote Russell Wiggins, his managing editor, who was still on leave in the Army Air Corps: "There is a tremendous job to be done for the peace of the world, not in this war, but against the next one. We are going to have to fight for peace in the future fully as hard as you fellows are fighting for victory in the present."[8] Fighting for peace required huge congressional budgetary appropriations, which meant continuing to combat Americans' isolationist attitudes, which had not simply disappeared during the war.

After the war, the idea of fighting for peace remained central to the diplomatic press corps' conception of its responsibilities. For it and the rest of the world, as the United States maintained permanent occupying forces around the globe, the war did not exactly end.[9] The state of being simultaneously at peace and not-at-peace affected law and policy, as the historian Mary Dudziak shows, as well as journalism, as reporters who had prided themselves on their responsibility in wartime continued to do so in the not-peace.[10] In this way, they blurred the line between objectivity and activism. Moreover, far from being the federal government's stenographers and suffering from government manipulation, they did their best in these early years to manipulate the government, especially the State Department, into providing more information.

The standard narrative about reporters during the early Cold War period is that they were passive, practicing a "journalism of deference."[11] In fact, they practiced intensive advocacy journalism on the side of internationalism. They did not call themselves advocates, as objectivity was their ruling principle, but they actively normalized the idea that the United States would need to be at the center of the postwar global order. A CBS producer's memo to the reporters covering the Italian elections of 1948 captures the dominant thinking. "The whole world knows that in the elections you are to cover, the United States Government, of which you are all nationals, is taking an active, partisan stand," he wrote. "But let it be clear that you go to Italy as reporters, not as agents. You will report this political contest with the same unbiased, fair and balanced manner you would use in reporting an election in the United States. As we are not advocates here, we will not be advocates there." The very next sentence reveals the crux of the tension: "It has been clear for many months that the United States faces the gigantic task of keeping a divided world from exploding into another world war."[12] In other words, the United States had no choice but to participate in global leadership to prevent the next world war—as it had failed to do after World War I—and that was considered objective fact.

Covering the Peace Negotiations

The peace conferences to plan the postwar world had begun before the war ended and lasted for years after—an extension of war and a crucial period for diplomatic reporters to set their standards of operation. These Washington reporters who covered foreign policy were constantly at odds with the State Department over access.

Diplomatic press coverage had changed significantly during the war. During the 1930s, only three newspapers had men working full time covering the State Department: the *Chicago Daily News*, the *New York Times*, and the *Baltimore Sun*. By 1945, twelve to fifteen men were cov-

FIGURE 5.1. This two-page spread in the *St. Louis Post-Dispatch* highlights Wallie Deuel's years as a prewar foreign correspondent and a member of the Office of Strategic Services during World War II. Newspapers during the postwar period promoted their diplomatic coverage, believing that Americans had developed a taste for international news during the war. Box 47, Wallace R. Deuel Papers, Manuscripts Division, Library of Congress.

ering the State Department full time, with another twenty to one hundred apt to show up at important press conferences.[13] Also, as the long run of Cordell Hull as secretary of state neared its end with the end of the Roosevelt administration in sight, it was assumed that his successor would wield a great deal of power in the cabinet of president-in-waiting Harry S. Truman, who had little foreign policy experience. (Roosevelt, by contrast, had led his own foreign policy initiatives.) Thus, the next secretary would require more news coverage. Another reason diplomatic coverage spiked was that during the war, Americans were thought to have developed a "news habit," craving more international news. Newspapers around the country promoted their diplomatic reporters to their readers, highlighting their reinvigorated coverage, and reporters felt pressure to provide the public with information on the new world order being made (fig. 5.1).

Disputes between newsmen and the State Department—as well as among reporters, editors, and publishers—over how to report on peace planning began at the Dumbarton Oaks conference of August 1944. When Allied nations met in Washington to plan a postwar peacekeeping organization, Hull was too ill to lead the negotiations, leaving it to Under Secretary of State Edward Stettinius Jr., who went on to serve as secretary of state from December 1944 to June 1945. Reporters considered Stettinius ill equipped for international negotiations. In fact, the diplomatic press corps viewed him as an uninformed dolt. In December 1945, Wallie Deuel, back at the *Chicago Daily News*, called him "only a precocious and well-meaning child."[14] His opinion grew harsher over time: in June 1947, Deuel simply called Stettinius "an idiot."[15] Scotty Reston of the *New York Times* had a similarly poor impression of Stettinius. During a January 1945 background dinner in the Shoreham Hotel apartment of Senator Harry Byrd Sr., Stettinius had struck the gathered newsmen unfavorably. In sharp contrast to the first time a group of newspapermen had held a background dinner with Admiral Ernest J. King, the reporters left the Shoreham thinking even worse of Stettinius. After the dinner, Reston wrote Arthur Sulzberger of the secretary: "Whenever he starts talking policy, his lack of background is overwhelming."[16]

Reston tried privately to advise Stettinius on information policy before Dumbarton Oaks, hoping to strengthen the prospects of a new international peacekeeping organization. After World War I, President Woodrow Wilson had been a guiding force behind establishing the League of Nations, but he neglected to get bipartisan congressional support. The US Senate refused to ratify the treaty that would have committed the country to a supranational organization.[17] The League failed not only in gaining the support of the United States but, the thinking went, obviously in preventing a second world war. Many of the older men in Reston's circle had witnessed its failure in the Senate firsthand, including the columnist Walter Lippmann, who had been an advisor to President Wilson. In explaining his conversation with Stettinius to Sulzberger, Reston wrote, "We talked about why the League failed and agreed that it failed, in part at least, not because the plan was bad or even because it was not approved by the majority of the people, but because the issue was confused by all kinds of irrelevant controversies." The messaging should be simple and clear, Reston believed. "Consequently, I urged him to set up his press relations on the conference in such a way that the minds of the people would be kept on the central issue, which is how to keep peace."[18]

Reston explained to the undersecretary of state that the only way to gain favorable coverage was to saturate the press with information, both to fill up the news columns and to appear transparent. He continued in his retelling to Sulzberger, "Particularly we agreed that it would be unfortunate to create suspicion that maybe somebody was trying to put something over on the people, and specifically I urged him not to create for the seventy-five reporters assigned to the conference a vacuum which would, under our system of newspapering, be filled by those who had a special interest in seeing that the conference did not succeed."[19] Secrecy ran counter to the interests of the United States, he believed, as well as his own interests as a reporter expected to break news. Correspondents had to file a certain number of words, and Reston wanted to be sure that those on the pro–United Nations side took advantage of the continuous news cycle as much as the opposition did.

Stettinius had appeared to agree with Reston, yet the State Department instead "clamped down complete secrecy on the conversations, threatened everyone on the delegation with an FBI investigation if anything leaked, and asked the visiting delegations not to discuss the conversations with reporters," as Reston privately recounted it.[20] Instead of support in print, the conference received criticism for being held in secret. And despite the information blackout, Reston's front-page article on August 23, 1944, still outlined the details of the peacekeeping plans proposed by the Big Three—the United States, Great Britain, and the Soviet Union. The article noted that the meetings had been closed to reporters but that the *New York Times* had obtained a digest of the three plans from an "unimpeachable source," later revealed to be an unhappily sidelined Chinese delegate.[21] Reston's aggressive reporting on the Dumbarton Oaks conference would earn him his first Pulitzer Prize. At the time of publication, the publisher wrote Reston that he was "much impressed" by the story, but he also gave a caveat: "I confess I was surprised to find that some of my associates here felt that our using it was not helpful or desirable."[22] According to a *Nation* profile of Reston twelve years later, Sulzberger was referring to Stettinius himself as among the complaining "associates."[23]

In response to Sulzberger, Reston defended his article by explaining the good-faith efforts he had made with Stettinius to get information from the US delegation directly. He also gave an account of the responsibility of newspapers to clarify issues rather than muddle them, and of the people's right to know what their government was planning. However, Reston concluded with an argument that was not about newspaper practices but about foreign policy, making evident how consciously he was aligned with the *Times'* editorial position on the UN. "We may, out of deference to the Administration, defer discussion of this issue of the press and, more important, of the fundamental facts of the American plan, but we must be very clear about one fact: the opposition Senators are not remaining idle, and are not hesitating to use the secrecy to their ends. I don't want to overstate this case, but you have in the Senate right now the beginnings of another conspiracy to kill an effective league, and the technique is not very different from the Lodge-Teddy-Roosevelt-Watson technique to defeat the League," he wrote, referring to the Republicans who had sunk the League of Nations treaty.[24] Isolationist senators were hoping to extricate the country from its wartime alliances once again, and Reston believed that a UN organization would succeed only if newspapers overcame the State Department's self-destructive information policies.

The Dumbarton Oaks conference solidified Scotty Reston's position in Washington's diplomatic reporting circles and proved to the State Department that he could get information with or without its cooperation. The issue was so important that Sulzberger and Reston ended up talking it through further on the phone, then again in writing. Ultimately, Sulzberger wrote Reston, "Once more let me say that I am quite certain our course was not only intelligent and correct but represented some damned good newspaper work."[25] Dumbarton Oaks established a pattern that the two men would repeat over the next decade and a half: Reston publishing articles the government found unhelpful, the government complaining to Sulzberger, Sulzberger complaining to Reston, and the men determining that "damned good newspaper work" was the most important news value. Quality reporting meant being an advocate not for the government but rather for "the Peace."

After the tense press situation at Dumbarton Oaks, in December 1944 the State Department created the position of Assistant Secretary for Public Affairs and Cultural Relations, with responsibility for press relations. ("Cultural Relations" was removed from the title in 1946.) The first person to hold the job, Archibald MacLeish, had recently been in the Office of War Information and was a favorite in progressive intellectual circles. However, he was also serving on the Commission on Freedom of the Press, a largely academic group that most reporters disdained.[26] MacLeish was not long for the office, which required dealing daily with members of the press on a practical rather than an intellectual basis.

Walter Lippmann met with MacLeish early on and laid out the problem. As famous as he was, Lippmann had been having no better luck than rank-and-file reporters at accessing State Department information on peace planning. He complained to MacLeish that he could no longer get high-level details on US policy from the department. Just as Scotty Reston had argued to Edward Stettinius and Arthur Sulzberger, lack of information was especially problematic for the Dumbarton Oaks proposal, which Lippmann told MacLeish that no journalist in America understood and therefore no American would understand or support.[27] For months in his "Today and Tomorrow" column, he had been criticizing the "fallacy" of the Allied policy of postponing all political issues of settling borders until after the war. He had also denounced what he perceived as the false division between the War Department, supposedly in charge of war, and the State Department, supposedly in charge of peace. Lippmann knew there would be no more peacetime. "The postwar era will not be an era of settled peace such as the United States enjoyed in the nineteenth century," he wrote in a December 1944 column. "It will be an era of pacification in which diplomatic action, military force, and also economic action, are inseparable."[28] The United States had proved that it had the military force and the economic action, but the diplomatic action was on unsure footing.

MacLeish and others in the State Department realized that they urgently needed to improve press relations, with both influential men like Lippmann and the lower level of diplomatic reporters like Reston. In February 1945, the news reporters collectively tried to address their issues by having the Executive Committee of the State Department Correspondents' Association make a formal complaint to the secretary. The association had been founded in 1932, after Secretary of State Henry Stimson tried to hand-select the reporters who could attend his press conferences. "He has been troubled by mavericks and foreign correspondents," the *Times'* Washington bureau chief, Arthur Krock, had explained to the managing editor.[29] Back then, reporters had been outraged that the secretary would be able to share information selectively, so they established an accreditation system like that used in the Congressional galleries and the White House, where journalists self-regulated. If anyone should be allowed to hand-pick the audience, they believed, it should be they. By the 1940s, they had grown comfortable eliminating the mavericks and foreigners from meetings themselves.

The reporters framed their 1945 protest in terms of not just information policy but international foreign policy. They argued that US foreign policy was being explained only abroad, while no one in Washington would go on the record, creating the impression among American news consumers that US foreign policy was determined in Europe. "This was disappointing and disheartening both for professional and policy reasons," the complaint read[30]—for professional reasons, because reporters could not produce the kind of copy their editors wanted; for policy reasons, because they wanted Americans to support an active role for the nation on the global stage. Americans would never accept a European-made peace settlement. Despite the United States' overall support for the war effort and intellectuals' support for postwar internationalism, the nation had deep isolationist roots.[31] But the Washington press corps—despite having been majority isolationist in 1937, according to surveys—now favored postwar international commitments.[32] This attitude had become so rooted in correspondents' worldviews that they could use as shorthand "policy reasons," on which the three members of the correspondents' executive committee agreed, in their complaint letter. Diplomatic reporters believed that the federal government was hindering US efforts through its secretive policies, which would embolden isolationists.

Taking this letter and the frequent grumbling into consideration, a new committee on information policy in the State Department recommended that the secretary start holding more and lengthier press conferences to explain foreign policy. "We worked out a new press conference schedule with the press boys here in the Department a couple of months ago," MacLeish wrote Stettinius on April 11, 1945, two months after the protest letter.[33] However, MacLeish's commitment to transparency was not as strong as he led the "press boys" to believe. Just five days after the State Department reporters issued their complaint, MacLeish wrote his own complaint to Arthur Sulzberger at the *Times* that Scotty Reston's articles on the Yalta Conference, lend-lease aid to France, and Russian credit applications had "caused this government grave embarrassment in its foreign relations and, specifically, in its relations with its Allies in the war."[34] It is no wonder that relationships between the press and officials were tense when officials so frequently went straight to their bosses.

The day after MacLeish's memo to Stettinius about the press boys' new understanding, Franklin Roosevelt died, making Harry S. Truman the president and putting Stettinius's job security in question. The entire department—both policy and information systems—remained unsteady as peace negotiations continued, without the demands of the State Department Correspondents' Association being satisfied.

President Truman decided that Edward Stettinius should remain secretary of state for the San Francisco conference, a continuation of the Dumbarton Oaks discussions, in the spring of 1945. Reporters' struggle for information continued as well. As at Dumbarton Oaks, there was a news hole that reporters had a professional obligation to fill with information from whoever provided it, whether or not those sources supported a UN organization. In response to continued quarreling between Reston and Stettinius, "using bad language to each other over Stettinius's tight news policy," as Arthur Krock remembered it, Krock convinced Stettinius to set up what he referred to as the ILO—the Intentional Leak Office—and suggested that their mutual friend Adlai Stevenson, special assistant to the secretary of state, run it. (Stevenson and Krock reminisced about this over breakfast in Washington in 1956 as Stevenson was running for president the second time.)[35] The *Times'* correspondents were not passive; they actively pushed to implement the information policies they believed in. If the State Department representatives bungled their message, it would at least not be the fault of the *New York Times*.

Reston and Sulzberger clashed again on what kind of news about the San Francisco conference could productively be shared with the public, despite their common goal. In late April 1945, Sulzberger chastised Reston by telegram for a front-page story that emphasized the difficulty of the Big Three reaching an agreement on Poland. "Please tell Scotty think his lead story today might have been based more optimistically," Sulzberger cabled his managing editor, E. L. "Jimmy" James, who had set up a news desk at the conference.[36] Sulzberger then added a disingenuous disclaimer, acknowledging the wall that was supposed to separate editorial judgment from news judgment: "That's difficult for me to say and I wouldn't if I wasn't certain you and he did not think I was attempting to color the story from here." However, as they all knew, coloring the story from New York was exactly what Sulzberger was trying to do. Finally, he asked, "Am I correct that Krock will do lead when he arrives and leave Scotty to scout?" The publisher trusted Krock to toe the line more than Reston, especially since Krock was Stettinius's main contact at the *Times*. James cabled back defensively that everyone in San Francisco thought Reston's story was very accurate, and that it was, in cable-speak, "hard to get optimistic about an affair which so far utter confusion."[37] As James doubtless knew, Sulzberger was not really questioning the accuracy, just the tone. "Don't misunderstand my reference to Scotty's story. I have no doubt it was accurate," Sulzberger cabled back. Accuracy was not everything, he was saying. "I liked this morning's statement however, 'Started with efficient determination but with full admission that difficulties lie ahead,'" he wrote, quoting Reston's latest article. "That's placing the emphasis encouragingly."[38]

The internationalist reporters, editors, and publisher of the *Times* wanted to give the delicate negotiations whatever support they could while maintaining a claim to independence. A wrong word at the wrong time could undermine the position of the United States. In one case, an editor in New York had asked the San Francisco team, Why so much coverage of Harold E. Stassen, the former Republican governor of Minnesota and a conference delegate? "That's a good question," a *Times*man replied, "but there's a pretty good answer which we can hardly print without causing dissention in the delegation and hurting the conference."[39] They believed that Stassen was the only competent member of the US negotiating team, a reputation enhanced by his access to and friendship with diplomatic reporters. And since reporters preferred not to highlight the incompetence of everyone else representing their country, they focused on Stassen.

There were moments of tension and disagreement among *Times*men and between reporters and officials, but their overall goal remained the one Sulzberger had expressed in 1939: to soften the US isolation shell through coverage and promotion of the UN, whether or not the State Department liked it. Meanwhile, the *New York Times* solidified its status as the most important newspaper for diplomatic circles by putting out a special facsimile edition of the paper in San Francisco: four pages released at two o'clock in the morning. That edition was sent by photographic wire from New York and distributed for free to the delegates. No other newspaper, including the *San Francisco Chronicle*, had the diplomatic sources as well as the financial resources to produce adequate timely news of the conference, so delegates and other reporters depended on the *Times* to communicate with—and understand—one another.[40]

The peace conferences would continue for years, and the *Times*, both promoting the United Nations and showcasing its own coverage, continued producing special editions. "I have just seen the first issue of the U.N. Edition of The New York Times which our people will enjoy reading within a few hours at the Palais de Chaillot," wrote a staffer in the UN Department of Public Information to Sulzberger in September 1948, from a Paris peace conference. "It is excellent from every standpoint, and adds another great service to the many the New York Times has been performing since the days of the San Francisco Conference to report on the activities and promote the ideals of the United Nations."[41]

After the San Francisco conference, Stettinius thanked Arthur Krock for the "constructive role which you have played in interpreting the work of the Conference and of the Delegation to the American public," which he believed was already evident.[42] The Senate did ratify the UN charter in August 1945, meaning that Truman and his supporters won a victory that had eluded Woodrow Wilson and had entered an era of bipartisan cooperation on certain foreign policy matters.

The survival and effectiveness of the organization was still in doubt, though, and keeping the press coverage positive was an ongoing concern for the State Department, now under the leadership of James F. Byrnes. Although Byrnes was more popular with reporters than Stettinius, the department's press relations through the peace conferences continued to be poor. The London conference of foreign ministers in the fall of 1945 went so badly from a public relations perspective that the State Department once again frantically reevaluated its operations. "The news policy of the Department is under severe attack," an official wrote in an internal memo in October 1945. "We are charged with secretiveness that is unnecessary and unwise." The memo cited several criticisms that had appeared in the press about the negative effects on US foreign policy if the State Department could not figure out a way to share its efforts with the American people. They included a quote from Scotty Reston, who had written in one of his stories that "what appears to be a lack of foreign policy is frequently a lack of press policy." The memo warned after the London conference, "The fifteen top State Department correspondents with whom we met were unanimous in their condemnation [of secrecy]."[43] These top fifteen reporters, or press boys, as Archibald MacLeish had called them, had a lot of influence. Between syndication and wire services, they reached nearly every media outlet in the country. What would appear to later critics as propaganda was usually the information reporters themselves had demanded, over objections of a bungling State Department.[44]

The State Department—whose officials during this period were caricatured as effeminate "lavender lads" and striped-pants-wearing cookie pushers—was an easy target for the rest of the government's and the nation's ire.[45] A joke that circulated among reporters and State Department staffers at the time went as follows: "You know how it is in Washington. A couple of friends run into each other in the Mayflower Bar one evening and one says to the other, 'What're you doing tonight?' and the other says, 'Nothing special. Why?' and the first guy says, 'Then let's go around and kick the hell out of the State Department.'"[46] That attitude never really changed, the beating up on the department merely becoming more programmatic under congressional investigation and the department's purges of "subversives" that lasted into the 1950s.[47] The State Department was constantly at odds with itself, other parts of the government, and much of the public. Many reporters saw themselves as the only way the department could survive the peace and promote internationalism in peacetime. Reporters were leading the efforts, with officials struggling to catch up.

Is It War?

As peacetime continued, so did a militaristic language of war that created tension within newspapers over their responsibility to serve their country. The old battles over the obligations of members of the press in times of war persisted, exposing the fault lines between the principle and the practice.

As he had been during the war, the *New York Times*' publisher Arthur Sulzberger was anxious to give reporters leaves of absence when men in government requested their service. When General George C. Marshall asked to borrow Tillman Durdin, the *Times*' East Asia correspondent, in the summer of 1946 for a stint in China, the managing editor, Jimmy James, expressed his annoyance to Sulzberger. "I don't like this at all," he wrote. "The war is over and we certainly did enough for the Government while the war was on."[48] (James knew he was likely registering a protest merely for the record and that it would not have any impact, and Durdin did take two months' leave to help Marshall.)

A revival of wartime language coincided with Harry S. Truman's announcement of US intervention in Greece and Turkey with a speech in March 1947 that became known as the Truman Doctrine, followed three months later by the announcement of aid to Europe through a European Recovery Program, known as the Marshall Plan. The tension between serving one's country and fulfilling one's ethical obligations as a journalist then continued with the advent of the Cold War. When the *New York Times* loaned Harold Hinton of the Washington bureau to the recently established Department of Defense in the summer of 1948 to help its staff set up a new, integrated information program, Hinton called it "this small draft in the Cold War."[49] The fifty-year-old had previously been on military leave for five years during World War II, serving as a colonel in the United States Army Air Forces, primarily as an intelligence officer in North Africa and Italy; before that, he had served as a pilot in France during World War I.[50] As Kenneth Osgood has detailed, most Americans experienced the Cold War as a real war, and for many journalists that meant being willing once again to serve their country.[51] "Of course I completely agree with [Secretary of State George C.] Marshall that we are still in a kind of war," the *Washington Post* chairman Eugene Meyer wrote in January 1948 to William Benton, recently of the State Department. "What people do not understand is that war doesn't begin with shooting and doesn't end with shooting. We are now in the business of idea shooting."[52]

Despite the differences of opinion behind the scenes, the public line of newspapers was that the nation was not at war and that their reporters must remain objective. The private line was a different story. In 1949, Paul Hoffman, the chief of the Marshall Plan's administrative body, the Economic Cooperation Administration, wanted Turner Catledge, then assistant managing editor of the *New York Times*, to become his information officer. When Hoffman first took the job, he had received Sulzberger's assurances that the *Times* wanted to help. "Please don't hesitate to call me on the telephone at any time if we seem to neglect doing anything that might be helpful," Sulzberger had written. "You know how much we on the Times are committed to the project."[53] A year later, Hoffman took Sulzberger up on the offer by asking for Catledge. But Catledge did not want to leave New York or the *Times*. When Sulzberger wrote Hoffman with the news, he cited lofty ideals of objectivity: "I think the strongest argument is that we do not wish to have any news executive of The Times associated with what necessarily is a propaganda agency—no matter how firmly we believe in the justness of that propaganda."[54]

Sulzberger was lying when he told Hoffman what the *Times* wished. In fact, he had urged Catledge to take the position, if only for six months, and offered to make up his difference in salary during his leave of absence.[55] He also continued to encourage other reporters and editors to accept the government's requests. At the same time, he knew well enough that leaves of absence in peacetime would be so counter to the principles of objective journalism that he could use objectivity as the public-facing excuse for Catledge. In the end, the job with Hoffman at the Economic Cooperation Administration went to Roscoe Drummond. He was the Washington correspondent of the *Christian Science Monitor*, who had been a regular in General Marshall's and Admiral Ernest King's background circles during the war and would later move to the Washington bureau of the *New York Herald Tribune*.

Other reporters were still experiencing what felt like wartime Europe as they traveled abroad to cover the postwar peace (fig. 5.2). The *Washington Post* reporter Ferdie Kuhn wrote his wife, Delia, in March 1947, "London was worse than you or I have ever seen it." As the first full-time diplomatic reporter for the *Post*, Kuhn had been sent to Europe to cover the Moscow Conference of Foreign Ministers. "When I got in at Waterloo Station the streets were almost as blacked out as in wartime, people shivered along the streets, and shivered in chilly restaurants over bad food, and shivered in their offices with overcoats on. In the daytime inner corridors in office buildings had to be lit with candles; life in general was as inconvenient and nasty as it ever was in wartime except that no bombs were falling."[56] Kuhn viewed London as still fighting the war

FIGURE 5.2. United States Army representatives in Frankfurt are shown briefing a group of visiting newsmen in 1948, including Scotty Reston (*front row, in the bow tie*). After the war, American newsmen traveled to Europe at greater rates than before as the United States continued its military and economic intervention. Box 137, James B. Reston Papers, Courtesy of the University of Illinois Archives.

that had shaped his view of the world. He returned to Washington with tales of the dire straits their European brethren were in.

Ideas about postwar rebuilding relied on existing transatlantic friendship networks, especially those developed during World War II. Eugene Meyer of the *Post* made his own scouting trip to Europe in August and September of 1947, in preparation for the Marshall Plan funding debate in Congress. Meyer had many close friends in Europe, especially England. In the privation of wartime and the postwar period, he habitually sent his friends packages of hard-to-obtain items like cigars, meat, and scotch. For this trip, Meyer took Al Friendly as his traveling companion. (Friendly was the young reporter who had taken a leave of absence from the *Post* to serve in the Army Air Corps during the war and who would later become the newspaper's managing editor.)

Meyer and Friendly visited London, Paris, Berlin, Frankfurt, and Coburg. Friendly took detailed notes and sent the diaries to Phil Graham, his publisher and Meyer's son-in-law, who then shared them with the newsroom and with Friendly's wife, Jean. Friendly warned his wife about the diaries: "You'll find almost all of it dull, in being exclusively devoted to economic phases, but it will give you an idea of whom we saw, and it contains a couple of pages of the [Winston] Churchill conversation, written as soon as I got back to London." Then, in language typical for its explicitness in the desire to keep secret the ethical compromises of the postwar news industry, he added this warning: "Please keep all of the diary confidential, the whole business was very much off the record and could seriously embarrass The Post were some of the remarks and interviewees passed about."[57] Among other things, remarks included candid comments about the political parties and personalities in Britain that would never see print, and Meyer's strong alignment with Churchill's Conservative Party over the Labour Party.[58]

Of course, publishers could implement whatever editorial policies they wanted. Their editorial pages were entirely at their disposal and expected to be biased. It was not inappropriate for Meyer to have had lunch at the Churchill family home of Chartwell with the former prime minister and Mrs. Churchill; Randolph; little Winston; and little Winston's governess. Nor was it inappropriate for Meyer to have asked Churchill's advice on editorial policy. But Friendly knew that their meetings throughout Europe amounted to more than mere editorial policy research. They were building a framework that would influence the totality of news coverage and would do so at a moment when the *Washington Post* was growing into a nationally important newspaper. There *was* something unethical about the trip they were taking, which they knew at the time, as Friendly's warning to his wife indicated.

Reporters in Washington traveled in circumscribed and constantly intersecting circles; their journeys through Europe were similarly narrow. For instance, Meyer and Friendly ran into Scotty Reston and his wife, Sally, in Paris, at the Hotel Ritz on the Place Vendôme. The group made a date for dinner. Friendly wrote his wife, "Later this afternoon we're off to an Embassy cocktail party, and this evening are having dinner with Scotty Reston and wife, who sends you her love." Unsurprisingly, Jean Friendly and Sally Reston were friends, another node in the network. The Restons had just spent six weeks in Germany, Poland, Czechoslovakia, and Italy and, according to Friendly, had "wonderful, if depressing stories," the circulation of which Washington connections and the Paris Ritz helped facilitate.[59]

During its initial passage as well as the bill's subsequent renewals, newspapers across the country ran series promoting the Marshall Plan. Those papers, including the *Washington Post*, that could afford to reprint the series as pamphlets did so, further widening distribution. For instance, the *Philadelphia Bulletin* reprinted a series it had run in January 1949 as a pamphlet entitled *The Marshall Plan—How It Works*. Before doing so, though, the financial editor of the *Bulletin* had sent the series to the Economic Cooperation Administration to find out whether republication would help or hinder the Marshall Plan effort.[60] The ECA was in favor of publication, and its information officer internally recommended that although the ECA should not officially sanction the series—since the newspaper could lose credibility that way by appearing to be less objective—his boss should privately phone or write the publisher to let him know how thoughtful and understanding the series was.[61] That information officer, not coincidentally, was Al Friendly (fig. 5.3).

"Washington Is Not America"

Whether newspapermen were propagandists or exemplars of objectivity was a source of tension between reporters, editors, and publishers, especially those outside Washington. In May 1947, Wallie Deuel and his *Chicago Daily News* editor Basil "Stuffy" Walters argued about it. Walters worried that the home office was not privy to Deuel's sources and that those sources also were not more explicitly revealed to readers. The dominant rules of attribution during this period were meant to protect reporters from accusations of bias or fabrication. If they quoted someone by name, they were no longer responsible for the accuracy of the quote. Deuel—and reporters and media critics for decades to come—thought that this lazy attribution was a poor substitute for objectivity and certainly for the responsibility he had come to feel during the

FIGURE 5.3. In May 1948, the *Washington Post* staff threw Al Friendly (*left*) a bon voyage party as he started his leave of absence to work for the Economic Cooperation Administration, the administrative arm of the Marshall Plan. Box 4, Alfred Friendly Papers, Amherst College Archives and Special Collections.

war. Deuel responded to Walters with skepticism, showing how the isolationist press used "objectivity" to argue its case. "There are various tricks for dressing up stories with ostensible sources. The Tribune people get some stooge to say the things Bertie wants said, and then quote the stooge," he wrote, referring by nickname to the famously isolationist publisher of the *Chicago Tribune*, Robert McCormick. "This is supposed to make the story look like objective reporting."[62] Deuel

believed that truly unbiased reporting was instead based on synthe-
sizing several sources and determining which were credible—a conception of fair reporting that would not become mainstream until the
1960s and 1970s, when objectivity came under public attack.[63] Deuel's
synthesis would always be internationalist, though, just as the *Chicago
Tribune*'s would always argue for "America First." His perspective—like
that of Reston, Ferdie Kuhn, Walter Lippmann, Joe Harsch, and the
State Department Correspondents' Association—defined the discourse
in the spaces of Washington and became the consensus about foreign
policy there. That was exactly the problem, Stuffy Walters thought:
"Frankly, I am giving you these views, not because I want you to slant
any stories my way but because I think you are exposed to one side in
Washington. Washington is not America."[64]

Walters worried that Deuel prioritized his sources over his readers.
"Your obligation is to the public and you must always be on the alert
not to let friendship or protection of contacts keep you from writing
the story," he warned.[65] Deuel was annoyed at the insinuation that he
was being used to disseminate US foreign policy or that he had practiced anything other than responsible journalism—as he and his cohort
defined and practiced it. He defended himself to Walters: "As for being
critically vigilant regarding the State Department . . . I have attacked so
many powerful elements on so many subjects vital to them, and made
so many of them so mad, that I have sometimes wondered how long
you and Mr. Knight would stand for it," he replied, referring to the
owner of the Knight Newspaper chain, which owned the *Daily News*.[66]
Just like Reston and others, Deuel *was* often critical of foreign policy.
The issue was not consensus on every issue but consensus on the one
issue that overshadowed others and had delayed entry into World War
II while Deuel was in Berlin watching the rise of Hitler, and Reston was
in London watching bombs fall: the fear that the United States would
retreat entirely from the world stage.

After receiving another letter from Walters, which criticized Deuel
for not having been harsh enough on a US diplomat in a recent profile,
Deuel wrote back at length with obsequiousness, acknowledging how
much he relied on his editors to point out to him when he was edito-

rializing. But he also responded with defensiveness: "To revert to the question of critical vigilance vis-a-vis men in office, I know that you have thought on various occasions I might not sound critical enough, and it occurs to me that it might be useful—or at least amusing—to cite all the occasions and all the issues on which I *have* been critical."[67]

The most common source of disagreement between Washingtonians and their bosses outside the capital were profiles. These brief biographical sketches could spotlight certain men and provide reporters with opportunities to ingratiate themselves with their sources, thus laying the groundwork for future information pipelines. Editors, meanwhile, feared that the profiles put reporters' credibility in jeopardy. In these same letters, Deuel defended himself for having gently treated the diplomat George Kennan—author of the initially anonymous *Foreign Affairs* article outlining the US strategy of Soviet containment— because he needed to keep Kennan as a source. Deuel had written in the flattering article, "The [State] department has a habit of calling on Kennan whenever there's a job to do that calls for the toughest and most brilliant career diplomat available."[68]

The specific profile that Walters thought was not critical enough was of Spruille Braden, an assistant secretary of state. Deuel said he had learned about Braden's policies from other people in the State Department before getting to know the diplomat personally. Braden had been criticized as a "bull in a China shop," Deuel wrote in the first of a series of articles that came to his defense. "Braden is built like a bull and has the strength and courage of one, but he has none of a bull's clumsiness, stupidity or blind rage. He is as light on his feet as a cat, both personally and politically."[69] In the letter to Walters, Deuel acknowledged, "I did become very fond of Spruille before the end, because he's a grand guy personally, quite apart from his policies, but that came after I had sized up the issues and begun to report them as I did all along."[70] (An old friend who had served with Deuel in the Office of Strategic Services had introduced him to Braden—the invisible wartime network still in action.)

Walters was not satisfied: "I don't like trying to spoon feed people with only the news that we think is good for them. . . . Having been a propagandist in the 1st World War, for the United States Army, I think it may be all right in wartime but I don't want to have anything to do with it in peacetime."[71] The problem for Deuel was that he, too, had been a propagandist, but in World War II. And to him, the country seemed to be not in peacetime but still at war.

When Wallie Deuel described the letters with Walters to his mother, he noted the confusion at being "the pampered darling of the management one week every month, the problem child another week." He was also cynical about the "long, involved and incoherent sermons on the highest moral plane about objectivity in the news columns. Since I'll never see things their way if I live to be a million years old, and since I can't write things any way except the way I see them, there's nothing much to be done about it except to be polite and go right ahead my way."[72] The relatively liberal *Chicago Daily News*, let alone the nation, had not arrived at an internationalist consensus. That there appears to have been one is a testament to Deuel and his cohort's commitment. (The next year, the *Daily News* fired Deuel, and he went to work for the *St. Louis Post-Dispatch*, which had an internationalist publisher and editorial page.)

Deuel's other problem was a common one: his sources were his livelihood. Reporters and sources relied on a rarely stated quid pro quo: policy makers and reporters needed each other. Deuel explained this deal, which journalists would not have admitted to their readers or even their own editors, in a letter to his mother. "I've wanted for some time to build up good contacts and sources in the [Senate Foreign Relations] Committee, but never gotten around to it," he wrote. "The best way of doing that is to write a good profile of the people you're interested in—assuming they turn out not to be such dopes that your profile, if honest, will alienate them, rather than making them like you."[73] Deuel was especially concerned about that committee because Scotty Reston was known to have a direct information pipeline to Senator Arthur Vandenberg, the Republican credited with bringing bipartisan support to the Truman administration's postwar foreign policy.[74] In May 1948, Reston wrote a *Life* magazine cover profile of the senator, under the headline "The Case for Vandenberg." His managing editor at the *New*

York Times, Jimmy James, promptly chastised him for jeopardizing his reputation for objectivity. Reston was less than contrite. Although he began his response with "I think I'll say 'uncle' on that Vandenberg piece without too much argument," he then went on to argue why the theory of objectivity should yield to the necessities of foreign policy reporting. After explaining that it was really Henry Luce, the publisher of *Life*, who had turned Reston's straight profile into an advocacy piece, he wrote, "One other point: in theory you are absolutely right" that he was now problematically identified as pro-Vandenberg. "There are two angles to this however: there may be a theoretical disadvantage to The Times in my close association with him, but I think you'll have to agree that there is an enormous practical advantage in that contact. The guy is in the key spot in my field; he gets tipped off in advance on almost everything; it is not, therefore, an accident that we were first with the [Paul] Hoffman appointment, the [Averell] Harriman appointment, the State Department's case against Russia, etc."[75] Losing a little theoretical credibility with the readers of *Life* magazine was worth the tradeoff for actual news coverage for the *Times*, which Reston believed had more important readers.

Reston's fellow Washingtonians accepted the quid pro quo more readily than did his editor in New York. When Deuel wrote his mother a few days after Reston's *Life* piece came out, he noted what a strategic move it had been on Reston's part, since at that point everyone in Washington believed that the Republicans would win the White House that November. "Scotty will be sitting pretty if Van gets elected or becomes Secretary of State," Deuel wrote.[76] The *Times*' Washington bureau chief, Arthur Krock, would also have understood Reston's motivations. After all, he and Vandenberg were so personally close themselves that two weeks after the *Life* story, the Krocks and the Vandenbergs had a party jointly celebrating their wedding anniversaries in the garden of the Krocks' Georgetown home. Krock's memo about it noted that the joint occasion was something the couples had done "several times before."[77] He also believed that the information he gleaned that night—about Vandenberg's views on his chance of being nominated at the upcoming Republican National Convention (slim) and being a symbol of party disunity—was so important that it merited a "private" memorandum. He asked Reston, who was also at the party, to correct and endorse it to save for his files.

Not just the practices of journalism but the very premise of US foreign policy seemed much less like a foregone conclusion to news-papermen outside the capital's echo chamber. Major newspapers from all across the country and the world had reporters there who operated as somewhat free agents. Apart from those working for the local Washington papers, the typical pressures of the newsroom did not affect most of the reporters in the capital in the usual ways.[78] Instead, a horizontal pressure—of not disappointing peers and sources who shared a particular vision for peace—shaped their behavior.

In August 1949, an editor at the *St. Louis Post-Dispatch* on an anti-Washington tirade wrote one of his Washington-based writers: "I thought you did very well with your piece on our bipartisan foreign policy, but personally I am again forced to the conclusion that US foreign policy, whether bipartisan or not, never did amount to very much." The editor went on to say that US policy did not prevent the spread of communism but merely encouraged nations to "blackmail" the United States into supporting their political regimes with the threat of going communist. But the news out of Washington, even from his own news-paper, was not acknowledging the obvious. "It seems to me that we might well re-examine the major premise on which our policy has been based," he wrote. "This premise, I take it, is that we can not afford to let the rest of the world go Communist and so fall under the control of Soviet Russia. I believed this just as strongly as anyone else at the start; but more and more I am coming to believe that we could, if we had to, face this question with a big, 'So what?'" Contradicting the consensus in Washington and even among his own staff, he continued, "Even with all the rest of the world Red, and I do mean all and I do mean Red, I'm still far from being convinced that we could not defend at least North America and perhaps even the entire Western Hemisphere if we were to spend some of the money on defense that we are now spending on Operation Rathole"—that is, the Marshall Plan, which some saw as throwing good money after bad, down a rathole. "This, of course, adds up to neo-isolationism," the editor concluded, revealing the genuine cracks in the supposed American postwar consensus.[79] The shell of isolation that Arthur Sulzberger had observed during the 1930s seemed once again to be hardening.

During the late 1940s, as the US emphasis on postwar economic recovery made the transition to an emphasis on military preparedness, the government began negotiating the North Atlantic Treaty of 1949, which established NATO (the North Atlantic Treaty Organization) and planned for permanent armed divisions in Western Europe. This was the birth of what one historian has called the "heart of the western security system for the entire cold war period and beyond."[80] In October 1949, President Truman signed the Mutual Defense Assistance Act, providing billions in military and financial aid to support the buildup of Western Europe's military defenses.

The American public had reluctantly supported US involvements in Europe during the 1930s, and that reluctance remained after the war. The cohort of diplomatic reporters responsible for writing about it remained largely enthusiastic about military interventionism. Scotty Reston noted in a January 1950 profile of Secretary of State Dean Acheson that while Acheson had skillfully pushed the North Atlantic Treaty through Congress, he had not gotten it "understood and approved in the country."[81] There was fear in Washington of the failure of the wartime alliances, as well as a fear that the rest of the nation had settled into peacetime, perhaps even isolationism. "We are going through one of our bad patches here," Reston wrote two months later to Jean Monnet, a French friend who had spent his career working toward European unification. Monnet's relationships in the capital greatly contributed to support there for a United States of Europe— what eventually became the European Economic Community and then the European Union. "The atomic explosions in the Soviet Union, the Communist victory in China, and the decision to proceed with the hydrogen bomb, have created a new sense of apprehension," Reston wrote. "I don't think the people as a whole are worried about it but the intellectuals in most cities are more disturbed now than they have been in some time." He wished people were a bit a more disturbed, or at least that the "average guy" be given "a sense of participating in something important and beyond himself." This critique resonated with the one in his profile of Acheson, though was far blunter. "Our capacity to learn, however, is very great and just as we have mastered the disease of isolation, so we will, I am sure, conquer the residue of isolation which still exists in certain attitudes of mind and political habits."[82]

Korea and a Time of War

In the summer of 1950, fighting broke out on the Korean peninsula, with US-led United Nations troops supporting South Koreans against the communist North Korea. The United States was in a clear time of war. Indirectly, NATO got a boost from the Korean War.[83] Because troops were now needed in Korea, the thinking went, there was new urgency to settling some of the outstanding questions in Europe. These issues included whether Germany would be allowed to re-arm, which France mostly opposed and the United States mostly supported, and how quickly the headquarters for NATO could be set up under General Dwight Eisenhower. Truman had selected Eisenhower in December 1950 to be the first commander at SHAPE (Supreme Headquarters Allied Planners Europe), just as during the war the general had commanded SHAEF (Supreme Headquarters Allied Expeditionary Forces). It already seemed to many of Washington's newsmen that World War II had never ended; seeing General Eisenhower back in uniform, back in Europe, in charge of Allied troops, reinforced that feeling. The Korean War then made it a reality.

Arthur Sulzberger believed that the Korean War was just what the country needed to stem its growing tide of isolationism. He wrote Arthur Krock in July 1950, "The one grain of comfort that I can offer you is that this trouble in Korea may prove to have saved our lives as a nation." The *Times*' publisher believed that the country would realize how unprepared its defenses were and continue to build up its military program. If it did learn that lesson and improve its defense establishment, the war in Korea would be, in his word, "worthwhile."[84] Krock likely relayed that sentiment to Reston and other trusted colleagues. Six days later, Reston wrote a friend (the cousin of Sulzberger's wife) who had asked for his opinion on Korea. He ended on a note that echoed Sulzberger's: "Meanwhile, cheer up, there are some good aspects to this thing. It may at least have convinced some people that the 'leadership of the world' which everybody talks about so glibly and accepts so blithely, cannot be achieved without sustained sacrifice. Or am I being too Calvinistic?"[85]

As usual, Reston *was* being too Calvinistic, and a nation that felt it had already sacrificed so much during World War II did not want to give up more. Rather than promoting increased internationalism, the Korean War threatened exactly what Sulzberger, Reston, and many of their compatriots had been trying to prevent for five years: the public's return to isolationism. That war opened the door for renewed "America First" sentiment, especially from the wing of the Republican Party led by Senators Robert A. Taft and Kenneth S. Wherry. The Truman administration's desire to prevent Soviet and further Chinese interference in Korea, as well as to curb "war psychosis" on the home front, led it to downplay its own bellicosity in wartime messaging. The US government ended up curbing public support from the outset of what remained an unpopular war.[86]

Isolationism seemed to be strengthening. In a widely covered radio address in December 1950, former president Herbert Hoover urged recalling US ground troops from around the world. He called for increased air and naval power and a reliance on the Atlantic and Pacific Oceans for protection. "These policies I have suggested would be no isolationism. Indeed, they are the opposite," Hoover claimed.[87] But of course, with the America Firsters of the 1930s a recent memory, everyone knew that Hoover was precisely describing isolationism. Joseph Pulitzer Jr., the publisher of the *St. Louis Post-Dispatch*, wrote his managing editor that Hoover had put "isolationism now in the open," as if he and everyone else knew that it had just been lingering under the surface of American politics but had been reluctant to say so in print.

That was no longer the case. "The Post-Dispatch may have a fight on its hands to defeat the instinctive American isolationist sentiments for which Hoover is a spokesman," Pulitzer concluded.[88]

The morning after the Hoover speech, the *New York Times*' editorial board responded, acknowledging the many points on which it and Hoover agreed, especially "the folly which prompted the free world to disarm." But it pointed out the disastrous effect that withdrawal would have on the world and on US economic prospects ("economic strangulation"). "Under these circumstances," the editorial concluded, "we prefer to follow the present American policy of building up strength wherever possible, as endorsed not only by a bipartisan coalition in Congress but also by the man who will shoulder this responsibility in Europe—General Eisenhower."[89] Focusing attention on Eisenhower, rather than Korea, put the spotlight where the *Times* wanted it: Western Europe. That Sunday's "The News of the Week in Review" section had a large triptych on its front page, with Eisenhower at the left, Harry Truman and Dean Acheson together in the middle, and Hoover at the right.[90] In a lengthy article, Scotty Reston made sure to call NATO forces "Gen. Dwight D. Eisenhower's international army."[91]

The fact that Eisenhower was at SHAPE made him an attractive potential presidential candidate to those Americans wanting to uphold the wartime alliances. The man running NATO presumably would not eliminate NATO. The other likely Republican candidate, Senator Taft, "Mr. Republican," might.[92] The *New York Times* had never before endorsed a candidate before the party nominating conventions, since the newspaper's modern founder, Adolph Ochs, did not want to be seen as interfering in internal party politics. The possibility of a Taft presidency, however, was enough for Sulzberger to break with his late father-in-law's tradition.[93] On January 7, 1952, the *Times* ran an editorial calling on the general to publicly declare his candidacy. The editorial praised Ike personally, criticized the right-wing Republicans who might endanger the country, and—despite there being no Democratic nominee yet—remarkably ended with the following promise: "If Dwight Eisenhower should be nominated by the Republican party as its candidate for President, we shall support him enthusiastically."[94]

Soon, Eisenhower officially resigned his post at SHAPE to run for president in earnest, a journey that would end at the Republican National Convention in Chicago in July, at a time when party conventions still held suspense. Just before the convention, the *Times* had continued its pressure, running a three-part series with the headline "Mr. Taft Can't Win."[95]

Once Eisenhower had secured the nomination, Sulzberger kept a close eye on news about him and his Democratic opponent, Adlai Stevenson. He grew annoyed when Reston's news coverage did not reflect his agenda, just as he had been annoyed during the peace conferences. This time, however, the two men were on different sides, since Stevenson was as good a candidate for internationalists as Eisenhower on foreign policy issues, and a better candidate for liberals, including Reston, on domestic policy. On September 24, 1952, Reston's article described how Eisenhower had started criticizing the Democratic administration, concluding that "the point is merely that the Eisenhower crusade is turning into just another political campaign, featuring all the old back-platform tricks, all the old debating points, all the old slogans, and all the old compromises."[96] Reston observed that Eisenhower would publicly praise only two of Truman's foreign policies—the Marshall Plan, and Greek and Turkish aid—since those had been passed by Republican-led Senates. NATO, which had been passed under a Democratic majority, did not get a mention, despite the fact, as Reston pointed out, that Eisenhower had run its operations. NATO was the whole reason the *Times* was supporting Ike.

Irked, Sulzberger leveled the worst insult at Reston he could think of for a straight-news reporter—that Reston apparently wanted to be an editorial writer, "to the extent that you write editorials for the news columns and that, very frankly, we find embarrassing." His letter continued, "Take for example, your statement that Ike didn't 'even mention the North Atlantic Treaty.' Do you believe for a moment that because he did not do so he has turned his back on it or that he feared to mention it? Personally I do not and I think that would certainly seem to be inferred in what you said." Sulzberger had all the same fears, he just wanted them kept out of his newspaper.[97] In fact, just five days earlier, he had sent Reston a telegram conveying the "feeling that Taft has swallowed Eisenhower" and that he hoped their candidate would make another foreign policy speech to dispel that feeling.[98]

When Reston replied, he emphasized that the *Times* was under additional scrutiny for not being objective when it came to Ike because of the paper's unprecedented endorsement. "I ask you to keep in mind that, even down here at the pick and shovel level, our actions are being watched with the most critical eye," he wrote. "Ever since we came out for the General, every Times' reporter on the political beat has been watched very carefully by the politicians and by the other reporters to see whether he pulls his punches. My colleagues know I have been writing interpretive dispatches on foreign affairs for years; they know I have been writing them on Stevenson. Surely against this background, I could not ignore [Eisenhower's] Cincinnati speech, which I still think was more representative of the prejudices of Harry Luce (who had quite a hand in preparing it and went out to Cincinnati to hear it delivered) than of the principles of Dwight Eisenhower."[99] Again, Luce was so disliked in Reston's circle that he was always an easy target in private correspondence.

Sulzberger knew very well that Reston had written accurately about what was happening with the Eisenhower campaign. The same day that he complained to Reston, he also sent a telegram to Sherman Adams, Eisenhower's campaign manager, urging him to stop playing politics. He cabled Adams that he was "in despair" at the news that Ike would share a stage with the red-hunting senator from Wisconsin, Joseph McCarthy.[100]

For the most part, Eisenhower supporters tried to ignore McCarthy during the election season so as not to hurt the Republican ticket. Since 1950, McCarthy in the Senate and his counterparts in the House of Representatives had brought to a frantic zenith the loyalty investigations that had been ongoing since the 1930s. Resentment toward McCarthy in liberal Washington circles was enough to sour many of these people on Eisenhower. The official Washington ("polite society") consensus on the senator was that he was a boor and a bully, whom they hoped Eisenhower would disavow.

Although McCarthy did not specifically target Washington reporters in the same way he did other high-profile groups, the newsmen all had friends and acquaintances affected by the Red Scare.[101] From a practical standpoint, they were disgusted by how much space and resources newspapers were giving to cover the senator's hearings as well as those hearings in the House Un-American Activities Committee. Many of them were forced to write up accounts of all interactions they had ever had with socialist or communist groups or people to submit to Congress. Some were questioned by Congress on any work they did tangentially for the State Department, such as broadcasts that the department's Voice of America had re-aired abroad. Most reporters in the public eye during this period received especially nasty hate mail from McCarthy supporters. Within Washington, so many officials and reporters disliked McCarthy so much that anti-McCarthyism quickly became the consensus view and could live alongside anticommunism. Many reporters had been criticizing the senator in print all along, and readers of all but the most conservative news outlets knew that McCarthy was considered, within the capital at least, a stain on the Senate. Television viewers may not have seen explicit anti-McCarthy reporting until the mythologized Edward R. Murrow takedown, but the world of print hardly treated the despised McCarthy with the kid gloves it was later accused of wearing.[102]

Adams and Sulzberger later spoke on the phone about the contents of Eisenhower's upcoming Milwaukee speech, which distressed Sulzberger for its omission of a planned line defending General George C. Marshall. The former secretary of state, along with everyone who was now or ever had been a member of Truman's State Department, was under attack from McCarthy. Eisenhower did not defend Marshall but did endorse McCarthy for reelection to the Senate. After the speech, Sulzberger followed up with a letter to Adams saying he was "sick at heart" that Eisenhower had not defended Marshall.[103]

Largely because he did not renounce McCarthy, Eisenhower was a disappointment to many liberal internationalists who supported him. The columnist Joe Alsop gave an assessment of the feeling in Washington in an October 1952 letter to his friend Isaiah Berlin, the philosopher at Oxford: "I have no news whatever that would interest you, except that Phil Graham is both defiant and violent in his continued support of the Republicans," referring to the publisher of the *Washington Post* who had also come out early for Eisenhower. "I would have thought he would have switched by now," Alsop wrote, reflecting the general disappointment in Washington that Eisenhower's campaign had moved rightward. "The NEW YORK TIMES has relapsed into uncomfortable silence, and almost all one's personal friends are going to vote for Stevenson. So there you are."[104] Even Walter Lippmann, who publicly supported Eisenhower, admitted to Wallie Deuel on Election Day and within the safety of the Metropolitan Club, while waiting to be seated for lunch, that in his heart he wanted Stevenson to win.[105]

Arthur Sulzberger had been jittery and a little defensive the day before the election. He was so absorbed in the race that he dated a letter to his friend General Alfred Gruenther at SHAPE: "The Day before Election, 1952." He wrote, "We saw in Taft a menace to all we hold dear and so we spoke and committed ourselves when we did."[106] He seemed to be answering the criticisms of the fifteen thousand readers who had written the *Times*, asking it to change its position and endorse the Democratic nominee, Stevenson.[107] From Sulzberger's perch, the general's chances of winning appeared slim, and the publisher wanted to justify his decision by reminding himself of its main purpose: saving the Atlantic alliance from the isolationists.

Sulzberger's anxiety proved to be without foundation. Ike received 55.2 percent of the popular vote compared to Stevenson's 44.3 percent, and he won in the Electoral College, 442 to 89. By one thirty in the early morning of November 5, the results were clear. General Julius Ochs Adler, Iphigene Sulzberger's cousin and the *Times*' business manager, dashed off a telegram to Eisenhower almost frightening for its implication that internationalism was part of America's Manifest Destiny: "Under your inspiring leadership the American people will be restored to the heights of our righteous destiny. Thrice congratulations upon your overwhelming and magnificent victory."[108]

After the 1953 Korean War armistice, the United States seemed to be technically at peace again. For as long as isolationism remained, though, so would the press corps' sense of duty for stamping it out. For Europe to recover from two world wars just twenty years apart, diplomatic reporters believed that the nation would need to play a greater role internationally than it had during the 1920s and 1930s. Preventing a retrenchment of isolationism and making it seem as if isolationism was not in the mainstream were as important to them as fealty to an imperfect ideal of objectivity.

6

COVERING IMPERIALISM
IN THE POSTWAR WORLD

"I am pretty sick of the whole theory of American self-righteousness," Joe Harsch, the Washington reporter for the *Christian Science Monitor* and commentator for CBS, wrote a friend in 1944 as the Allies were planning the peace. "We are the pretty innocents of the world who never grab anything while naughty Britain and wicked Russia look after their own self-interests and security. Nonsense! We aren't going to get anything out of this war. No? We are just going to take all the islands in the Pacific which happen to be all we need to guarantee our naval and air control of that Ocean."[1] Harsch was not a radical leftist but a liberal internationalist—socially and ideologically in the mainstream of his cohort. He was born in Toledo, attended Williams College, joined the *Monitor* in 1929, and was assigned to Washington in 1939. His newspaper was among the most highly regarded in the nation, and his radio spots gave him a broader national audience. His involvement with Christian Science did put him out of the mainstream of Washington religiously, but the only noticeable effect the religion seems to have had on him was a crushing guilt about smoking.[2] He continued in the 1944 letter, "My only contention is that we have the appearance of greater morality only where we can afford to be more moral—which isn't as often as we like to believe. Sometimes I think that we are the world's greatest hypocrites."[3]

Like Harsch, Wallie Deuel of the *Chicago Daily News* kept a larger critique about hypocrisy for his private journals, letters, and conversations. Several times in his postwar notes and letters, Deuel compared Americans' attitudes about foreign policy with their attitudes about sex—that is, that they "do the same things everybody else does, but they honestly don't realize/think they do." He wrote in private notes in February 1946, "Americans have no idea what their conduct looks like to other people, and are sincerely outraged when the others call things by their right names." Deuel and Harsch had both been based in Europe before the war and were especially attuned to international attitudes, as were most of their fellow diplomatic reporters. These newsmen spent as much time on Washington's Embassy Row developing foreign sources as at the State Department, much to the chagrin of the State Department. "The others, for their part, see little but the rankest kind of hypocrisy in the American attitude," Deuel wrote, referring to foreigners' perceptions. "You can do anything you like, provided you don't call it by its right name or give your real reasons for doing it. This is particularly the case with regard to power."[4]

As reporters gathered to discuss the United States' position as a new kind of imperial power, they created one conversation within Washington and another for public consumption, which has had significant repercussions for how we have come to understand the Cold War. Historians initially thought of this early period of the Cold War as one when both mainstream liberals and conservatives believed that political ideology trumped economic concerns: that the nation cared more about combating communism than acquiring markets and raw materials.[5] The United States was a force for good, the mainstream thinking supposedly went, if only people around the world could be made to understand that fact, through subtle propaganda to counter the Soviet charge of Western imperialism.[6] In 1959, the revisionist historian William Appleman Williams in *The Tragedy of American Diplomacy* developed the idea that "open door imperialism" had driven US foreign policy for a hundred years, and still did so in the Cold War. Williams's argument for economic determinism and criticism of the United States' ongoing imperial ambitions did not become accepted until the social revolutions of the late 1960s and 1970s, and then primarily within academia. Yet those ideas were discussed at the time within diplomatic reporting circles. The revisionist academic critiques of US foreign policy that emerged during the late 1950s and 1960s often made it seem as if mainstream liberal intellectuals and journalists had not understood or fully appreciated the economic imperatives behind postwar foreign policy. Or they might have been deceived by US government officials. Or they were blinded by patriotism into believing that the United States was a moral force for good in the world.

Yet archival sources suggest that few people, in Washington at least, held illusions about the country's goals—official rhetoric and their own faulty memories notwithstanding. Reporters recognized a hypocrisy in America's postwar power grab that they kept to themselves for professional reasons, so as not to alienate readers and newspaper executives, and for personal reasons, to demonstrate their trust and loyalty within a closed group.

The affinity that reporters and foreign policy elites felt for Western Europe and the importance placed on maintaining strong ties with Atlantic allies had roots in a worldview that privileged whiteness and considered *civilization* to refer to white democratic nations, valuing Western Europeans over colonial peoples.[7] Reporters believed that the survival of Western Europe depended on its continued access to the resources of its former and current colonies, highlighting the tension between the anticolonialism the United States ostensibly supported and its friendly relationships with Great Britain and France. Both in print and in private, newsmen emphasized the multiple, sometimes contradictory, naturally self-interested reasons for the pursuit of foreign policy. However, the blatant hypocrisy of certain policies or the fact that policy makers spoke differently in private to the American people than they did publicly was not part of their public discourse. Only reporters for Black-owned newspapers and "rebel" journalists like Izzy Stone were willing to point out the contradictions in foreign policy in print. Meanwhile, the newsmen of Overseas Writers and the Gridiron Club kept themselves in segregated spaces in which saving white civilization—embodied by Great Britain and France—trumped concerns about self-determination and independence.

"British Empire Here We Come"

In late February 1947, Secretary of State George C. Marshall spoke off the record to Overseas Writers at the Statler Hotel about one of the main hypocrisies the United States was facing in its postwar task: imperial power. Wallie Deuel summarized Marshall's assessment in his notes: "Long critical of the British Empire, the U.S. must now accept responsibilities for doing at least some of the things the British have done in the past." Deuel then quoted Marshall directly as having said, "It causes quite a wrench in your thinking."[8]

A few days later, on March 4, 1947, General Dwight Eisenhower, then serving as United States Army chief of staff, had an off-the-record lunch at the home of Eugene Meyer, chairman of the *Washington Post*. Meyer had invited twenty-two newsmen, many who had just seen Marshall at Overseas Writers.[9] The conversation focused on raw materials and realpolitik, and Eisenhower reiterated Marshall's talking points about the importance of the British Empire. The attendees all wrote memos and sent them back to their editors. Carroll Kilpatrick of the *San Francisco Chronicle*—later of the *Washington Post*, with a stint in between as an assistant press chief in the State Department in 1951—paraphrased Ike. "No matter what we may think of Great Britain we must consider the Empire as our defensive outpost," Eisenhower had said. "We are not going to take over where Britain pulls out but we want to be sure we have friendly relations throughout the Empire."[10]

Eisenhower then explained the domino theory of communism, but in the same breath he expressed the seemingly incongruous idea of flexibility in dealing with the Soviet Union, for the sake of access to raw materials. If one country, such as Greece, fell to communism, Ike said, others might follow, and this would be problematic for the West's access to oil. "The brigands are communist-controlled, and to permit Greece to fall into the Russian orbit would be serious business not only for Turkey but for the whole Middle East," Kilpatrick wrote. "We must remember that Russia has legitimate rights to a warm water port and perhaps we should support her in that ambition as one way of relieving tension. But we also must remember that Iran and Iraq are the major sources of oil."[11] Eisenhower made it clear that material considerations, like oil, were just as important as ideological arguments about how much power the Soviet Union should have.

Marshall and Eisenhower were laying the groundwork for the announcement of a massive aid package to Greece and Turkey. On March 12, 1947, President Harry Truman gave the speech famous for outlining the Truman Doctrine, an interventionist policy that called for defeating communism wherever it emerged. He asked for $400 million for aid to Greece and, without naming Russia, made it clear that US foreign policy was now anti-Soviet.[12]

In a front-page *Christian Science Monitor* article in late April 1947, Joe Harsch characterized the Truman Doctrine as an "uneconomic and ideological struggle with Russia," which fortunately, he believed, was already being abandoned six weeks later in favor of an economic and nonideological one. He wrote about the "major shift" from a weak and costly plan to a focus on "the heart of western civilization, which is western Europe."[13] A reader—a World War II veteran living in Princeton, New Jersey—wrote Harsch that Americans were not being told the real story of *why* the country was opposing Soviet expansion in Western Europe. He doubted that what the United States really had in mind was improving the conditions of Europeans. Instead, it was its own interests, which could lead to backing "regimes which will first protect their and our interests," rather than improving political and economic conditions. The nation had done this in the past, he noted. "If we do it in the future, our hypocrisy will one day become evident, and I fear for our nation in the storm which will break."[14]

Harsch did not address all the reader's concerns, but he replied with a frank discussion of the difference between what leaders said publicly and privately. "May I say that so far as I have been able as a reporter to determine the real reason in the minds of Washington's top diplomatic planners for our resistance to communist expansion it is the conflict of economic and political interests. The ideological argument is used for the purpose of obtaining Congressional action and popular approval, but in talking privately to the men who make policy I find this issue usually played way down and frequently ignored all together." Harsch went so far as to say that the United States would be having similar concerns about stabilizing Russia's borders if it were ruled by Peter the Great instead of Joseph Stalin. This trope of an unchanging "Eternal Russia," though ahistorical, downplayed communism and would become a common part of journalists' public appraisals of the Soviet Union during the 1970s.[15] For now, it was private. Harsch's response—that "the anti-communist crusade is a device" and that even if Truman did not understand that point, Secretary of State Marshall did—was likely of little comfort to the reader, who may have hoped for a similar frankness on the front page of his newspaper.[16]

Daily newspapers covered the many variables that went into foreign policy, and often did so well, but only outsiders, like Izzy Stone, stated the hypocrisy outright. "Only naivete and ignorance can accept Mr. Truman's pharisaical self-portrait of American policy," Stone wrote in 1949. "A government which constantly bypasses the UN, curries favor with [Argentinian vice president Juan] Peron, does business with any number of military dictators in Latin America, deals under the table with [Spanish dictator Francisco] Franco, interferes in Italian elections, and supports reactionaries in Greece has too many motes in its own eye to preach a dubious freedom in Eastern Europe and China."[17] Harsch was neither naive nor ignorant.

There still is no consensus on the extent to which anticommunism motivated foreign policy makers and whether ideological concerns were genuine, rhetorical, or, as is most likely the case, a combination. Truman and his successors' public and private statements include those that emphasized the practicality of access to raw materials as well as the less tangible ideals of freedom and democracy. At different moments, different policy makers had multiple and sometimes contradictory beliefs, and the many policy memos that the new National Security Council, established in the summer of 1947, produced can provide support for any number of arguments about the "official" policy directions. Reporters were privy to the day-by-day, on-the-ground discussions of what was "in the air" in Washington, though, and that was *not* ideological concern about anticommunism.

Anticommunism has indeed been a dominant and sometimes virulent strain in US domestic politics, from the Russian Revolution through at least the end of the Cold War. Many groups promoted domestic anticommunism and wove it into beliefs about the "American Way."[18] The liberal newsmen who dominated foreign policy reporting were typically not among those groups. Perhaps some Americans read the most emphatic of Joe Alsop's "cold warrior" columns and came to anticommunism through them. Most Americans reading about foreign policy news saw fairly muted discussions of communism, however— what only the most extreme publications and commentators would have called a red menace.[19]

On May 10, 1947, two months after the announcement of the Truman Doctrine, the Gridiron Club held its spring banquet. If there was one thing the Gridiron did well, it was putting the hypocrisy of the federal government on private display, usually while ignoring its own. This spring banquet had all the elements that made those dinners special to the club's members: attendance by nearly every top government official, a dress code of white tie and tails, attendance exclusively by white men, terrapin stew, performances in blackface, and jokes about foreign policy that revealed the depth of understanding of the limits—even demerits—of US foreign policy that these same men did not acknowledge in public writings.

In 1941, the Republican Senator Arthur Vandenberg, later famous for expanding the internationalist wing of the Republican Party, wrote a story about the history of the Gridiron for *Liberty* magazine. In it, he praised the Gridironers and made a case for their importance. "It is doubtful whether any other group of fifty private citizens have wielded a greater indirect influence upon the public questions which the glow of the Gridiron has illuminated—although any conscious thought of 'exerting influence' is farthest from the Gridiron thought or purpose," Vandenberg wrote. "But one of these Gridiron 'skits,' as they are called, may succeed so conclusively in projecting the innate absurdity of something in the national prospectus that even its sponsors may conclude not to risk a national reaction in kind. I think I have seen exactly that thing happen more than once in the twenty-six consecutive dinners which I have been lucky enough to be invited to attend."[20] The dinner was an opportunity for five hundred of the nation's elites to come together in Washington, in the midst of a foreign policy sea change, and work through the acceptable ranges of dissent while at the same time shoring up the US racial order.

The men who attended Gridiron Club dinners had access to one another, to the many cocktail parties before and after the dinner, and to off-the-record political speeches of national consequence. Gridiron tradition dictated that the president and a member of the opposition party were the two keynote speakers. But even the extroverted Franklin Roosevelt begged more than once in his twelve years in office to be released from the obligation. Dwight Eisenhower got away with just a toast, leaving other men to deliver the speech. The Gridiron members bestowed the other speaker spots as favors. "We consider that in asking a public man to speak, we are paying him an envied compliment; and affording him a precious opportunity," noted one member in 1947, in a letter of advice for that year's opposition speaker, Earl Warren, then governor of California and later a Supreme Court justice. "We try to pick our speakers with care," he explained. "We owe them much for their appearance, but we think they owe us for the chance. Men can be made or broken by a Gridiron speech. In my own membership of fourteen years, I have seen this. Harold Stassen was coming up fast in the political world, as a Minnesota Governor, but I believe his Gridiron speech of say ten years ago, really started him on the national stage." (Stassen was that Republican representative at the 1945 San Francisco UN conference whom reporters had covered so favorably.) "Conversely, I saw, in recent years, a speaker show such ineptitude and such poor taste, that his chance as a national figure was damaged for the time, at least," he continued, likely referring to the reactionary Republican senator John Bricker, whose speech of December 1946 had been famously terrible.[21] At the time, one White House aide had commented to a member of the Gridiron that Bricker had crucified himself. "Why do you think we had him?" responded the Gridironer, a supporter of Bricker's rival, Tom Dewey.[22]

During the May 1947 dinner, the foreign affairs skits poked fun at the Truman Doctrine, with Truman and George C. Marshall at the head table. One of the chief criticisms of that policy was that the more communist a country was leaning, the more money it would receive; it behooved a country to pretend to be more susceptible to communism than it was. Communism *was* a laughing matter. The skit took place in the fictitious kingdom of the cannibals, the only land where Truman Doctrine aid had supposedly yet to reach. The stage had a man-sized kettle over an electric fire, a gaudy throne for the cannibal king, and a palm tree with a pay phone in it. The chorus of cannibals for this skit were all wearing blackface, a common Gridiron costume. Amateur minstrelsy was a tradition in white men's fraternal organizations and, as the historian Rhae Lynn Barnes argues, was also "integral to domestic and international imperialism."[23] Skits like these seamlessly connected domestic racism to the racism of procolonial foreign policy. The scene opened with the cannibal king, played by Lewis Wood of the *New York Times*, saying to the cannibal treasury secretary, played by Peter Brandt of the *St. Louis Post-Dispatch*: "Mister Sekatary of de Treasury, you look lower dan a Chinese dollar."[24]

"Chief, I aint any lower dan de royal trashury. We is plumb broke," Brandt responded, in the dialect written out in the script.

The secretary of the treasury then informed the king about the Truman Doctrine, prompting all the cannibals to sing about getting "paid just to keep the Reds away / Soak Uncle Sam for a billion bucks or so" and to make a plea: "Massa Truman, save us please from Old Red Joe," making a connection between the stereotypes of the US slaveholding South and the global South.

The Gridironer playing Joseph Stalin then entered to sing about the glories of the Soviet Union, until the Gridironer playing Secretary Marshall arrived for a duet with Stalin to the tune of "Anything You Can Do, I Can Do Better" from the popular Broadway musical *Annie Get Your Gun*. Here is Marshall, halfway through the song:

I can drop a rocket into your hip-pocket.

I can bounce uranium right on Russia's cranium.

Stalin: I can use a Trojan horse.

Marshall: You mean THAT GUY HANK?

Stalin (spoken): Da!

Marshall: We think he's rank.

"Hank" referred to Henry Wallace, part of the late President Roosevelt's Brains Trust and lately persona non grata in Washington. Wallace was seen as someone reciting the Soviet propaganda line that US economic aid was politically menacing. The realities of imperialism were not meant to be spoken out loud, as Wallace was doing, but only in off-the-record luncheons and songs.

A Wallace character soon entered the scene dressed as a Boy Scout and sang "You Can't Win the Peace with a Gun" to the tune of "You Can't Get a Man with a Gun," also from *Annie Get Your Gun*. Wallace was supposed to be regarded as a ridiculous, naive dupe, since the common agreement by now in Washington was that guns—or missiles— *were* necessary to winning the peace. Peace was waged, as war was, with uranium, on Russia's cranium, so to speak.

The skit ended with the arrival of a Gridironer playing the State Department advisor John Foster Dulles. He was still six years away from becoming secretary of state but at the time was being mentioned for that job in the Republican administration that was predicted to win in 1948. The columnist Mark Childs, playing Dulles, sang that the United States was coming after the British Empire to the tune of "California Here I Come":

The Turks and Greeks said, Don't be late,

Save us from an awful fate.

Leave your dollars at the gate.

British Empire here we come.

When the skits were over, Harry Truman gave the customary presidential speech, which included thanking journalists for supporting the Truman Doctrine. "As I have said before, our press has done a particularly fine job in making clear to people the full meaning of our policy of aid to Greece and Turkey," Truman said. "It can take some share of the credit for the resounding majority which the Greek and Turkish aid bill has just won in the House of Representatives. I am not here just to butter up the press. I don't think it is perfect. But, it is the best press in the world and it is a doing a fine job. It is an integral part of our democracy."[25] Diplomatic reporters certainly believed themselves to be integral, and special occasions like this one helped reinforce the idea that they were doing important work in the struggle for democracy, at home and worldwide. At the same time, they were in privileged enough positions to be able to lampoon those same policies and discuss them more frankly behind closed doors than they would in print.

Less than a month later, in a June 1947 commencement speech at Harvard University, Marshall announced the second major foreign policy initiative of the Truman administration, which Joe Harsch of the *Christian Science Monitor* and others had foretold in their news articles: an increase in economic aid to Western Europe. In selling the Marshall Plan, or European Recovery Program (ERP), to white reporters, the undersecretary of state, Robert Lovett, emphasized, according to Wallie Deuel's notes: "The Europeans are 'first class people.' 'The fundamentals of life are still there.' The land is there, technology is advanced, etc. 'Damn it all,' he can't see why it can't be saved. It was 'one of the nicest places in the world.'" The Marshall Plan was envisioned as aid only for these first-class people. Lovett also framed the ERP as a way for the United States to export surplus capital, a distinctly revisionist historical understanding. He explicitly put the British Empire analogy into the context of a search for markets, the heart of what the historian William Appleman Williams later called the "tragedy of American diplomacy." Deuel wrote detailed confidential notes of the meeting, noting that Lovett had said, "America's position now is analagous [sic] to that of Britain after the Napoleonic wars. Capital is accumulating in the U.S. at a terrific rate. The British exported capital then, we can do it now. But fiscal stability is required in the places to which capital could be exported."[26] Indeed, conversations during this period shared more similarity with Cold War historians' revisionist discourse of economic determinism than with the traditionalist narrative they ostensibly reflected.[27] That is, reporters helped maintain the fiction that the United States was *not* building an empire, or searching for markets, or seeking investments, even when they discussed those motives among themselves. The administration was not propagandizing them into patriotic anticommunist submission, however. Indeed, in this early phase, the government's propaganda efforts were barely developed, and the institutions developed to support Cold War foreign policy still nascent.[28]

The Marshall Plan was about saving a first-class people, since it would be ridiculous to prioritize those uncivilized peoples who barely had "sekataries" of "de royal trashury," as the Gridironers had just mocked. Developing nations did receive aid from a separate allocation of funds in 1949 with the Point Four program. That program assisted nations where the technology and institutions were not advanced enough, the reasoning went, for the economic aid then being given to civilized nations. Seventy years later, many remember the Marshall Plan but few recall Point Four assistance, which reflects the amount of funding and press coverage each received.[29] The legacy of the Marshall Plan was one of European recovery, while the Point Four program resulted in a less savory narrative of access to raw materials and developing industry for the West, with little of the promised infrastructural uplift or poverty relief for the recipient nations.[30]

Diplomatic reporters, who had a genuine desire for Europe to recover from the war, framed their news stories in ways that promoted the Marshall Plan and ongoing US intervention in Western Europe. They wanted to save the heart of civilization. In November 1947, the *Washington Post* ran a much-publicized sixteen-page pull-out section on the Marshall Plan entitled "This Generation's Chance for Peace."[31] In this special supplement, the *Post* emphasized how important the plan was to Americans, with the first story headline proclaiming that "Our Mutual Interests Dictated Marshall Plan." A boldfaced paragraph in the opening article accentuated the point: "The situation we face is difficult and possibly perilous. We must approach it with hard-headed concern for our own well-being. But we should not forget that our welfare is geared into the welfare of other peoples, particularly those of western Europe."[32] The United States had a special bond with the peoples of Western Europe, the *Post* writers believed. In addition to being widely read within Washington, two hundred thousand copies of the supplement were distributed nationwide through the Committee for the Marshall Plan to Aid European Recovery, a group of eighteen hundred US leaders with deep and wide media ties, who charged themselves with promoting acceptance of the ERP.[33]

If any journalists later said they had considered the United States a selfless power, seeking only to do good in the world or introduce democracy abroad, they misremembered the experience of actually living and working in Washington in 1947 and 1948, when a different conversation circulated. They knew at the time that Americans were building a new kind of empire that conflicted with the rising decolonization and anticolonial movements. They heard that narrative at Overseas Writers and reiterated it in their daily reporting. ("Also we have a keen interest in the development of European colonial resources of raw materials," the diplomat Averell Harriman reminded reporters in April 1948.)[34] In notes from one meeting that Deuel, now reporting for the *St. Louis Post-Dispatch*, had with three State Department officials during the fall of 1949, he revealed the clarity with which the United States saw its postwar mission—that is, as an economic one to revitalize its Western European allies. He and his sources discussed an agreement that the colonial Dutch and the Indonesians had reached with the help of the United States. "Indefinite prolongation of the hostilities there would probably have resulted in Indonesia's going Communist," Deuel wrote in his notes on "BACKGROUND," as he emphasized for himself. The State Department men then drew a direct connection between Indonesia's natural resources and the Marshall Plan: "Indonesia is vitally important because of its strategic position, its production of vital raw materials— which are especially important for the success of ERP—including foodstuffs [and] rubber and tin and sugar."[35] Indonesia going communist mattered mainly insofar as it had economic consequences for Western Europe. The Marshall Plan could work only if the structures of colonialism remained intact, despite the United States' publicly committing to self-determination for all peoples and consistently condemning the Dutch for its police actions against its colonies.[36]

The discourse around raw materials from nonwhite colonies and former colonies, and a belief in "civilization" existing only in the white metropoles, remained strong into the 1950s. In January 1951, when Dwight Eisenhower was supreme allied commander at NATO, the *New York Times'* Washington bureau chief, Arthur Krock, wrote a summary of a "very small confidential meeting today at luncheon" with the general at the Statler Hotel. He sent it to the *Times'* managing editor in New York "for the Publisher's private eyes and yours." Krock wrote that Eisenhower had spoken of the necessity of building up fifty or fifty-five NATO divisions in Europe: "That is because only Western Europe and its colonies, possessions and related allies in the Eastern Hemisphere can furnish the things we need, and Western Europe is the cradle of our civilization. If it goes India will follow soon, for example, and where will we get our manganese?" White reporters did not acknowledge unsavory facts, out of fear of being accused of disloyalty not to their government but to one another and to the Western civilization they cherished—not to mention to the readers on whom their livelihood depended.[37] In November 1947, Ferdie Kuhn did have a front-page story in the *Washington Post* based on a report by the President's Committee on Foreign Aid, Averell Harriman's committee, that ended with a list of nine resources necessary to the United States in alphabetical order, from bauxite to tungsten, and specific locations where those resources could be obtained. The headline read: "U.S. to Seek Rare Minerals from Europe," but the article specified in its first paragraph that the materials were from "Europe and its colonies," the most important of which was Belgian Congo. Of those nine specific materials, only one actually came from Europe—tungsten, from Portugal, the cost of which was deemed too high to make it attractive to the United States anyway.[38]

A Segregated Sphere of Consensus

The discourse that was largely private among the white male journalists who made up the diplomatic press corps was clearly visible in the Black press, whose reporters had no Overseas Writers or Gridiron invitations to lose out on and very few exclusive social functions with State Department dignitaries. In fact, the capital's hotels and restaurants remained segregated until 1953, after which de facto segregation and discrimination continued for decades. Washington had become an international city, but it was still Southern. For instance, in 1946, the New York–based Overseas Press Club—a more public-facing group than Washington's Overseas Writers—hosted a dinner in Washington honoring decorated war correspondents. The Washington-based organizers worried when they found out that some of those correspondents were African American, since the venue, the Hotel Statler, normally served whites only. Just two years earlier, the Statler had actually fired a white supervisor who had insisted on eating with members of her staff, who were predominantly Black.[39] For this event, however, "the hotel agreed to serve provided there were not too many and no disturbances," according to the notes of Ruth Cowan, one of the organizers and a reporter for the Associated Press.[40] Ultimately, fourteen Black guests attended, when Cowan had expected four. "We had hoped that the $10 a piece ticket charge would hold them down," she wrote in her notes, revealing a strategy that white clubs often used to maintain de facto segregation: pricing out anyone who was not white, since salaries for reporters of color were systemically lower. Cowan rearranged the tables to put anyone who looked Black to her in the second, overflow room. The executive secretary of the Overseas Press Club, a New Yorker, began raising objections to the segregation, "not fully understanding this town's tense feeling," as Cowan put it—a sentiment highlighting that the capital was indeed a Southern town and that whatever norms held among reporters in New York or other cities did not necessarily obtain in the capital.

Kept out of many public spaces and barred from all the press clubs, thirty-five African American men and women reporters and government public relations workers formed the Capital Press Club in 1944. The club held weekly luncheon meetings with guest speakers at places like the Club Bengasi or the Dunbar Hotel in the U Street area, the main artery for Black theater, restaurants, and civic life. For larger events, like their fast-growing annual awards banquet, members met in spaces at Howard University, the Black university founded in 1867 that was an important hub of Washington intellectual and civic life.

The Capital Press Club served a central function to the internal networking of Black newspapers. However, the white press, which controlled access to news events in Washington, did not even register its existence. In 1951, when Princess Elizabeth of England and the Duke of Edinburgh visited the capital, a committee that represented "the ten organizations of the press" planned the reception.[41] The committee members presumably thought that this covered everyone. The ten organizations were the Radio Correspondents' Association, the American News Women's Club, the White House News Photographers' Association, the Periodical Press Galleries, the White House Correspondents' Association, the Department of State Correspondents' Association, Overseas Writers, the Standing Committee of Correspondents, the National Press Club, and the Women's National Press Club. No Capital Press Club. Since 1947, Black reporters had been allowed to be members of the Periodical Press Galleries and would have still been able to attend some of the events held in public desegregated spaces, but their club did not rate formal representation in the event planning.[42]

Editors and publishers who could have hired Black reporters and broken the color barrier were reluctant to do so, in part because reporters of color did not have the same access to segregated private spaces. In 1950, the *Washington Post* was trying to figure out how to "meet our all-around objectives of fulfilling a social obligation to the Negro community without affronting the white community," as the managing editor, Russ Wiggins, wrote the publisher, Phil Graham. Perhaps they could "consider taking a bright young local boy of demonstrated aptitude, and start him out in sports." By hiring a young reporter instead of someone established, they could fire him without creating backlash if it did not work out. Also, certain sports had already been integrated, so the assignment would presumably be less offensive to white readers. However, Wiggins warned that this move could still "get us into some trouble with some of our most prejudiced communities." He suggested the best option might be to hire someone who worked only inside the building, like a library clerk or assistant, and had no public-facing interactions. "Any Negro reporter in this city is going to have limited usefulness and encounter a great many rebuffs, both for himself and the paper," he wrote.[43] Wiggins—a member of the all-white Gridiron Club, Overseas Writers, and National Press Club—knew firsthand how limited a Black reporter's usefulness would be.

The next year, the newspaper did hire one Black reporter, Simeon Booker, who had recently completed a prestigious Nieman Fellowship at Harvard, available for reporters to study any subjects they wanted at the university for a year. Booker, who had most recently covered issues of housing discrimination against African Americans for the *Cleveland Call and Post*, had written directly to Graham asking for a job. He stayed two years at the *Washington Post*, until the accumulated barriers and slights—especially the fact that the paper assigned him his own bathroom—led to his leaving to work as Washington bureau chief for Black-owned Johnson Publishing, which published the magazines *Jet* and *Ebony*.[44] The *Washington Post* did not hire another Black reporter until 1972.

Black reporters in Washington were at a disadvantage in another, less obvious way as well: less leisure time. In 1953, Ethel Payne (fig. 6.1) moved to Washington to work for the *Chicago Defender*, one of the nation's leading Black newspapers, as its only reporter there. Because she wrote solo for an underfunded Black paper, she worked around the clock and had little time to socialize.[45] Similarly, regional white newspapers around the country often had one-person bureaus in Washington, but those papers usually also subscribed to wire services—the Associated Press or the United Press—for general news coverage from the capital. White newspapers had prevented Black ones from joining the wire services, leading them to start their own in 1919: the Associated Negro Press, which still did Payne no good, since the *Defender* at that time did not pay for any wire services. So Payne covered every news

FIGURE 6.1. Ethel Payne, the Washington correspondent for the *Chicago Defender*, and Senator Paul Douglas at a Capital Press Club event in 1958. Thirty-five Black reporters, who were barred from joining all other Washington news clubs, had formed the club fourteen years earlier. Credit: Maurice Sorrell, Prints and Photographs Division, Library of Congress.

beat by herself: breaking news, longer feature pieces, the White House, the State Department, Congress, and the Pentagon. She remembered working out of her apartment, since the newspaper could not afford an office, pounding on the typewriter until two or three o'clock in the morning, and then taking a cab to the post office to send in her stories. "I just was determined to try to do a job, and that took all my energy, all my thoughts, and took all my time. I didn't have time to be social," Payne recalled in 1987. Even with more time, she still would have had two strikes against her as a Black woman in her profession. Payne, who wrote an essay on the Black press that was aptly titled "Loneliness in the Capital," was doubly excluded.[46]

Moreover, bringing up racism as a problem at all was dangerous for both Black and white reporters. In 1954, the White House press secretary, James Hagerty, threatened to withdraw Payne's press credentials after she asked at a press conference about an Interstate Commerce

Commission ruling on segregation that sparked an outburst from Eisenhower, the official transcript of which apparently does not convey the harsh tone that Payne recalled.[47] She remembered that the president's wrath had been so intense that Eddie Folliard of the *Washington Post* had consoled her afterward.[48] Her newspaper ended up publishing a story about the incident on its front page ten days later under a banner headline: "Defender Query Angers Ike." Hagerty looked into Payne's background to see whether there was a basis for taking away her press credentials, which he believed that he found: work she had done for the CIO, a labor organization, that could compromise her reportorial objectivity. Payne recalled that Hagerty only dropped the issue a year later, once the syndicated columnist Drew Pearson ran a story that touched on several issues, including Payne's being silenced at press conferences. He framed these issues in terms of press freedom, which the administration could not be viewed as going against, and Payne kept her credentials.[49]

The Black press, with its history of public activism, of course treated the racialized foreign policies of the postwar United States, like European recovery, differently from the white press. A front-page headline from September 1946 in the *Atlanta Daily World*, "Africans Stay Poor while Europeans Rob Rich Mines," ran with a story from the Associated Negro Press, which meant that it had wide distribution.[50] The article began with the explanation that "poverty stricken Ashanti people must remain poor while their wealthy mineral mines are robbed by the British." No white newspaper could have run a similar story and had its reporter ever again invited to an off-the-record or background session that dealt with the British. The Black press's critique of US foreign policy as imperialistic did find a white audience, but not until it was raised by white revisionist historians decades later.

Similarly, the Black press characterized from the beginning the quest for oil in the Middle East as a project of US-British imperialism. A columnist in the *Chicago Defender* wrote in May 1946, "The truth is that behind the curtain of Kremlin-baiting lurked a couple of unsavory characters who were engaged in a little drama of their own. They could be named Wall Street and London City, respectively identified as US and British imperialism. Their joint aim is to plunder as much of the wealth and resources of the Near East as they can."[51] Joe Harsch of the *Christian Science Monitor* acknowledged in private that anticommunism was a rhetorical ploy, but he was unlikely to have used a phrase so controversial—either publicly or privately—as "Kremlin-baiting." Nor did he and his cohort of reporters frame resource extraction as "plunder," even as they acknowledged US imperial practices.

Those articles had been written before the Marshall Plan, legislation that most high-profile Black organizations, like the National Association for the Advancement of Colored People (NAACP), ultimately endorsed, though not without registering disapproval of its inherent racial bias. Even with overall support, the language of the ensuing coverage by the Black press sometimes remained quite critical. W. O. Walker of the *Cleveland Call and Post*, in a column that was then also excerpted in the *Baltimore Afro-American*, declared, "The Marshall plan is nothing short of being the biggest appeasement effort ever put forward by the American government to save England and several other European countries in which American banks and investment houses have large financial holdings. . . . As I see it, the Marshall plan simply is trying to provide a breathing spell for these European nations until they can better organize themselves to take more wealth out of the hides and lands of their exploited people."[52] Walker was a fairly radical columnist, but even influential Black activists in the mainstream who supported the Marshall Plan spoke of its discrimination, which was entirely overlooked in the published writings of the white press.

During Senate Foreign Relations Committee hearings on the funding of the European Recovery Program in February 1948, Walter White, the executive secretary of the NAACP, testified that while he supported the Marshall Plan, he thought it should be applied more broadly to non-European countries also affected by the war.[53] The page-one headline in the *Atlanta Daily World* proclaimed, "Aid Others beside Europeans—White."[54] "Let Marshall Plan Help All, Senate Told," was the *Baltimore Afro-American*'s more subdued version. The story seems to have appeared in every major Black newspaper over the next ten days. White's testimony was not mentioned by the white press at all, except at the end of a story by Al Friendly in the *Washington Post* noting simply that White had "urged the Marshall Plan as a step in 'human kindness.'"[55] White was simultaneously trying to get an antilynching bill through Congress, so his name did appear in the white press in that regard, including as the author of columns in the *New York Herald Tribune*, but not in relation to the critique of the Marshall Plan or foreign policy. Meanwhile, the *New York Times*, whose publisher, Arthur Sulzberger, was friends with the financier Bernard Baruch, printed Baruch's testimony in favor of the Marshall Plan in full around the same time. Baruch's statement is one of the only times that *colonies* appears in the same story as the Marshall Plan in a major white newspaper, and the context was not one of racial critique. Instead, Baruch said that the United States should take measures that would indicate to the world: "We stand ready to assure a market for the productive labor of all peoples for the next five years. Bring out the resources that lie in the ground. Go out into your colonies and the far reaches of the world and tap their riches. Produce! You will be able to sell it all."[56] Otherwise, the *Times* seems to have been silent on the colonial issue. The critique of the Black press did not seem to penetrate the "sphere of consensus"[57] built out in white Washington, even though both groups acknowledged the same facts: that the United States was trying to save Western Europe using the raw materials of poorer nations.

Researchers at Northwestern University during the early 1950s found twenty-eight themes in white newspaper coverage of the Marshall Plan from mid-1947 to mid-1948 and divided them into "Pro themes" (typified by the *New York Times*), "Left-anti themes" (typified by the *Daily Worker*), and "Right-anti themes" (typified by the *Chicago Tribune*). The racist or procolonial nature of the plan and its neglect of nonwhite nations were not identified as themes, though the researchers may have been coding those subjects under the category of "capitalist-imperialistic scheme," which was one of the Left-anti themes.[58] Either way, race did not factor enough into the coverage of any of these newspapers to merit a category, these researchers believed, nor did Black newspapers merit inclusion in the study at all. Present-day digital searches of a cross section of the white press reveal hardly any mention of nonwhite nations in relation to the Marshall Plan, beyond a three-sentence Associated Press squib on page 11 of the *Christian Science Monitor*—which the *New York Herald Tribune* got down to two sentences—noting that an English-language Ethiopian newspaper was critical of the Marshall Plan for leaving out Ethiopia.[59]

In March 1948, the *Chicago Defender* decided to take the same line as the NAACP: to endorse passage of the Marshall Plan, with the caveat that "some effort must be made by our government to extend this foreign aid to the non-white nations who have suffered as much from the ravages of war. . . . The Negro republics and the colonial peoples should be counted in the budget for world peace."[60] The caveat was not one the white press embraced or seems even to have covered, apart from noting the necessity for Western Europe to increase production from its colonies to be able to take full advantage of American plans.

The Marshall Plan was controversial in Congress, which is why there was such a huge promotional effort to pass the legislation, but these debates usually did not highlight the racist implications of US policy.[61] Critics on the floor of the Senate most often made anti–Marshall Plan arguments based on potential disadvantages to domestic labor and domestic consumers or on an isolationist foreign policy. Less well remembered are the rare congressional critics who echoed those in the Black press. For instance, when the isolationist senator William Langer of North Dakota said that Great Britain was using American dollars to "exploit further colonial Africa," the only large-circulation white newspaper to cover it was the *Chicago Tribune*, already against the Marshall Plan.[62] At one point State Department officials discussed whether they could simply omit the *Tribune* man from a luncheon they were organizing to discuss the Economic Cooperation Administration, which was administering the Marshall Plan. They decided that they could not, since he wrote for a major daily: "I don't see how we can gracefully leave him out."[63]

The Truman Doctrine and the Marshall Plan together had the effect of curbing criticism of US foreign policy in the Black press, so anticolonialists turned to anticommunism in their messaging, as the historian Penny Von Eschen has shown.[64] Though fears of being charged with radicalism clearly muted their criticism, Black journalists were still far more disapproving of colonial exploitation than were their white counterparts. And even though Black editorials grew less militant during the 1940s, Black public intellectuals like W. E. B. DuBois continued their criticism and were covered by the Black press.[65] Their critique, therefore, was still part of the mainstream public conversation among African American newspaper readers. DuBois also had a regular column in the *Chicago Defender*, which he used in November 1947 to discuss the Marshall Plan: "The report of the European conference on the Marshall Plan brings forward again the role of colonies. If we are not careful we will fail to realize how the value of the raw material in colonies in this new era of capitalism, may easily stop the broad plan for colonial emancipation laid down by the charter of the United Nations at San Francisco."[66] The "sphere of legitimate controversy" was wider in the Black press than in the white press, although each group recognized that raw materials in colonies were valuable, not yet to the colonized but to the colonizers.[67]

Even those many Black journalists who distanced themselves from radicals like DuBois and his alleged communist affiliations agreed with his main points and were not afraid to say so in print. DuBois gave a speech in April 1949 in which he said if the US government's lies about Soviets were "similar to the lies which Americans have been taught to believe during the past three hundred years about the Negro, God help America!"[68] Arthur Fauset, in a column in the *Philadelphia Tribune*, commented, "One need not be a Communist to agree with Dr. DuBois. And no man should be accused of being disloyal to our country for pointing out such a telling fact. It is time for us Americans to be willing to face the truth and to do something about it other than point the finger of blame in the other man's face."[69] In 1949, with the anticommunist crusade in the United States reaching its fever pitch, Black newspaper writers still engaged in critical discourse.

Again, that idea of American hypocrisy, so commonplace in the Black press and the Black experience, occurred only in private for the white press. And in that context, the acknowledgment of hypocrisy is often breathtaking. One of the most striking examples, from a man who can sometimes come across as obtuse, is a 1942 letter that Arthur Sulzberger wrote—but did not send—to *Life* magazine. *Life* had been critical of Britain's trying to maintain her Empire, arguing that it was preventing the Allies from opening a second front in the war. Sulzberger wrote, "If the British were to use the same method we employed in solving our own Indian question it would produce photographs for Life even more circulation-building than slaughtered Chinese or Nazi executioners at work. But that isn't quite fair; times have changed since we cheated and tricked and finally mowed down the men, women and children that we called Indians."[70] If we imagine the mainstream liberal internationalists of the 1940s and the 1950s to have been somehow less jaded or more patriotically naive about the United States and her history and motives, we are not taking into account the opinions they chose to keep behind closed doors or in the letters that remained in their files unsent.

Struggling with Postcolonialism

While the consensus opinion was that Americans were against colonialism in principle, anticolonialists constantly struggled to get the US government on the side of sovereignty for developing nations. The April 1955 meeting in Bandung, Indonesia, of twenty-nine African and Asian nations has come to be seen as a crystallization point for the postcolonial world order, as well as a reckoning for the United States to recognize the necessity of incorporating a "Third World" into its global vision.[71] Previously, the freedom-versus-slavery binary had allowed only for those "free" from and those "enslaved" by communism. Nations at Bandung rejected the Cold War division of the world into those countries aligned with the Soviets and those aligned with the United States. Secretary of State John Foster Dulles had framed the meeting in the mainstream press as a referendum on the Cold War, but as the foreign news committee of the Associated Press Managing Editors wrote in its annual review, "Some editors felt the coverage of the important Bandung Conference was so concerned with the search for pro-West and anti-West sentiment that we failed to catch the true relationship among the nations represented."[72] The APME review reached its thousands of member newspapers—another example of the press being self-critical during this period. However, their criticism remained largely internal, later obscuring their conscious complicity, more than passive compliance, in maintaining global white supremacy.

Two weeks after Bandung, and on what happened to be the morning of the spring 1955 Gridiron Club dinner, Chal Roberts, who covered foreign policy news for the *Washington Post*, wrote a column assessing the conference's impact. He acknowledged that Chinese premier Chou En-lai had "successfully made Red China's debut on the world stage." Chou, the United States' enemy, had "won" at Bandung. By extending an olive branch to the West, the premier had placed the diplomatic burden on the United States "to disprove the widely held belief that this country is aggressively inclined."[73]

Roberts, who during the war briefly had been Scotty Reston's assistant at the Office of War Information in London, was one of the most influential diplomatic reporters of the 1950s and 1960s. Not only did he write for the *Washington Post*, which in 1954 had a circulation of more than 381,000 for its daily paper and more for the Sunday edition, but he also was a frequent contributor to the magazine the *Reporter*, which was closely followed by fellow reporters. The *Reporter* was important for connecting the internationalists of New York, where the magazine was based, to Washington, where many of its contributors were. (Reston even had helped come up with the idea for the magazine with its publisher and editor, Max Ascoli, when the two were discussing "the subject of promoting world peace" in November 1946. Early memos outlining the parameters of the *Reporter*, sometimes referred to as an "American *Economist*" and later "an organ for the Marshall Plan era," included Reston, Wally Carroll, Eric Sevareid, and Arthur Schlesinger Jr., who all had become acquainted during the war.)[74] Additionally, Roberts wrote the "Washington Roundup" for the *Guild Reporter*, the publication of the Newspaper Guild. And finally, from 1955 to 1963, he was the anonymous author of the Washington section of "The Atlantic Report on the World Today" in the *Atlantic Monthly*.

Despite its being a Saturday, typically a low newspaper readership day, many of the Gridiron's guests, in from out of town, would have taken the opportunity to read the *Post* and likely would have read Roberts's piece as well as the editorials. The editorial on Bandung stated, tongue in cheek, "We are glad that Secretary Dulles appreciates the usefulness of the recent Bandung Conference. If he and his associates had a sympathetic attitude toward the conference all along, however, as he testified on Thursday, he managed to conceal his feelings with great skill. There was what appeared to be sound reason to believe at one point that the Secretary was anxious to play down the Afro-Asian meeting as much as possible; and the State Department, judging by normal standards of observation, seemed to undergo a succession of chills at the very thought of the conference."[75]

In fact, the month before the conference, at a secret dinner with members of the press, the secretary of state had privately told Russ Wiggins, the *Post*'s managing editor, that "he rather hoped the conference would not be as energetically covered by the Western press as the Bangkok Conference," the Southeast Asia Treaty Organization conference Dulles had organized two months prior. "In fact, he said, it would suit him all right if the press of the free world sort of boycotted the Bandung meeting. He felt this way because he felt that the meeting was primarily a tub-thumping propaganda meeting at which the Soviet countries hoped to put out a drumfire that would divide the West from the East. The greater the coverage, the more the facility with which this propaganda would be distributed throughout the world."[76] In reality, Dulles did not want China to gain the upper hand in negotiations in the Formosa Straits, or for Chou to appear like the peace-loving hero, while he, Dulles, seemed bellicose—as the editorial writers, Roberts, and everyone else in Washington knew.

That night, Chal Roberts attended the Gridiron dinner as a guest.[77] The May 1955 banquet celebrated both the seventieth anniversary of the club and the tenth anniversary of Victory in Europe Day, a sign of the ever-present war memories in the capital and a nod to the dinner's guest of honor, the onetime Allied commander in Europe, President Dwight Eisenhower. The dinner program also shows us how the door could be open for reporters to offer a more public critique of US foreign policy while at the same time they reinforced the racial hierarchy that undergirded colonialism and a free-slave Cold War framework. Nowhere can the division between white foreign policy and Black activism be seen more starkly than in a ballroom of five hundred white men in white tie and tails having a conversation about world peace while watching a Gridironer perform a skit in blackface. This was the dinner that included the song "When the Stags Go Marchin' In," poking fun at Eisenhower's tendency to throw stag dinners for wealthy businessmen. In the script, a Gridiron member "attired in knee breeches and doorman's waistcoat, black-face, white gloves" says to the Eisenhower character, "Mr. President! Mr. president, dere's a big night tonight at de White House, yes, sir. All us doormen is workin' over-time. We got one ob dese here stag dinners. Dat means no women millionaires. And here comes de first one. De president of American Cyanide!"[78]

The 1955 Gridiron happened at a moment when racial discrimination at home, as well as its connection to US reputation abroad, was of paramount concern to the State Department.[79] For the next year, Bandung remained a prism through which observers all over the world saw US foreign policy. As Joe Harsch described the conference a year later in a *Christian Science Monitor* article, Bandung had "fortified" the argument "that anticolonialism was the only policy which could compete successfully with Moscow." The article, however, was about the United States' not really being that committed to anticolonialism after all, as anyone at a Gridiron dinner might have guessed. Harsch led his story by stating, "It would not be accurate to say that the foreign policy of the United States shifted over from an anticolonial to a procolonial position this week." He then went on to explain that this was not accurate only "because the United States never did take an outright and consistent anticolonial position."[80] The news peg for the story was Washington supporting France over Algerian nationalists. Changing power dynamics in the Middle East, especially since the rise to power of Gamal Abdel Nasser in Egypt, inaugurated a time of confused US policy, culminating in January 1957 in the Eisenhower Doctrine, which stated US support for the independence—against Soviet encroachment—of Middle Eastern nations.[81]

At an Overseas Writers meeting in April 1956, Allen Dulles, the director of the CIA, spoke of the "new wave of nationalism abroad" and acknowledged the CIA's central barrier in carrying out its "hearts and minds" campaigns in developing countries. "Many nations look to Russia in part because the U.S. is tarred with the colonialism brush due to our ties to European colonial powers," Dulles acknowledged. "We can't cut these ties and go all out for anti-colonialism. But we've got to find a more understanding way to deal with problem."[82] The agency didn't find one, of course, and the tar of colonialism only grew stronger as the United States became more enmeshed in Indochina and the Middle East over the next several decades.

At a background dinner at the Carlton Hotel ten days later, Secretary of State John Foster Dulles spoke to correspondents on the condition that "no fill-in are to be given, ESPECIALLY to foreign press men." Dulles emphasized the importance of Middle Eastern oil and its passage through the Suez Canal to the survival of Western Europe and NATO. "If that were lost or the pipe lines and the Suez route cut, W Eur would be in an 'extremely grave position,'" Chal Roberts wrote in his memo about the dinner. Dulles returned to the subject later in the evening, citing the two main objectives that the United States had in the Middle East: "1. To maintain the existence of Israel as a state. 2. To maintain the flow of oil to West Europe."[83] While it later became seen as a leftist critique to say that America would go to war for oil, it was one of the main narratives during the 1950s, as oil was frankly recognized as one of two of the United States' chief interests in the Middle East.[84]

The crisis in the Suez created a moment of clarity for newsmen and foreign policy makers. In October 1956, three months after Nasser had nationalized the Suez Canal, Israel, followed by France and Great Britain, invaded the Gaza Strip and Sinai Peninsula. Dulles publicly condemned the invasion and theoretically supported Egyptian self-governance. Privately, he had acknowledged the more realistic and less ideological arguments. Dulles did not, in fact, support Nasser, because Nasser threatened Europe's oil, and Europe was the heart of Western civilization.[85] The Eisenhower administration even frankly briefed congressional leaders as well as journalists on oil at the time.[86] And that oil, of course, was related to the Cold War, not because of communism but because whoever had oil had power in an industrial global economy.[87]

Reporters, commentators, and foreign policy officials had varying reactions to the administration's policies regarding Britain, France, and the Middle East in general. Harsch was disappointed that the administration had not stood up for its Allies and had affected a hypocritical anticolonial posture. His columns were measured, as always, but he expanded on his beliefs in letters responding to readers. To a reader in New Jersey, Harsch wrote, "Suez is one of the great strategic centers of the world. In losing Western military control over Suez it seems to me that we have paid fair [sic] too high a price for our 'anti-colonial purity.'" Since the United States was far from pure on that issue anyway, he implied with his quotation marks, it should stop posturing. What mattered was Western Europe. They had all believed so strongly in the Marshall Plan nine years earlier; they could not see Europe fall to "Moscow" for lack of oil. "The recovery of Western Europe which was achieved by the Marshall Plan would all be wasted if that were to happen," Harsch told the reader.[88]

While white reporters often questioned their own objectivity, they did not interrogate their whiteness—perhaps a result of the wider society, which had yet to understand race or gender as cultural constructs. White reporters quite simply had more sympathy for Europeans and did not let anyone into their circle who might challenge that sympathy. Still, the hypocrisy of a nation promoting anticolonialism in words but colonialism in deeds was not lost on these journalists, who reported frankly if not frequently on the necessity of exploiting European colonies for their raw materials.

But they had an affinity for France and Great Britain, for reasons of preference, convenience, and what they believed their American readers were interested in. Newsmen did not simply abandon their war-born identification with those countries because the US government was now supposedly in favor of independence for former colonies. In December 1956, as the Suez Crisis was being resolved, Ralph Bunche, the Nobel Peace Prize winner who was then working at the UN, began a correspondence with Arthur Sulzberger, finding fault with the *Times'* coverage of the UN. Sulzberger responded, "I confess to being very troubled in my thinking about the United Nations these days." He recounted that before leaving New York City recently, "knowing that I would be away for a while, I called together a group of my chief associates and told them that as they knew we had always backed the League and the U.N. and that I wanted to continue to do so and to do everything up to the point where it took us away from our two major allies. Then I proposed that we stick with them."[89] The two major allies, as the majority of diplomatic reporters would have agreed, were Great Britain and France. (Joe Harsch bluntly told a reader in 1954, "To me, the western alliance means first Britain, and second France.")[90] Sulzberger continued with the high-minded rhetoric he liked to employ when discussing his affinity for white civilization: "I added that so far as I knew I had no French or English blood in me but that the spirit of Liberty had come to me from France and the law of Freedom I had inherited from England—that so far as I was concerned we were at war with the U.S.S.R. and I hoped to stick with the Allies upon whom we could count."[91] In other words, the United States could count on other trustworthy (white) nations, not backwards cannibals who would not know how to spend US dollars and had neither the spirit of liberty nor the law of freedom in their blood.

White male reporters created a segregated sphere for themselves in the physical spaces of Washington that allowed them to speak frankly to one another while marginalizing voices of dissent. In those spaces, we see a fairly clear-eyed understanding of the hypocrisy of US postwar foreign policy, and a recognition of perhaps the greatest myth of all: that the Cold War was foremost an ideological struggle about communism.

7

THE BREAKDOWN BEGINS

One of the understandable fallacies perpetuated by some leftist press critics during the 1970s and 1980s was that there was no conspiracy between the press and the US government; there did not need to be, this line of thinking went, since both groups supposedly agreed on foreign policy, and the press did not doubt that the government was telling the truth. In 1970, looking back on a 1951 *Collier's* magazine piece that took the government's line on North Korean intransigence, the journalist and press critic James Aronson wrote, "Was there collusion between government and the magazine? There did not need to be any. The magazine simply assumed, like the rest of the press, that United States policy is pure, and that information from the United States is honest."[1] While I cannot speak about the staff of *Collier's*, a New York publication, most of the Washington press corps never assumed that US policy was pure, instead operating under the assumption that information was skewed, only partially true, or an outright lie. This does not mean they did not function primarily as a "voluntary arm of established power," as Aronson argues, for they did.[2] But there was far more contention and dissent on the ground than is often remembered.

During the 1950s, reporters' growing discomfort with government lies—especially those coming from the State Department and the CIA, respectively run by the brothers John Foster Dulles and Allen Dulles— combined with their frustration with the government secrecy that had developed in World War II. During this tense period, reporters tried to navigate what was best for their careers and best for their readers. Even as they were reluctant to trust the government, they relied on one another to do their jobs and maintained the trust and fellowship that kept that sphere of consensus intact. Reporters did collude with one another, at least, to determine the best way of framing issues, and this was hardly an effortless process. There was nothing inevitable about the daily decisions these reporters and editors made in their coverage of the newly permanent national security state. We see complicity, guilt feelings, and occasionally outrage, but we do not see mindless acceptance of the government's word, which lost its value during the reign of the Dulles brothers, or the so-called purity of its foreign policy.

The Growing Tendency toward "Totalitarian" Secrecy

A tendency toward secrecy around weaponry grew organically out of wartime information policies and anxieties, especially those concerning the atomic bomb. The reporting on the bomb was itself a product of the World War II revolving door of government service. William Laurence, known as "Atomic Bill"—to distinguish him from his colleague at the *New York Times*, the political reporter Bill Lawrence—was one of the few Americans who had known about the atomic bomb before it was used.[3] The War Department selected Laurence, a science writer, to be the only reporter to witness the tests in New Mexico as well as the dropping of the bomb over Nagasaki, Japan, from an airplane. By bringing him inside, paying him, and heavily censoring his copy, the United States Army ensured that its version of events would prevail. The army even asked the *New York Times* to grant him a few months' leave of absence to write the War Department's press releases on which all the subsequent newspaper and magazine stories were based.[4] The department gave the first release to the press corps on Monday, August 6, just after the first bomb dropped. Laurence was among those reporters who wrote about the bomb for the *Times*, based on his own press releases. His series of articles was then reprinted as a pamphlet, ensuring even wider distribution. A White House press officer at the time noticed with some surprise that the stories produced the day after the first bomb deployment were about the development of the bomb, the attendant secrecy, and the tests, with little news about the weapon's effects.[5] That framing was intentional. Indeed, the devastating effects went largely unpublicized until John Hersey's reporting appeared a year later in the *New Yorker*.

Except for "Atomic Bill," the press's understanding of the new era of atomic warfare was just beginning after the annihilation of Hiroshima and Nagasaki. No newspaper or newspapermen could know yet where their responsibility lay. The lines of what could be reported were not established. In the summer of 1947, at the Bohemian Grove in California (fig. 7.1), Arthur Sulzberger, the publisher of the *New York Times*, ran into Vannevar Bush, who then headed the government's Office of Scientific Research and Development. This office had overseen the development of the atomic bomb during the war. The Bohemian Club, a gentlemen's organization founded in 1872 to hold summer encampments in the woods of Northern California for influential men, provided—and provides, operating in 2021 and still only for men—opportunities for the male power elite to spend time together in a camplike atmosphere of fellowship and fraternity. Members and their guests put on musicals and skits, heard lectures, ate, drank, smoked cigars, and did favors for one another year-round. Former presidents, current secretaries of state, and publishers all met and could subtly shape what happened in the outside world based on the off-the-record conversations they had and the relationships they built at the Grove, as they called it. As the sociologist G. William Domhoff writes of the Bohemian Grove, "Upper-class retreats . . . increase the social cohesiveness of America's rulers and provide private settings in which business and political problems can be discussed informally and off the record."[6] At such places, the elite of the government and the military, along with the elite of the newspaper industry, came to understandings, sometimes against the desires of the reporters on the ground.[7]

The Grove encampment in 1947 provided a forum for Bush to complain to Sulzberger that the *Times*' chief military writer, Hanson Baldwin, had revealed classified information about a proving ground for

FIGURE 7.1. The Bohemian Grove is an elite men's summer encampment in the redwood forests owned by the San Francisco–based Bohemian Club. After a 1946 session commemorated in this photograph, Eugene Meyer, chairman of the Washington Post, wrote his host, "I cannot but believe that it must be the spirit of those wonderful trees that pervades and dominates the thinking, the feeling and the good fellowship of the gathering." Box 166, Eugene Meyer Papers, Manuscripts Division, Library of Congress.

weapons in New Mexico. Bush convinced Sulzberger there had been a breach of security. As Sulzberger wrote his managing editor when he returned to New York, in his typical understated and good-natured tone, "You can imagine that I felt pretty bad when Vannevar Bush told me that one of Baldwin's articles had spilled the beans."[8] Baldwin and the rest of the staff made their case to Sulzberger for having published, arguing that newspapers should be allowed to print whatever they could ascertain. Then the editors and Baldwin spoke to and wrote one another at length before drafting a four-page response to Bush over Sulzberger's signature. That response made a lasting impression on the *Times* staff and would be remembered and retrieved from the files fourteen years later, during the failed Bay of Pigs invasion, when the government again complained about the *Times'* "spilling the beans" and the *Times* again pushed back.[9] "I think the protection to be afforded such secrets is the responsibility of the government, not of the press," Sulzberger wrote Bush. "For newspapers can hardly be expected to accept the thesis that, in peacetime, when the United States Army or Navy, or any other governmental agency, simply labels something 'Confidential,' or 'Top Secret,' the obligation extends automatically to them."[10] Over the next few months, Bush and Sulzberger continued to exchange confidential letters and even met again in person, until the publisher had what seems to have been the final word, in January 1948. In that letter, he reiterated the *Times'* position and warned Bush against the tendency toward secrecy that was not only characteristic of but also "the greatest element of weakness in the totalitarian states."[11]

With greater secrecy on the part of the US government came increased press scrutiny about what information the government was classifying as secret and whether, like the authoritarian governments it sought to defeat, the secrecy had a political, rather than a military, basis. The press's concerns about government secrecy worsened after September 1951, when President Harry Truman issued Executive Order 10290, "prescribing regulations establishing minimum standards for the classification, transmission, and handling, by departments and agencies of the Executive Branch, of official information which requires safeguarding in the interest of the security of the unit." Basically, any civilian department could classify any document it wanted to as restricted, confidential, secret, or top secret by claiming that the release of the information would compromise national security.[12] Truman's actions had precedent. Franklin Roosevelt on March 22, 1940, in Executive Order 8381, had allowed for classification in civilian agencies doing war-related work. (The noncivilian departments had long had classification schemes: the army since 1907 and the navy since 1909.)[13] But Truman's order went well beyond Roosevelt's, designating seventy-two civilian agencies with classification authority. At a press conference ten days later, the president justified the order by citing a CIA-commissioned Yale University study claiming that that 95 percent of government "secrets" had already been published in the American press.[14] The government believed that it needed to be more vigilant.

The press widely and publicly denounced Executive Order 10290 as formalized news suppression and inimical to freedom of the press.

Individual White House reporters registered complaints with Truman's press secretary as their home offices prepared editorials criticizing the order. Many journalism groups publicly opposed the order as well, including the American Society of Newspaper Editors and the Associated Press Managing Editors, which wrote that it "opposes as a dangerous instrument of news suppression the President's executive order of September 24, 1951, extending the cloak of military secrecy to the civilian establishments of the government."[15]

Despite the criticism, something to which Truman had long grown accustomed, the president did not modify or rescind the order. At the press conference announcing the policy, he specifically brought up the issue of *Fortune* magazine having published maps of atomic energy plants. The notes that Truman's press assistant Eben Ayers took reveal the president's irritation with the press and willingness to blame it for any future nuclear war. When a reporter pointed out that a government department had provided the information on which the *Fortune* article and others were based, Truman retorted that the publishers still should not have used it. Pete Brandt, the bureau chief of the *St. Louis Post-Dispatch*, then said that the wire services had, in fact, attributed the story not just to government departments but to the military agencies. Surely, that meant that the information was safe to print. "If the military agency gives you that, and an atomic bomb falls on you on account of that, at the right place, who is to blame?" the president asked, in a manner that was unfair but that touched a deep fear reporters shared.[16]

The controversy continued into 1952, a year in which the phrase "news suppression" was a buzzword. That April, the *Washington Post's* managing editor, Russell Wiggins, leading the Associated Press Managing Editors' freedom of information efforts, represented the press's perspective on a radio program called "Town Meeting of the Air." The subject was: "Does the President's Security Order Threaten the People's Right to Information?" The initial audience may have been considerable, since 278 ABC-affiliated stations ran the program. In addition, a transcript of the discussion was published as a pamphlet after the broadcast. Wiggins stressed that the press's opposition was to secrecy, not in matters of true military security but in nonmilitary information. "We object to the use of the term 'national security' throughout this order," he said. "We have found in the past decades that this is an integral part of a vocabulary of every totalitarian regime."[17] Wiggins and his colleagues, having just fought in a war against totalitarianism, never had Adolf Hitler or Benito Mussolini far from their minds during the 1950s and so were especially suspicious of government secrecy. The assumption that the government would try to hide damaging information was common in the mainstream press.

Perhaps secrecy would diminish with the Eisenhower administration taking office in 1953, reporters hoped. The December Gridiron Club dinners in election years were occasions to start forging relationships with the incoming administration. At the December 1952 dinner, Wiggins had as his guest Milton Eisenhower, the president-elect's brother and president of Pennsylvania State College, who had worked at the Office of War Information during the war and was friendly with several Washington newsmen. After dinner, Wiggins caught up with General Hoyt Vandenberg, the Air Force chief of staff and an Eisenhower advisor, at a cocktail party. "I got to talking to Vandenberg after the dinner about Ike's public relations," Wiggins wrote Eugene Meyer, chairman of the *Washington Post*. Vandenberg then called Wiggins two days after the dinner and asked him to see Eisenhower in New York City the next morning at ten thirty. Wiggins flew up, spent thirty minutes with the president-elect, and returned to Washington. "I had a very interesting half hour with him," he noted to Meyer. "He is basically right in his view of the right of citizens to know about the government. I got the impression that he overestimated the difficulty of, and under-estimated the importance of, Presidential Press Conferences, and I think was under some misapprehension about them."[18]

Wiggins then wrote Milton Eisenhower that he had some restrained hope. "As you know, it is my ever present anxiety that the people's right to know about their government will be impaired by (1) the real needs of security, (2) the sheer size of the government, and (3) changes in the structure of government which have transferred legislative and judicial functions from courts and Congress, where they have been openly conducted, to executive offices and independent agencies where they are often secretly conducted."[19] Here Wiggins succinctly described the major changes in the federal government since the rise of the New Deal administrative state and linked them to problems of reporting. That is, journalism was necessarily changing during this period because the government was changing—growing larger and more secretive. "I expressed the hope that the General would not become a victim to the disease that has over taken every President since Washington—a progressive hostility to the press," Wiggins wrote, foreshadowing eight years of unsatisfactory White House press relations and a deterioration of press support for the administration's foreign policy measures.

Lies, Denials, and the Dulles Brothers

On April 3, 1953, Overseas Writers held its first background lunch with Eisenhower's new CIA director, Allen Dulles, at the Statler. Joe Harsch of the *Christian Science Monitor* presided and warned against any breaches of Dulles's confidence. He reminded his colleagues that when General Walter Bedell Smith had spoken as CIA director, there had been a leak, and no one from the CIA or the Joint Chiefs of Staff had come to Overseas Writers since. "If we can't have security, says Joe, we might as well go out of business, and he for one would be disposed to resign if there should be another breach of security like the one of which Beedle was the victim," Wallie Deuel of the *St. Louis Post-Dispatch* wrote in his notes, using the general's nickname.[20]

The notes that the *New York Times* reporter Walt Waggoner took at the Dulles meeting made it into the files of the CIA, where they were then sanitized. In other words, the agency blacked out information that every Overseas Writers member had access to at the time, but that the public would not see until approved for release in 2001.[21] Diplomatic reporters in Washington usually knew more than we might assume they did, and they certainly knew more than the CIA was willing to tell the public.

At the luncheon, the men tried to work out the rules of the new world of national security reporting, determining as a cohort how the game should be played. They also acknowledged how difficult it would be "trying to work out problems of news indiscretions and public relations in general," Deuel wrote, paraphrasing Dulles. During the question and answer period, one of the reporters asked about the 1952 revolution in Egypt, during which Muhammad Naguib and Gamal Abdel Nasser had overthrown King Farouk. At the time, Allen Dulles had served as General Smith's deputy.

"Q: CIA helped drive out Farouk and put in Naguib. Would a news story on that have been OK?

"A: We never like to be mentioned at all. Every time we see 'CIA' in print we tremble a little bit. We prefer anonymity. It harms our relations with other intelligence agencies. I think you flatter us a little bit in the Egyptian thing."[22]

Dulles then outlined the procedure the CIA would follow if requesting a newspaper to withhold information. "Sometimes he [Dulles] learns in advance of an intention to publish a story about some CIA operation, and gets in touch with the publication and asks that the story not be used," Deuel wrote. "He does not, however, want to employ this procedure. He understands perfectly that if a reporter is not satisfied by Allen's explanation of why the story ought not to be published then of course the reporter is perfectly free to go ahead and print it."[23]

While this was Dulles's stated policy, the reality in newsrooms was that reporters felt less than "perfectly free." As the *Times'* soon-to-be Washington bureau chief, Scotty Reston, wrote three weeks later to the paper's managing editor in New York, Turner Catledge, about sharing sensitive, national-security-related information with the home office, "We are obviously in a period when it is not always easy to be a good newspaper man and a good citizen; therefore, some information will have to be withheld." What "period" was Reston referring to? Did he mean the last few months of the Korean War, where major fighting was long concluded and armistice was just months away? He likely meant the entire postwar, nuclear era. In fact, the information he shared with Catledge was not about Korea but about Laos. General Smith, who had just stepped down as CIA director and was headed to the State Department, had "told me confidentially that we are now 'lending' quite a few transport planes to the French in Indo-China in order to air-lift supplies to the French garrison defending the Capital of Laos," Reston wrote. "We are also arranging pilots for these planes. These pilots are being paid out of unvouchered CIA funds, and for the time being some of the pilots are American civilians."[24] Reston said that it was up to the New York office to decide whether to publish this information; unsurprisingly, it was withheld.

Withholding controversial information, or simply not probing a source, was considered an acceptable way for foreign policy reporters to deal with the new intelligence apparatus. The complicity of the press became clearer as the CIA's covert actions under Allen Dulles became bolder. Both because reporters felt responsible for national security and because of Dulles's personal relationships within the Washington reporting community, the CIA had an unusually long honeymoon period with the press, until about 1960. Around that point, the accumulated deceptions would grow to be too much. The *Times* abruptly increased its coverage of the CIA and for the next few years continued to cover the agency at double the rate that it had during the 1950s.[25]

On Monday, April 6, 1953, three days after the Overseas Writers meeting with Allen Dulles, Wallie Deuel and about twenty other newsmen hosted a background dinner for Secretary of State John Foster Dulles in the basement of the Carlton Hotel: cocktails, steak, and strawberry ice cream sundaes at one enormous table.[26] Then the gentlemen of the press began their questioning and remained until about a quarter past ten o'clock, by which time the room had grown unbearably hot. Among other not-for-attribution revelations that fell under the Lindley Rule, Dulles said that if the Soviet Union really wanted to take all of Western Europe, the United States could not stop it.

Deuel revealed in his notes how dependent reporters were on discussions with one another to reach consensuses about what should or should not make it to print, and it had nothing to do with trust in Dulles. "It is agreed informally afterwards among the newspaper men present that it would be a mistake from our own selfish point of view and quite possibly from the point of view of the national interest for us to rush into print with much of this stuff and it is left rather vaguely that we will confer tomorrow before anybody writes anything about it," he wrote. He noted that some of the men had left by the time this was decided, which led to a controversy.

Walt Waggoner, the *New York Times'* State Department correspondent, was one of the men who had left early. He had assumed that his newspaper would not expect a breaking news story from a background dinner. However, the next day, Tuesday, the *Christian Science Monitor* carried a story about new administration policy in its afternoon edition, followed by the *Wall Street Journal* on Wednesday morning. So on Wednesday afternoon, with Waggoner covering the visit of the German chancellor, his editors asked him to hand off his dinner notes to a fellow reporter, Anthony Leviero. Secretary Dulles had said that the new administration's policy on a Korean truce was to consider settling for a division at the "narrow waist" of the peninsula. He also said they would entertain a UN "trusteeship" for Formosa (Taiwan). Leviero wrote about both of these but did not include everything Waggoner had learned. As Leviero read the notes he could not believe some of the claims that Dulles had made. In summarizing the incident for Washington bureau chief Arthur Krock, he wrote, "In the circumstances I believe we were circumspect. You will recall that I expressed amazement over some of the things that Mr. Dulles had said and I recommended that the New York Times should not publish without attribution his statement that Russia could take all of Western Europe and that we could not stop her. You agreed out of a sense of responsibility for national security we should not publish that when so much peace talk was in the air."[27] Recently, the Soviet premier Joseph Stalin had died, and his successor, Georgy Malenkov, had been making peace overtures to the United States. Leviero did not want to be the reporter who started World War III.

The White House quickly denied the news on Formosa and Korea that *had* make it into the newspaper, which was not surprising to the reporters. "It was perfectly obvious at the time that one of Dulles' purposes in talking in these terms was to float a trial balloon," Deuel explained to his editor, "and I therefore spent considerable time and effort writing my story in such a way that it would stand up in spite of any official denial."[28] Such contortions to reflect an official record but obscure the reality known in Washington were common. The White House press secretary, Jim Hagerty, made the official denial the following morning at a press conference: "The reported administration policy on Formosa and Korea is without foundation of fact. No consideration has been given by the Administration to a United Nations trusteeship for Formosa. Likewise, the Administration has never reached any conclusion that a permanent division of Korea is desirable or feasible or consistent with the decisions of the United Nations."[29] Both of these statements, of course, were false. Both proposals had at least been considered, and although Formosa did not become a UN trusteeship, the Korean peninsula was later permanently divided at "the waist." This fracas was simply the first in a long line of official lies and denials that reporters came to expect from their deceitful government.

Two days later, which happened to be the morning of the spring 1953 Gridiron Club dinner, Reston, after talking with his colleagues, wrote an article explaining how the federal government had employed "the technique of denying the truth without actually lying," which he called an art "as old as the government itself." He still referred to Foster Dulles only as the "man who came to dinner," but he acknowledged that "almost everybody in town knew the identity."[30] The readers of the *Times* still did not get to know.

The dinners and secret meetings with Dulles continued, but so did the skepticism that attended them. After a confidential background conference in June 1954, Joe Harsch inserted a comment at the end of his summary memo to his editors. He began it with a caveat: "If all D. said is taken at face value then there would be two writable stories out of the above." Then he explained why Dulles's words could not be taken at face value. "Thus, since all such gatherings are for the purpose of inspiring news stories, the two stories which this session was designed to promote would be phonies."[31]

By the time the Eisenhower administration was in office just two months, the press had started seeing as routine the lies and denials, not to mention the phoniness of the public-facing Cold War philosophies. "We are fond of saying we never interfere in the internal affairs of other countries," Reston said in a private meeting at an agency within the

State Department in September 1953. "As you know, that is complete nonsense. We are interfering and intervening, politically and economically, all over the world. We are up to our eyes in the Philippine election, for example."[32] In addition to these broader lies, the quotidian denials continued, as in September 1956, when the State Department denied that Dulles sent the Yugoslavian government a warning cable after President Josip Tito had visited the Soviet Union. Elie Abel, the *Times'* reporter in Belgrade, wrote that Yugoslav sources had confirmed the message, but his editors in New York dutifully printed the State Department's denial along with Abel's article and even called his information "circumstantial."[33] In cables that revealed their mutual annoyance, Abel asserted to a Foreign Desk editor that Dulles was lying to stay out of trouble with Congress and the electorate in an election year. The Yugoslav issue was a "hot potato in view impending elections," Abel wrote, in cable-ese. His final cable on the matter delicately referenced the State Department's propensity for lying whenever needed: "We printed truth for which we needn't apologise and should I feel let matters rest. I seem recall its not first time state has dissembled when in tight spot. Hope you agree."[34]

Again, the convoluted series of articles, denials, and follow-ups that these lies often entailed would hardly have been clear to readers at the time. They were barely clear to the publisher of the *New York Times.* As Turner Catledge explained to Arthur Sulzberger, when Sulzberger asked him to decode an elaborate packet of evidence that an indignant Arthur Krock had sent him, with articles marked A, B, and C: "I think what Mr. Krock means to call to your attention is the disposition of the State Department to deny as a matter of policy things which later turn out to be true."[35] Exhibit A was a front-page article by Scotty Reston on the administration's willingness to negotiate a truce with China and North Korea on terms that the Chinese premier Chou En-lai had proposed. His attributions in the article, which ran on April 15, 1953, included "it was understood here tonight," "It was generally assumed," "were understood to have been," and "no announcement was made here tonight of the new instructions, but it was known."[36] The State Department then denied parts of the story, a denial printed in the

Times on the sixteenth, only have to have the story confirmed as true on the eighteenth.[37]

The State Department denying truths became a matter of course and no small annoyance to the reporters who constantly had their integrity impugned. This especially happened when reporters overseas observed something inconvenient for the State Department, as Abel had. Sydney Gruson, the *New York Times'* reporter in Guatemala, had made enemies with the government there, which had already expelled him once, in February 1954, for "unfriendly" stories, before letting him back in the following month. In late May 1954, Gruson wrote privately to his Foreign Desk editor in New York about his deteriorating relationship with the US ambassador to Guatemala, John Peurifoy. He partially attributed the tension to the fact that he, Gruson, was sending news dispatches that contradicted what Peurifoy told the State Department. "I think our editorial writers (and the State Department) should know that there is a very strong feeling among intelligent, non-communist Guatemalans that the U.S. has made two basic mistakes here recently," Gruson wrote. One mistake was promoting the United Fruit Company's claim against the Guatemalan government for $16 million in damages over land it had seized. His sources thought that the claim "could only exacerbate US-Guatemalan relations and could only lead people here to feel that perhaps the Guatemalan government is right in claiming that the communist issue here has been raised by Washington simply as pretext for intervention on behalf of the fruit company"—referring to concerns that the Cold War would provide ideological cover for the United States to interfere politically on behalf of United Fruit. Gruson wanted his bosses at the *Times* to believe him that average Guatemalans were not buying the Cold War pretext for imperialistic US policy, and that this did not mean they were communists. He worried that soon the only supporters of the United States in Guatemala would be the right-wing reactionaries who looked back fondly on the dictator Jorge Ubico's time "and all that went with it," as he euphemistically put it.[38] That included the dominance of United Fruit, a client of the New York white-shoe law firm Sullivan and Cromwell—where Foster Dulles had made his fortune as a lawyer before becoming secretary of state.[39]

Gruson's reporting in Guatemala was the last thing either Foster or Allen Dulles had needed before staging a coup, which the CIA had been planning under the code name Operation PBSuccess. In late May, Allen Dulles talked with General Julius Adler, the general manager and second-in-command at the *New York Times* and Dulles's fellow member of the Princeton University class of 1914. He alerted Adler and then Sulzberger to supposedly "disquieting reports" that Gruson was a fellow traveler of the Communist Party. "You told us that Foster was also disturbed and requested us to keep the correspondent away from sensitive areas," Sulzberger later wrote Allen. "This I agreed to do because of my respect for your judgment and Foster's. I also know that neither one of you subscribes to the apparently growing theory in American life that a man is guilty until proved innocent," he continued, referring to the false McCarthyite implications that Gruson was a communist. "I know also that you are as disturbed as I am by the thought that government should exert any control over the press."[40] Here Sulzberger was being coy; he knew as well as the Dulles brothers that controlling the press was precisely what they wanted to do. Yet at the time, Sulzberger had capitulated. On May 29, 1954, Gruson arrived at his home base of Mexico City, where he planned to stay two days before returning to Guatemala. His Foreign Desk editor asked him to "sit tight."[41] On June 18, CIA-backed armed forces began the coup that deposed the democratically elected Guatemalan leader, Jacobo Arbenz, and installed the authoritarian Carlos Castillo Armas. Gruson missed the coup. (Another reporter, Paul Kennedy, stepped in to cover Guatemala in the meantime.)

It took Gruson only a month to figure out that the US government had been behind the "sit tight" message and become angry enough to write the *Times'* management about it. "As you know I had covered the Guatemala story for more than two years until the final blow-up," he wrote the deputy managing editor, Robert Garst, on July 14. "I wrote it honestly and, I think, well, and I angered the Guatemalan government far more often than I did the State Department. But I had only one rule for covering the story—to find out whatever I could, to judge and analyze the information as honestly as possible and to write it as well as I could. I grind no one's axe in my reporting." He continued with a sober critique: "It seems to me that American newspapermen are getting very close to dangerous ground if they must consider beforehand whether or not their stories will have an unfavorable reaction at the State Department, or in other government agencies."[42] Reporters in Washington would have supported Gruson's position in theory, but they also would have been—and were—entrusted not to endanger national security in a way that Gruson, outside the capital, was not. Sulzberger asked Garst to tell Gruson that his sidelining was Sulzberger's fault and not the government's. But Sulzberger lied about his reasons: "I had received a tip (which proved to be a false one) that Mexico City would be involved in the incident, and consequently I did not wish to leave it uncovered." He continued, "Of course, as soon as the abrazo had taken place and no more fireworks were to be expected, I should have advised you that my story was a dud and that Mr. Gruson was no longer required to go through a period of watchful waiting. Please pass word of this on to him."[43]

This letter was blind-copied to Allen Dulles, accompanied by a somewhat bitter note from Sulzberger defending Gruson as "a good newspaperman who happened upon some stories which the people reporting to you did not like."[44] Gruson remained at the *Times* and had a long, successful career there. In 1956, when Gruson was based in Warsaw, Scotty Reston wrote him a complimentary letter about his coverage and noted with amusement, "In the days when the boys at CIA were calling up to find out what you were going to say on the following day I had the pleasure of reminding them they were asking for information from the guy they tried to destroy during the Guatemala fiasco."[45] Reston did not say that he never gave them the heads-up they asked for, but he did know how duplicitous the US government was. Gruson's reporting on Guatemala had been accurate, as both the *Times* and the CIA could admit to each other over the phone when the "boys at CIA" called up the boys at the *Times*.

In his history of the Guatemalan Revolution, Piero Gleijeses cites Reston's column from two days after the coup, in which Reston wrote, "If somebody wants to start a revolution against the Communists in, say, Guatemala it is no good talking to Foster Dulles. But Allen Dulles, head of the Central Intelligence Agency, is a more active man. He has been watching the Guatemalan situation for a long time."[46] Gleijeses notes, "Reston quickly moved onto other, less contentious subjects. The discreet works of the CIA were of no concern to patriotic journalists."[47] This is perhaps an oversimplified dismissal of a group for whom concern about the CIA was quite high. Though much of the concern was so far kept private, Reston's column was public.

Excessive patriotism can no longer be the reason we indict journalists from this period. Patriotism alone does not lead to lack of critique. (*Patriotic* in fact is the word William Appleman Williams, the revisionist historian of the "Wisconsin school" of diplomatic history and a vocal critic of US foreign policy, called himself in a 1959 letter to the influential syndicated columnist Mark Childs.[48] The language of patriotism was ubiquitous and did not necessarily mean blind faith.) Reporters understandably did not want to trigger the next world war, even as they were ambivalent about the national security state that was impinging on their ability to report straightforwardly on their government's actions.

A discussion between the Washington and New York offices of the *Times* a few weeks after the coup demonstrates how Reston justified the newspaper's behavior in terms of journalism ethics: it was committing sins of omission rather than commission. But he was becoming increasingly disturbed by what the CIA expected of the *Times*. He wrote a lengthy memo to the New York office in August 1954 on the issue. "For a long time we have been conscious of the difficulty of reporting information which has to do with the activities of our own secret service agents (CIA) here and abroad. Since we are clearly in a form of warfare with the Communist world it has not been difficult to ignore information which, if published, would have been valuable to the enemy," he wrote, indicating the extent to which the *Times* staff was knowledgeable of operations and complicit in keeping them from the public. "Thus we left out a great deal of what we knew about U.S. intervention in Guatemala and in a variety of other cases involving the capture of some of our agents and the shooting down of some of our planes over Communist territory. In all of these cases, however, officials here were willing to take responsibility for what was published and we published what they said as official statements. So far, as in the case of Guatemala, we have been merely leaving things out of the paper."[49] Withholding information and knowingly quoting the government's lies—not as dupes but as accomplices—were considered ethical in this time of quasi war.

A sin of commission would be journalistically unethical, though, Reston believed, and that was what the government now wanted in the case of Otto John, the head of West German counterintelligence. In late July 1954, John had defected to East Germany, or possibly been kidnapped by the East Germans, as the West German and US governments claimed for a time.[50] "The CIA is, of course, very embarrassed by what happened in the John case," Reston continued in his memo to the New York brass. He noted that the agency was "furious" about a front-page *New York Times* story by Tad Szulc, which, after several days of stories in other newspapers speculating about whether John was kidnapped or tricked, said that the defection was both voluntary and made sense to those who knew him—the opposite of what the CIA wanted to be written.[51] "I am sure you noticed that [the CIA] inspired several articles in the last ten days by the Alsops [the columnists and brothers Joe and Stew], all of them on the theme that John did not defect but was tricked into going to Communist Germany," Reston wrote. He also noted that officials were "playing the agencies hard," meaning leaning on the Associated Press and the United Press, since the wire services' articles were printed so widely and since editors outside Washington, including those at the *Times*, tended to believe the wire reports over their own reporters.[52] Two days after the Szulc story, an AP story printed in the *Chicago Tribune*, *Boston Globe*, and other papers quoted a source who said that John had been drugged.[53] By contrast, Reuters, the British wire service, whose story the *Christian Science Monitor* ran on the same day, included the following line, meant to undermine the official story: "many newspapermen said privately the evidence, contrary to [the source's] . . . statement, indicated Dr. John had defected of his own free will."[54]

The John story stayed in newspapers for the next two weeks, and the

CIA continued to pressure reporters not to print articles stating that John had defected, or at least to show the CIA and Allen Dulles in a favorable light. In that spirit, the AP sent out a lengthy, flag-waving profile of Dulles for Sunday editions. The article ran in hundreds of newspapers under adulatory headlines that included "Why There'll Never Be Another Pearl Harbor" (*Boston Globe*) and "Free World's Survival Hangs on Secrets Gathered by Master Spy Allen Dulles" (the *Atlanta Journal* and the *Atlanta Constitution*).[55] The *Washington Post* ran the story but under the more critical headline "Nation's 'Master Spy' Runs a Shadowy Show."[56] The paper's readers, living in Washington, would have been skeptical of the putatively patriotic spin, or at the very least, its headline writers were.

When Scotty Reston wrote his memo about Otto John, he was angry that the night before, the New York desk had believed the Associated Press over the *Times*'s own reporters in Bonn, Berlin, and Washington. The paper had inserted a story with no byline and a Washington dateline that led with "Two letters written by Dr. Otto John, West German security chief, after his disappearance July 20 have strengthened the belief of officials here that he was 'lured' by Communist agents behind the Iron Curtain."[57] The dateline made it look as though the Washington office had come up with the story, which was embarrassing to Reston; he did not want to mislead readers or look like a chump within his circles, where no one believed that John had been lured. Reston and Felix Belair, his right-hand man, had specifically urged the *Times* not to print such a story. They were vindicated when John himself gave a press conference the next day explaining he had purposefully defected.

At this point, the CIA approached Reston to plant false information, "and to do so on our own authority without any attribution to them or anybody else in this government," as Reston described it to Robert Garst, the acting managing editor in New York during August vacations. "They are now asking us to publish a 'projection' of probabl[e] Soviet exploitation of Dr. John which is extremely interesting but which they admit is entirely speculative and for which they are not prepared to take any responsibility." Reston advised that he personally was against publishing "articles which we would not normally publish but which might be very useful to the government." But he also noted that it was one of the *Times*' policies "beyond my authority to decide."[58] He sent a carbon copy of the Garst letter to Arthur Sulzberger as well as the chiefs of the foreign bureaus, who would all be on his side against the New York executives and the CIA. (Foreign correspondents worried that inaccurate information about their host countries would hurt their credibility with sources.)

Garst supported Reston and reminded the New York editors that Reston and Belair should have the final word on CIA stories. "I think the interview this morning shows conclusively that the CIA was trying to sell us a bill of goods," Garst wrote to "all concerned."[59] Sulzberger replied separately with his own support for Reston, writing, "You are, of course, entirely correct in the position that you take. We cannot permit ourselves knowingly to pull chestnuts out of the fire even for our own Government or any administrative agency of it, if we know in advance that the chestnuts are no good." But he then went on to make a declaration that seems remarkable for the man who ran the "paper of record": "We are, of course, prepared to print any statement made by the Administration if they will permit themselves to be quoted and we will do this whether we believe them or not."[60] Sulzberger and men like him did not consider themselves to be deferring to the government; they were actively standing up for what they considered to be the principles of an independent press, which must exercise its own good judgment for the cause of national security. In their minds (and memos), they distanced themselves from the Alsops of the press, whom they considered to be distorting the news. The *Times* took seriously its position as the "paper of record," and that included printing government lies—unchallenged—as long as it could attribute them to the government. *Readers* would need to take some responsibility for then judging whether what the government said was truthful.

That weekend, Reston was still seething when he made his Sunday column a critique of the State Department for trying to publicize its own defector, Yuri Rastvorov, at a last-minute Friday evening press conference that the department had pressured two hundred reporters into attending. Reston noted that he had been called twice, once personally by an assistant secretary of state, who said, "Don't miss this one. Big show." He poked fun at the department for making such a to-do of the "'surfacing' of a genuine straight-up-and-down Soviet spy," describing Rastvorov's unveiling in the State Department auditorium in this way: "He came up blinking in the midst of a highly suspicious audience whose members wanted to know if there was any connection between the sudden appearance of Mr. Rastvorov at this time and the 'surfacing' earlier in the week of Dr. Otto John, the West German security chief who skipped to the Communists in East Berlin. Henry Suydam, the State Department's press officer, was indignant. Certainly not, he said. No connection whatsoever." Reston continued sarcastically, "Thus the reporters found themselves in attendance upon the most remarkable coincidence of the cold war." The column even carried the ironic title of "A Remarkable Coincidence in the Cold War," making it clear to all his readers it was not a coincidence but rather another manipulation by the State Department and the CIA, which he mentioned by name in the article and with whom he was tired of playing along. He spelled out for readers what he had written his bosses: there were items that could not be printed, such as when "our agents are captured and our planes shot down from time to time in circumstances that cannot be put into the press without great benefit to the Communist cause," foreshadowing the exact circumstances of Gary Powers's U-2 flight six years later. After this caveat, he presented the problem to the readers as he had internally: the government was planting lies. "There is a growing tendency here, however, to expect the press to go beyond this: not only to leave things out of the papers but to put things in which may be advantageous to some particular agency but which are not true."[61] (This criticism made it into the FBI's top-secret background file about Reston, and although the file makes it clear that the FBI considered him a thorn in its side, the bureau ultimately believed a source, the politician Harold Stassen, who said that Reston was sufficiently anti-Russian so as not to merit action.)[62] Reston had grown tired of keeping his complaints about the CIA in private and then lying to the reading public.

He then shared all the correspondence between the Washington and New York offices with his friend and mentor, the columnist Walter

Lippmann, who was on vacation in Maine. Lippmann replied with the indignation that Reston had counted on. "The issues have to do with the fundamental principles of an honest press and are so important they deserve, it seems to me, a fulldress discussion with Allen Dulles himself on where the line is to be drawn," Lippmann wrote back. "The line, it seems to me, must be drawn against articles which do not have on them the label giving either the source or clearly warning the reader that the sources are not identified and that he must not regard the reports as more than guesses. The basic principle is sincerity and candor between the newspaper and the reader, and no government bureau should be allowed to ask a newspaper to participate in anything which could mislead its readers. When I read the Alsop piece, I knew that obviously it was inspired and I had no trouble guessing by whom it was inspired. The unprofessional reader is entitled to be alerted too."[63] So much of what was printed in the newspaper during the 1950s was legible only to those in Washington, already in the know. Lippmann and Reston, who believed that the press should not lie, were dissatisfied with the federal government's behavior. Change comes slowly and gradually, though; the circumstances that would enable the printing of the Pentagon Papers in 1971 were years in the making.

The next six years of the Eisenhower administration were a tense time for reporting on foreign policy, as Dwight Eisenhower preferred covert operations under CIA purview to outright military intervention. Consequently, newspapers faced frequent dilemmas about what to publish. Newsmen continued to voice their concerns cautiously in print, as Reston had done. The syndicated columnist Mark Childs wrote a December 1954 column that led with "Among working reporters in Washington there is a growing concern over what appears to be a concerted effort to suppress legitimate news—with a system of rewards and punishments to see to it that only news which is favorable or reported in a favorable light is given to the public."[64] Childs was especially outraged that a Senate committee investigating "subversives" was maligning the extremely well respected correspondent Homer Bigart for his reporting on Greece.[65]

Reston also continued to air his dissatisfaction publicly, as in a September 1955 column. "There has been a growing tendency in Washington since the war for the government to put out not what it knows to be true but what it wants people to believe is true," he wrote, admitting what everyone in Washington knew: the government lies. The *Times'* headline was "Of Truth and Fantasy: An Assay of U.S. Habit in Foreign Affairs of Claiming Victories That Ring Hollow"—a near parody of the *Times'* penchant for cautious wording. The real substance of the article was reflected in the *Atlanta Constitution*, which ran the column via the *Times'* wire service but under a more straightforward headline: "Government Tends to Slant the News."[66]

The Beginning of the Credibility Gap

Although it did not yet have a name, the credibility gap within Washington was growing, invisible to all but the most astute and thorough newspaper readers. (The term *credibility gap* would emerge only during the early 1960s as a takeoff on "missile gap.") The mid-1950s were a critical turning point—when newspapermen were fed up with secrecy as well as with lying for an administration that was becoming increasingly unpopular around the world for its heavy-handed interventions. Censorship, classification, and leaks were frequent topics of conversation as well as congressional testimony.

During the mid-1950s, reporters were starting to let their cynicism show to their readers, especially in coverage of the "spirit of Geneva," which referred to a summit meeting held in Switzerland in the summer of 1955. "Whatever the President does now is automatically wonderful," Scotty Reston wrote bitingly in a September 1955 *New York Times* column. "If he goes to Geneva and cries peace, even when there is no peace, he is proclaimed throughout the world. If he counters the optimism of Geneva six weeks later with stern warnings to the Communists, nobody asks why he didn't think of that before but hails him as a scourge of the appeasers."[67] Two months later, when the foreign ministers of the "Big Four" (the United States, France, Great Britain, and the Soviet Union) were back in Geneva, Elie Abel's (fig. 7.2) front-page *Times* story discussed the US government's attempts to explicitly

FIGURE 7.2. In 1955, Elie Abel (*second from left*) covered the Geneva Summit Conference, where he had lunch with (*left to right*) fellow *Times*men Drew Middleton, Scotty Reston, and E. Clifton Daniel. Abel covered Eastern Europe for the *New York Times* and often found himself at odds with Secretary of State John Foster Dulles. Accession Number: 2016–418, Harry S. Truman Library.

manipulate reporters. "Reporters Advised to Hint Success" was part of the subheadline, strongly implying that Foster Dulles was spinning the news so that the administration could look as though it had scored a foreign policy win before the 1956 elections. Abel gave the "latest distillation of the 'Geneva Spirit'" in bullet-point form and then wrote, "If these views faithfully reflect the opinions of Secretary of State Dulles, there has been a significant change in his thinking about the old familiar problems."[68] Abel was highlighting Dulles's hypocrisy. Before the conference, the secretary of state had emphasized "deeds, not words" and that the United States intended to take a "forward step" toward German reunification. When the conference ended without that step and with only more words, not deeds, he tried to claim it as the victory he had intended all along.

Felix Belair, then in the Geneva office of the *Times*, wrote Reston that he had heard from a friend "that Dulles is screaming ma[d] at Abel for his handling of that back-grounder in which Foster played the starry-eyed Pollyanna better than the author wrote about it."[69] He wanted Reston to know that he, Belair, should take the blame for any fallout, because he had written the lead paragraph and the headline, and that Abel should be spared. The deceit at Geneva rankled Reston so badly that it was one of the examples he gave of "managed news" to the Moss Committee—a House subcommittee chaired by Rep. John E. Moss, a first-term Democrat from California—which was investigating complaints that the Eisenhower administration "has been withholding or suppressing" information.[70] Eleven years later, the Moss Committee prevailed on Congress to pass the 1966 Freedom of Information Act, which Lyndon Johnson signed into law.[71] Again, the change came slowly but had deep roots.

Meanwhile, *Time* and *Life* magazines continued to do puff pieces on Dulles—accounting perhaps for the more positive views of him outside the capital, where the magazine's readership lay, than within it. A controversial *Life* story from January 1956 called him the best secretary of state since Thomas Jefferson.[72] Mark Childs took particular exception to that piece in a letter to his *St. Louis Post-Dispatch* editors, explaining why they should not play the same game that the Luce properties were playing. "The connection between Dulles and Ambassador Clare Boothe Luce and the Luce publication hardly needs to be pointed out. The Luce publications have become virtually propaganda organs for the Eisenhower administration. Time a year ago chose Dulles as 'man of the year' and had a piece of fulsome praise about him," Childs wrote. "He apparently needs and desires this crude kind of flattery and the people around him know where he can get it."[73] He had recently written an appraisal of Dulles at Geneva that he thought had been fair. But after Dulles's assistant Carl McCardle (whom newsmen in private memos called Chowderhead and Bubblehead) passed along the secretary's appreciation of the piece, Childs worried he must not have been critical enough.[74] "That made me feel that probably I had been wrong," he wrote.[75]

A week after the *Life* story, Reston had a piece in the *Times*, "Officials and the Press," in which he lamented "the failure of public officials and the press to reach a common understanding about their obligations to one another and to the public in a time of world crisis." He cited Harold Nicolson, a British official at the Versailles conference after World War I, who had said there were only two appropriate ways to deal with a democratic press: tell it nothing, or tell it everything. "The worst method is to tell them half-truths in the form of conciliatory leakages," Reston quoted Nicolson.[76] Dulles, he said, had unfortunately chosen this unadvisable third way.

Even Arthur Sulzberger, a supporter of Eisenhower to the bitter end, was skeptical of Dulles. Instead of chastising Reston for that critical piece, as he had sometimes done in the past, the *Times'* publisher passed a joke along to him: "In view of your article this morning I wonder if you have heard that Foster Dulles is the only bull who carries around his own china shop?"[77]

"That's a good one about Foster and his china shop," Reston wrote back. "I have been talking to the Ambassadors and the crockery is all over the place."[78]

One of Secretary of State Dulles's most controversial stances among newsmen and the one that created the most acrimony with them was his refusal to allow them to report from mainland China. In 1955, with China reestablishing diplomatic ties under its communist government, its leadership began inviting specific newsmen to visit for the first time since having expelled foreign correspondents in 1949. Dulles banned American journalists from doing so, denying visas when they applied either to visit or to reopen bureaus there. He said the reason was that ten Americans were still being held in Chinese jails and would first need to be released. Newspapers formally challenged these rulings and privately lobbied Dulles to change his mind. Believing they had a personal friendship, Sulzberger spoke with Dulles about it several times by letter and by telephone, with Dulles consistently telling the *New York Times* not to defy the travel ban. In April 1956, Sulzberger tried to circumvent Dulles when the secretary of state was out of town by writing the Deputy Undersecretary of State Robert Murphy that he disagreed with Dulles's position. "I am not certain at all, however, that the responsibilities of the Department and the responsibilities of a great organ of public opinion like The New York Times are not quite different,"

Sulzberger wrote, stating a position that seems like it should have been obvious but had been in question over the previous decade and a half. "We have a duty to get the news wherever it breaks and whenever we can. The more I think of it, the more I believe we are falling down on our responsibility if we do not take advantage of the opportunity that is now afforded us."[79] That language of responsibility used in wartime to justify keeping news from Americans was recovering its prewar meaning, that of responsibility to readers.

The State Department continued to refuse visas, leading Eric Sevareid in September 1956 to record a radio news segment about it for CBS that his producers believed crossed the line into editorializing. (He had been similarly chastised in the summer of 1941 for criticizing isolationists.) This time, Sevareid said that the government was practicing censorship as surely as if it were wielding an editor's blue pencil. His language in response to his producers' negative reaction was passionate: "This strikes, fundamentally, at the whole premise, principle and worth of our own professional mission in life which is to get all the truth possible. What has happened here is an arbitrary government fiat governing the free press and radio, without accepted precedent or legal justification. I cannot feel detached or neutral about it, so maybe I should have left the subject alone."[80] Sevareid clearly did not feel remorseful.

Not surprisingly, the first reporter to defy Dulles's travel ban outright, with the support of his editor at the *Baltimore Afro-American*, was William Worthy, then a Nieman Fellow at Harvard University. He had no particular relationship with Dulles and could dissent publicly, while the rest of the press corps grumbled in print or tried to take stands on the radio but could not act without their publishers' approval. When Worthy went to China in December 1956, he did so with assurances from the American Civil Liberties Union that it would support a legal test of the State Department's travel restrictions on noncommunists.[81] Two days after Worthy's arrival, *Look* magazine challenged the ban by sending its reporter based in Moscow and a photographer based in New York into China.

Yet when Sevareid tried to address the issue again in February 1957,

CBS kept his commentary off the air altogether. The fact that he had been "blue-penciled" himself created even more of a stir in his reporting circles, where other reporters were able to cover news items more frankly than could the correspondents at CBS. ABC, a newer network that did not have CBS's stringent editorial policy, allowed Bill Costello to raise the same issue the following week, tying his broadcast to the news peg of three senators confronting the State Department on the matter. He began, "At long last, we seem to be coming to grips with the question whether the press and radio in the United States can properly be used by the government of the United States as an instrument of diplomacy."[82] It took several more months of public and private pressure as well as, perhaps incidentally, a change of Dulles's public affairs man (Andrew Berding, formerly at the United States Information Agency, took Carl McCardle's place) for the State Department to announce in August that a limited number of newsmen could start traveling to mainland China.[83]

A Reckoning for the CIA

By the time John F. Kennedy (fig. 7.3) took office, the press had become increasingly unhappy with the secrecy and lies that were the standard operating procedure of the Eisenhower administration. Journalists were less willing to "pull chestnuts out of the fire" for the government, as Sulzberger had colorfully put it. They soon recognized that the Kennedy administration was just as bad as its predecessor in its overall attitude toward freedom of the press as well as in trying to get reporters removed from sensitive areas. (It would attempt this with David Halberstam of the *New York Times* in Vietnam in 1963.) Kennedy also entered the presidency with one final Allen Dulles–directed covert operation under way, the Bay of Pigs invasion. The CIA operation involved training anticommunist Cuban forces in Guatemala to land in Cuba for the purpose of fomenting rebellion and overturning Fidel Castro's regime.

Public memory of the Kennedy administration as a time of government-press cooperation—a memory informed by television's love affair with the First Family and personal Georgetown friendships

FIGURE 7.3. President John F. Kennedy attended the March 1961 Gridiron Club banquet escorted by the president of the club, Robert L. Riggs of the *Louisville Courier-Journal*, who wore his gridiron-shaped medallion. Just a month later, relations between the White House and the press soured over coverage of the Bay of Pigs invasion. Credit: Abbie Rowe. White House Photographs. John F. Kennedy Presidential Library and Museum.

between Kennedy and individual influential members of the press, such as the *Washington Post*'s Ben Bradlee—has obscured the reality of a difficult period. In terms of secrets, lies, and press tension, the Kennedy administration was of a piece with both the Eisenhower administration and the more famously contentious Johnson administration. Some reporters hoped Kennedy's New Frontier would initiate a new era of openness and cooperation, but the opposite happened. Tom Wicker of the *New York Times*' Washington bureau remarked in a 1983 oral history interview, "It's not well-known now in the glow that surrounds that Administration 20 years later, but they were very hostile to the press in many ways if the press wasn't playing the game the way they wanted it."[84] The Kennedy glow has since faded, but the false memory of good press relations has persisted.

Even before the April 17, 1961, landing at the Bay of Pigs, the US press had reported on the Guatemalan bases and on the US role in providing training and equipment to Cuban rebels. In 1960, the story was already in the public realm after first being printed in an academic journal and then picked up by the *Nation* magazine. On January 10, 1961, the *New York Times* published its own article about the training in Guatemala by Paul Kennedy, putting it on the front page and above the fold, with a large headline ("U.S. Helps Train Guatemalans at Secret Guatemalan Air-Ground Base") and a map that ensured almost all its readers would take note of the story.[85] In what seems to have been a continuing gentlemen's agreement with Allen Dulles, the article respected his exhortations not to put his agency's name in print. It did make clear, however, that the US government was playing a major role in the operation. The article seems to have had no effect on the incoming administration's plans, nor did it inspire much outrage from the public. The majority of Americans believed that nearby Cuba was in the US "sphere of influence," and if the government was going to suppress communism in faraway places like Greece, it made sense to do so closer to home.

In the next two months, the *Times* editorial writer Herbert Matthews, who had reported widely (and controversially, because of his affinity for Fidel Castro) on Castro's rise, wrote at least two memos warning the publisher and top editors about the danger of the CIA's activities.[86] After meeting in February with an assistant secretary in the State Department, Thomas Mann, he wrote, "Mann agreed with me that the role which the C.I.A. is playing in trying to overthrow the Castro regime is dangerous and could get us into a great deal of trouble."[87] Three weeks later, on March 6, he wrote more urgently with confidential information. "I pass this information along because I believe this intervention by the CIA in the Cuban Revolution is bound to come out with a great explosion one of these days and perhaps result in great harm," he warned. "Those of us who follow the situation closely believe that the CIA is handling this unintelligently and is relying upon men who will be entirely unacceptable to Cuba, whatever happens after the Castro revolution." Matthews was trying to be a good citizen, giving his government a warning through executives at the *Times*, as Sydney Gruson had tried to do from Guatemala in 1954. But he also wanted to be a good newspaperman, so he concluded, "I think it is also necessary from the news point of view that we all keep up with this development as well as we can so that when it breaks out, we will not be caught by surprise."[88] His framing of his memo in terms of preventing the CIA from making a mistake demonstrates that even the leftist Matthews knew that this was the best way to get the attention of the *Times'* publisher and editors. It worked. Sulzberger told Matthews that he would be forwarding the memo to Scotty Reston in Washington with instructions to show it to Secretary of State Dean Rusk. "I do not think that we should have this type of information which affects the standing of our government and not give them an opportunity to do something about it," Sulzberger wrote Reston.[89] Reston did present the memo to the State Department, but it did not prevent the invasion or even stop the Kennedy administration's post hoc claim that the *Times* should have been more helpful, as we will see below.[90]

Meanwhile, Tad Szulc was now the *Times*man on the ground in Cuba. In the first week of April, he was ready with his story on the planned invasion, which he said would take place in about ten days. Scotty Reston worried that pinpointing the date, or even calling the invasion "imminent," went a step too far in interfering with national security. He called Allen Dulles, who advised that removing the timetable as well as any references to the CIA would be in the national interest. The *Times* printed the story with the alterations but still did so on the front page, where it would be widely read.

The story of what happened at the *Times* that night became journalism legend.[91] Four years later, the historian Arthur Schlesinger Jr., in his book on the Kennedy administration, *A Thousand Days*, got the story wrong. He wrote that on Reston's advice, the newspaper canceled Szulc's story altogether: "It was another patriotic act; but in retrospect I wonder whether, if the press had behaved irresponsibly, it would not have spared the country a disaster."[92] Schlesinger needn't have wondered, of course, because the *Times* did print Szulc's story as well as having already published Paul Kennedy's in January. But because of the popularity of Schlesinger's book, combined with an appearance on *Meet the Press* in which he repeated the story, it became part of the public memory. In 1966, E. C. (Clifton) Daniel, an editor at the *Times*, tried to correct the record at a speech at a meeting of the World Press Institute but ended up cementing the idea that the Bay of Pigs represented a failure of the press to be "diligent."[93]

President Kennedy went forward with the Bay of Pigs invasion, which failed, bringing embarrassment to the president and Allen Dulles, who was not long for his position as the CIA's director. The CIA's dirty laundry was being aired, and so was the press's. On April 27, 1961, speaking before the Bureau of Advertising of the American National Publishers Association, the new president took a substantial step toward alienating newspaper publishers. He implied that by printing information on Guatemala and Cuba, publishers had not been concerned with the national interest. He proposed self-censorship. "If the press is awaiting a declaration of war before it imposes the self-discipline of combat conditions, then I can only say that no war has posed a greater threat to our security," Kennedy said, referring to the Cold War. He continued, "Every newspaper now asks itself with respect to every story, 'Is it news?' All I suggest is that you add the question: 'Is it in the interest of national security?'" Kennedy was scolding publishers for not doing something that they already did, and most were indignant that he suggested they had done otherwise. When the next month Secretary of State Dean Rusk told Cyrus Sulzberger, the *New York Times'* chief European correspondent, that the *Times* should have a "guilty conscience" over Cuba, Dryfoos responded that they had shared Matthews's memo with him back in March, placing the blame back on the administration, where it belonged.[94]

The Bay of Pigs marked a new era for the CIA-press relationship, one defined by the end of the Allen Dulles era and the agency's first public defeat. As the agency outgrew its original mandate as well as its offices— in the spring of 1961, the CIA was in the process of moving into its enormous new headquarters in Langley, Virginia—the press worried that it had abdicated its watchdog responsibility and so placed the agency under increased scrutiny. Journalists were embarrassed by their own compliance, and many were now adversarial to the administration. In addition, they resented the fact that the CIA had started asking report-

ers more often to lie. On May 11, 1961, Wallie Deuel, who had been working at the CIA since 1954, wrote his son, Michael, describing the public
relations issue from the agency's standpoint. (Mike Deuel later joined
the covert operations side of the agency and died while on a mission in
Vietnam.) "We've been living—I won't say in a fool's paradise, but we've
been living charmed lives all this time until now," Deuel wrote, referring to the CIA. "Our immunity from exposure and attack has been
partly luck, partly due to the laziness and lack of imagination of some
editors and publishers, partly to self-restraint imposed by patriotism
on the part of others, partly to trust in the Old Man," meaning Allen
Dulles, "partly to the Old Man's skill in handling his public relations—
and, above all, to the fact that we've had a series of fantastic successes.
We've had a few failures too, but they either haven't amounted to much
or we haven't been found out." Deuel blamed indiscreet colleagues for
the agency's current predicament: "Some of these people have got careless and arrogant and have deliberately promoted publicity for themselves and their achievements, not in the least realizing that if you seek
good publicity you also court the bad; a few have undertaken to lecture the press on where its duty lies with reference to us; one or two I
have actually heard argue that the press should print anything we ask
them to and refrain from printing anything we ask them not to print;
and some dear colleagues have been known to plant deliberate false-
hoods on the American press."[95] If there was one thing reporters hated,
it was being lectured on their duty by those outside the profession.

Complaints about the CIA now comprised the common chatter of
Washington. A week after Deuel's letter to his son, Walter Lippmann
phoned Scotty Reston "very disturbed," as Reston told the *Times'* deputy managing editor, Clif Daniel, the next day. Lippmann had recently
written a column about improper CIA interference in internal French
politics and believed that the agency should face a reckoning—that it
was "beleaguered" and that "our people have a right to know this."[96]
Privately, he told Reston that he "felt that the misdemeanors of the
C.I.A. were so vast and so wide-spread that only a great news organization like the New York Times could properly investigate them. He
did not think his own paper," the *New York Herald Tribune*, "could do

the job." That same day, Allen Dulles was scheduled to come to the New York headquarters of the *Times* to plead with the editorial director, John Oakes, for better publicity. "He felt the C.I.A. was in danger of being dismembered and of losing the confidence of the American people," Clif Daniel wrote in summarizing the meeting. "He wanted to do what he could to stop that process. . . . My honest opinion was that Mr. Dulles made a very poor case." Ultimately, Orvil Dryfoos, who had just taken over as publisher, "assured Mr. Dulles that we were highly conscious of our responsibility, that we had no desire to damage the interests or endanger the security of our country, but that we didn't know exactly where our responsibility lay." Daniel captured the tension well: "The whole affair was very inconclusive."[97]

A few years would pass before the *Times* ran the kind of "takeout" series on the agency that Lippmann had envisioned. Then in April 1966, it printed a series of five articles run over several days, beginning with a prominent, front-page story that took up three columns and was placed above the fold.[98] Because it was the *New York Times*, though, the series was cautious. "I might say that never in my history with The New York Times has a series of articles been prepared with such great care and such remarkable attention to the views of the agency involved," the *Times*' editor and reporter Harrison Salisbury wrote Clif Daniel. He chastised his colleagues and drew out the persistent tension that responsible organs felt between their duties to readers and to the nation.[99] Reston reflected on the problem in a January 1966 diary entry, as the series would have been in preparation: "In the old days of our country's innocency [*sic*], we could follow the old gutty principle, Publish and Be Damned; now it is not so clear, for if you publish at the wrong time or don't publish at the right time, the country can be damned, and that complicates the exercise."[100]

The Press's Responsibility in a Nuclear World

In mid-September 1962, a year and a half after the Bay of Pigs incident, President Kennedy invited Dryfoos to the White House to discuss the problem of the press and national security. To prepare, Dryfoos asked for a briefing from his managing editor, Turner Catledge. He wanted to defend the *Times* against the charge that the newspaper had threatened the public interest by printing leaked material—in the most recent case, a story by its longtime military editor, Hanson Baldwin, about Soviet missile sites. ("We've got an awful lot about Baldwin," Kennedy ominously told Dryfoos in the meeting, during a discussion of the FBI's surveillance tactics.)[101] At the same time, Dryfoos needed to reassert the *Times'* right to decide what news was fit to print. "In any discussion of freedom of the press versus national security, I suggest you take a positive role in favor of the press and its obligations to the public," Catledge wrote. The public he referred to meant their readers, to whom they had an "essential obligation to inform," as he put it. But, he continued, "any deviation from that course must be made only in the conviction that certain information would be plainly inimical to the public interest and national security." At this time, "the public interest" was invoked for national security reasons but seems not to have driven arguments for transparency. Nonetheless, Catledge emphasized who had the right to determine the public interest: Dryfoos. "No government official, from the President down, can possibly have any greater awareness of the public interest than you have as the publisher of one of the world's most influential newspapers," he declared.[102] Given the *Times'* impact on setting other newspapers' agendas and its matchless position among policy makers in Washington, Catledge's sense of the publisher's importance was not that inflated.

Before the meeting, Baldwin had provided a five-page memo of his own, entitled "Notes on the Problem of Freedom vs. Security." He wrote in depth about when a reporter should quote directly from secret documents and how important it was for newspapers to have the final word on publication. Point number five began, "A sense of responsibility should be the North Star of every newspaperman." Baldwin knew that the word *responsibility* was vague in this context. It had been the most desirable quality for a newsman since World War II and could never be defined. On when to withhold stories, he even wrote, "There cannot be any general rule." He noted, "It is not enough to determine whether or not the story would hurt the country, or even, in time of war, aid the enemy. The real scales in which the problem must be weighed is whether or not the aid to the enemy or the hurt to the country outweighs the favorable results of the story's publication; i.e.—the 'general good.'"[103] Again, Baldwin could not define the "general good," but he gave examples of when stories published had led to positive change, and when stories withheld—especially specifics about weapons—had been withheld for good reason. His resentment of the Kennedy administration and especially the Pentagon and its lead spokesman, Arthur Sylvester, was especially clear in the memo.

Dryfoos confidentially recounted his meeting with the president to his top editors the following day. He told them, horrified, that Kennedy had suggested that John McCone, the new CIA chief, and Robert McNamara, the secretary of defense, could institute a system whereby the CIA would receive a report each time someone in the Pentagon spoke to a reporter.[104] The suggestion was so antithetical to the idea of press freedom that Dryfoos cautioned his staff twice not to repeat it. He realized that Kennedy may have been floating a so-called trial balloon, but they had met for over an hour and the president seemed to think he had a valid proposal. The publisher spent thirty minutes arguing against this kind of unprecedented surveillance of the press. He presented the argument in terms the president would find favorable, though, pointing out that more openness with the press would actually help Kennedy get more support for foreign policies. Rather than the president's imposing additional restrictions, Dryfoos favored continuing the current system, whereby, as he assured Kennedy, "if [the editors] have any doubt they check with you."[105]

Just four weeks later, the United States obtained intelligence of Soviet missiles being set up in Cuba, beginning what became the Cuban Missile Crisis, thirteen days in October 1962 when the United States and the Soviet Union appeared to be on the brink of nuclear war. The administration had admitted since September that there was a Soviet buildup of defensive weapons in Cuba. While some speculation about offensive weapons had made it into print, nothing definite appeared until Friday, October 12, in a syndicated column by the "scoop artists" Robert Allen and Paul Scott. In their first paragraph, they flatly stated, "Russia is stepping up its arms shipments to Cuba."[106] The columnists wrote that their figures contradicted the report that the State Department had given to Congress. A few days later, the unpopular Pentagon spokesman Arthur Sylvester denied the Allen-Scott story. "That answer was the lie that has rankled ever since—the one paragraph mimeographed statement that the Pentagon had no information on the presence of offensive Soviet weapons in Cuba," wrote a reporter for the *Miami Herald* in a private letter four years later.[107]

Reporters in Washington already mistrusted Sylvester, and by Friday evening, October 19, they knew that he had lied. Secretary of State Dean Rusk canceled a speech that night, as did the chairman of the Joint Chiefs of Staff, General Maxwell Taylor. Reporters continued working their contacts throughout the weekend as Kennedy canceled his appearances at a series of midterm campaign rallies across the country because he had a "slight upper respiratory cold," which none of the reporters believed. Within forty-eight hours, the *Times*' bureau had independently verified that there were indeed offensive weapons in Cuba, and the bureau chief Scotty Reston phoned the president to let him know what the newspaper planned to publish. Kennedy requested that the *Times* not print anything specific about US knowledge of the missiles or the planned blockade, or else "[the Soviet premier Nikita] Khrushchev could beat us to the draw."[108] Reston lodged his objection to suppression of the news but said that the decision would be Dryfoos's. After at least one additional phone conversation between the president and Reston, during which Kennedy had assured Reston there would be no chance of bloodshed before his planned televised address to the American people (as there had been during the Bay of Pigs invasion), the *Times* agreed not to print details. The paper hardly kept silent, though. Its front-page headline the next morning, Monday, October 22, merely stated, "Capital's Crisis Air Hints at Development on Cuba; Kennedy TV Talk Likely." But the article, which ran without a byline, noted that the United States Navy and Marine Corps "are staging a powerful show of force in the Caribbean not far from Cuba. . . . The Administration denies that there is any connection between the anxious mood here and these maneuvers, which involved about 20,000 men, including 6,000 marines. But the speculation in Washington was that there had been a new development on Cuba that could not be disclosed at this point."[109]

The development was now common knowledge among members of the press, but the public had not explicitly been told. The White House sent a memorandum to all news outlets over the press association wires, describing a policy of voluntary censorship regarding information that the Defense Department was not officially releasing but that the press was finding out anyway: "During the current tense international situation, the White House feels that the publication of such information is contrary to the public interest."[110] The White House denied that this counted as censorship, which had been the controversial policy during World War II and the Korean War. In its article about the memorandum, which again had no byline, the *Times* commented drily, "Newspapermen who were in Washington during those two wars found it difficult to see where the difference lay."[111]

Still, on national security grounds—and, as the White House put it, in "the public interest"—the *New York Times* postponed publication about the missiles for a day. Even Tad Szulc, who felt that his newspaper had mishandled his Bay of Pigs reporting, supported the decision, saying later, "We were talking nuclear war here, not some little Cuban exercise."[112] Kennedy sent Orvil Dryfoos a personal note later that week, thanking him for his cooperation. "Events since then have reinforced my view that an important service to the national interest was performed by your agreement to withhold information that was available to you on Sunday afternoon," the president wrote.[113]

The truce between government and press was short lived. On October 30, Arthur Sylvester worsened his press relations even further by defending his lies of the previous week, telling a reporter that news handling was "part of the arsenal of weaponry" of the Kennedy administration. The problem was less in the content of what he said than the fact that he said it on the record, for public consumption. After all, members of the press and the government were all still figuring out where responsibility for national security lay. But as a *Washington Evening Star* editorial put it, "Mr. Sylvester is to be commended for his frankness, at least. But he has let an ugly cat out of the bag."[114] That is, everyone within Washington knew that the federal government manipulated the press and used it as a weapon, with the press's tacit cooperation, but the public was not supposed to know that.[115] The editorial pointed out that now, everything that Sylvester said would be suspect. Moreover, reporters were now obliged to say so.

The *New York Times* editorial of the same date took a loftier angle: "There is no doubt that a democratic government cannot work if news of and about that government is long suppressed or managed or manipulated or controlled." It acknowledged the "sense of responsibility" the press must feel in a time of crisis. "But to attempt to manage the news so that a free press should speak (in Sylvester's words) in 'one voice to your adversary' could be far more dangerous to the case of freedom than the free play of dissent, than the fullest possible publication of the facts."[116] The Kennedy administration had forced the *Times* into taking a public position on the issue. For the first time since World War II, it would be difficult for newspapers to cover for the government when it was lying—even when doing so was, as Turner Catledge once put it, in the "so-called public interest."[117]

CONCLUSION

DISRUPTION AND CONTINUITY

Scholars tend to make assumptions about what journalism was like during the 1940s and 1950s. At times, of course, it was stenographic, but it was hardly monolithic. Reporters had motives more complex than patriotism. Negotiations behind the scenes that reveal the genuine tensions over reporting on foreign policy help complicate a story of the 1960s and 1970s as bringing with it "an end of innocence."[1] Attention to the lived experiences of a cohort of foreign policy reporters in Washington, DC, allows us to question some of our ideas about consensus, as well as understand how much the appearance of consensus depended on a gendered and racialized community.

We expect newsmen to respond to workplace pressures. During the 1950s, the political scientist Warren Breed was one of the first scholars to study social control in newsrooms. He provided a nuanced account of how journalistic norms and practices combined with a publisher's editorial policy to produce conformity. The "socio-cultural situation of the newsroom" that he described became even more complicated within the sociocultural situation of Washington.[2] The newsrooms in that city were typically bureaus detached from their home offices, which meant that the horizontal pressures of functioning in Washington society among responsible peers were as important, if not more so, as the vertical pressures from publishers. The conformity, then, was not just within a single newsroom but appeared to the public as a consensus across all newspapers with a reporter stationed in Washington.

Reporters also did respond to pressures from their hometown publishers, but often with defiance, as Scotty Reston of the *New York Times* so frequently did with Arthur Sulzberger. One of the reasons he felt entitled to do so was the sense of self-importance so common in this group of men who believed they truly were writing the "first rough draft of history"—a phrase popular in the *Washington Post* newsroom at the time and therefore likely popular within the capital.[3] They wrote for posterity. "I can never get out of my mind yon chalky pedagogue thumbing through The Times or peering into the lighted microfilm box in some dim college library thirty years from now when we are all gone," Reston wrote while in a philosophical mood one Sunday morning in 1959 to "Mr. Gus," one of his pet names for Sulzberger from World War II. Sulzberger had complained about Reston's unflattering portrait of President Dwight Eisenhower in an article. "You are my boss, but so is he," Reston noted of the future historian. "I have to tell him the plain unhappy truth: the nation faltered in 1956–1957 because it lacked energy at the political core. This has been the topic of private conversations here throughout the last year. It has to be reported; otherwise, those who know the truth and who know we know the truth will properly say we are not doing our job. And when my dusty little professor goes back to the files of the only paper deemed worthy of keeping the daily record, I don't want him writing that, out of personal kindness or consideration for the President, The New York Times ignored what almost everybody knew to be the truth."[4] Scholars have judged both the *Times* and Reston much more harshly than he would have anticipated, but they have done so without yet having the complete and complicated story.

Washington journalism during World War II and the early Cold War era certainly had much that set it apart from the reporting that came before and after it, but reporters' trust in the federal government and in the rightness and morality of US intentions abroad were not immutable factors.[5] As we have seen, the Cold War itself—at least in its traditional formulation as an ideological struggle against communism—was not actually that important to on-the-ground foreign policy reporting in Washington. In 1992, just after the end of the Cold War, the communication scholar Daniel Hallin identified some of the political, economic, and institutional changes that marked the end of an era he calls "high modernism" in journalism.[6] One of them was the Cold War itself. "It was the Cold War above all that made a relatively passive, state-centered model of journalism appear reasonable. Truth and power seemed united in the Washington headquarters of the free world, and the basic job of the reporter, in a phrase I have often heard from reporters covering national security policy, was to 'reflect the thinking' of official Washington. . . . As foreign policy consensus has broken down, reporters have had to think for themselves much more, about which voices to listen to, for example, and how to synthesize for their audience a political reality that is not black and white."[7]

There was no single Cold War mindset among newsmen, though, and they certainly did not "lap up" the US government's lines as enthusiastically as we sometimes assume or remember.[8] Wally Carroll, the North Carolina newspaperman who worked for the government in psychological warfare during and after World War II (and later returned to Washington to help run the DC bureau of the New York Times), gives a more representative perspective of this cohort. In a March 1953 memo that he submitted confidentially to President Eisenhower's committee on psychological warfare (and shared with Scotty Reston), he declared, "We might stop to consider whether anybody wants to be involved in a cold war, and whether anybody wants to be a target of psychological warfare, and whether anybody is eager to be manipulated by Americans." He recommended that the administration "bottle up the 'cold war' talk—get it out of the official vocabulary."[9]

Reporters covering foreign policy from Washington had always been thinking for themselves, but also, the foreign policy consensus to which they subscribed never quite broke down, even after the Cold War. The broader internationalist consensus—that the United States has a major role to play in keeping world peace, and that our strongest allies are in Western Europe—has persisted. As president, Donald Trump was in the minority in official Washington for his apparent disdain for NATO and other agreements with Europe. He was certainly at odds with the majority of the press corps, which remains internationalist in its outlook. At the grass roots, isolationist voices that have been downplayed since the late 1930s have found renewed purchase, especially those that call for "America First."[10] But these public opinions had existed alongside what we think of as consensus, which was rarely as solid as newsmen made it appear. Ultimately, the end of the Cold War did not bring with it the end of NATO, or even the end of US-Russian tensions. Just as Joe Harsch predicted in a 1948 letter to a reader, the United States remained on guard against Russian expansion, whether its leader was a communist Stalin or a tsarist Peter the Great—or, presumably, a Vladimir Putin.[11]

What *was* different about this period, and why do we continually return to the 1940s and 1950s as exceptional decades in the history of journalism? For one, the fear of nuclear holocaust—"the fear that would be the constant companion of Americans for the rest of their lives," as the historian Paul Boyer puts it—was pervasive.[12] The anxieties of average Americans who hoarded canned goods as their children participated in duck-and-cover drills in their classrooms were no less acute for the newsmen of Washington. As time passed without nuclear warfare, and especially with the signing of the Nuclear Test Ban Treaty in 1963, those anxieties subsided. Nuclear war seemed less imminent. The possibility of World War III also seemed to grow more remote. The great fear that the peace after World War II would be as short lived as the peace after World War I lessened after World War II's twenty-year anniversary came and went. The next total war in Europe had grown increasingly unlikely, and with it, reporters' fear that they might trigger it.

Another reason that journalism appears to have changed by the 1960s and 1970s is that the agonizing soul-searching and complaining—about colleagues, publishers, and sources—that reporters had long done in memos and at dinner parties, behind the scenes, they began to do more often in print. Walter Lippmann wrote in a 1947 column that the public critique of journalism and the airing of dirty laundry would create "hard feelings . . . out of all proportion to the public benefit it causes." Feelings mattered in a small-town atmosphere like Washington's. "For there is a fellowship among newspapermen as there is in other crafts and professions," Lippmann continued. "They are not lone wolves. They have to see each other, meet together, and work together, and life would become intolerable, as it would in a university faculty or an officers' mess, if they practiced vigorous mutual criticism in public."[13] Twentieth-century press criticism had a distinguished history, including the famous muckraker Upton Sinclair's *The Brass Check* (1919) and Lippmann's own "A Test of the News" (1920). But press critics at midcentury—including George Seldes, the CBS commentator Don Hollenbeck, and even the Hutchins Commission, which reactionaries tried to brand post facto as radical—fell victim to red-baiting.[14] Regardless of the time period, perhaps life does become intolerable for the loudest critics. But public criticism—such as that which appeared in the *Columbia Journalism Review*, founded in 1961, the *Chicago Journalism Review*, founded in 1968, and the dozens of magazines of journalism criticism founded in the next two decades, like *(MORE)* (1971–78)—has now become part of the profession.[15]

The sociologist Michael Schudson calls this the "critical culture" hypothesis and demonstrates how transformations in the wider culture help explain similar tendencies to critique and dissent within journalism.[16] Criticism during the 1960s became more pervasive as well as more mainstream, part of a broader counterculture of antagonism to institutions that a new generation brought into the public discourse. However, the critique becoming public did not mean that reporters had not struggled over issues of objectivity and credibility in the preceding decades, merely that we need to look beyond the published record and remembrances to understand the parameters of the disagreements and the incentives journalists had for downplaying dissent.

Third, demographics shifted, both within Washington and within journalism. By 1960, Washington had a majority Black population.[17] The town continued to integrate, and the spaces that the white press operated in became less exclusive—more open to voices once considered outsiders. Around the same time, both the *Washington Post* and the *New York Times* experienced abrupt changes at the tops of their mastheads. In May 1963, the *Times'* fifty-year-old publisher, Orvil Dryfoos, died of a heart attack, making his brother-in-law, the thirty-seven-year-old Arthur O. "Punch" Sulzberger, his successor. In August 1963, the *Post's* publisher, Phil Graham, died by suicide, leaving his wife, Katharine, to begin moving into that role. Punch Sulzberger and Kay Graham were hardly revolutionaries, but they at least had different life experiences than their predecessors and brought somewhat new perspectives. Their staffs began changing over as well. Many of the newsmen in this book remained in the profession, but the tightly knit network of friends that had relied on one another so much to survive the anxieties, frustrations, and tedium of World War II was aging out of daily journalism.

A fourth reason journalism seems to have changed so much is the retrospective shadow of the Vietnam War. On the face of it, the actual business of reporting on Vietnam was not so different from the reporting before it. As we have seen in this book, journalists had not so much been advocates for the government as champions of Atlantic power. The war in Vietnam did not serve the internationalist agenda that prioritized US leadership in an Atlantic world, as Lippmann frequently wrote in his columns, making him—not to mention most of the press corps—a pariah with the Lyndon Johnson administration.[18] The manner in which the war was covered, in print at least, was often critical.[19] The war also created acrimony in the Washington community. The excitement of the New Deal that had brought Lippmann to Washington in the 1930s was a far cry from the rancorous political atmosphere of the Vietnam War era. In 1967, Lippmann left. He moved back to New York City, saying, "I simply can't stand Washington. It's impossible to breathe or think in this town."[20] The Washington of this book—the Lippmann era—was one that had been more congenial for reporters.

Finally, the relationship between presidential administrations and the press covering them changed. The executive branch had been acquiring more administrative power for decades, to such an extent that by the time Lyndon Johnson came to office in 1963, reporters had become wary of an imperial presidency. As presidential power increased, so did the press's sense of its watchdog function. In a December 1956 letter that Scotty Reston sent to Secretary of State John Foster Dulles expanding on an argument the two men had had, he wrote: "I said that the American press in my judgment was doing what I felt it must always do, namely to regard Government power with considerable skepticism and to make sure that its skepticism was kept in relationship to the amount of power exercised by the Government." He explained that the skepticism must increase with power. This attitude helps illustrate one of the reasons for the increased watchdog function of the press as Lyndon Johnson and his successor, Richard Nixon, took more and more foreign and domestic policy into their own hands. Reston continued to Dulles, "Furthermore I said that it was no longer adequate or fair to the readers merely to turn the newspaper into a transmission belt for whatever public officials wanted to put out. This we have done for a long time but in recent years our governments and politicians and great businesses had brought all the arts of modern publicity and public relations to bear in order to try to take advantage of the old techniques of merely reporting what was said without putting it into proper perspective."[21] (Reston's concern is the same one that his mentor, Lippmann, had outlined in his 1922 book *Public Opinion*.) Putting news in its proper perspective meant a major increase of what Schudson and Katherine Fink call "contextual" journalism—more interpretive stories that provide readers with explanatory contexts.[22]

The men in the White House, of course, changed too. The 1950s and the Eisenhower administration—especially Foster Dulles's State Department, which frequently lied to the press—laid the groundwork for the deterioration of the press's trust that we usually attribute to the Nixon administration. And of course, Richard Nixon's having been the vice president in the Eisenhower administration did not help reporters trust his own administration. They remembered Nixon. As Robert Allen, the leftist columnist and cynical diarist, wrote in December 1952, "Heard a very interesting story about Vice-President-elect Nixon, one of the prime jerks in American public life. He is a devious, crooked and treacherous son-of-a-bitch—as he has already repeatedly demonstrated and will be a big headache to Eisenhower before they get through together."[23] Reporters hated Nixon during the 1950s, and they hated him again during the 1970s, because some things never change.

Of course, these are not the only shifts and disruptions to have occurred during the 1960s and 1970s. Television news became much more dominant in American life. Technology changed reporters' daily work routines and environments.[24] But these shifts help give us a sense of why the period and the newsmen in this book were unusual.

What happened to get us from that period to the present merits its own book, as does the question of what the present is really like. But we can now see the origins of certain concepts, like pack journalism, the boys' club, and the appearance of a liberal internationalist consensus. We have known that those structures were central to midcentury journalism, but we have not known how they were created. We can also point to the parts of the culture that endure. The National Press Club is hardly the social necessity it once was, but reporters still travel in packs and eat and drink with one another. They still abide by off-the-record and background rules, and they even hold background dinners, especially when it comes to the two areas where material is especially sensitive: national security and the financial markets.[25] There are far more women reporters and reporters of color in the present day, but to remain competitive, especially in reporting on foreign affairs and national security, they abide by the gendered and racialized rules of responsibility that have obtained since World War II.

The world in this book is certainly specific, grounded in a particular historical moment, when foreign policy reporters worried about the future of what they called civilization. This period was not static, beginning with reporters covering peace settlements, frustrated that their State Department would not give them enough information to generate support for new international systems. It ended in the heyday of CIA secret operations and reporters' resentment that their government primarily fed them half-truths and lies. Nevertheless, similarities between that town and present-day Washington persist. Even referring to "this period" is not quite right, since some aspects of it have had no finite ending. Washington remains a fairly insular town in which it is possible to keep a secret from the rest of the nation, at least for a short time.[26] "This town," as its residents have been known to derogatorily call it, is still a peculiar city.[27]

ACKNOWLEDGMENTS

I began this work in Princeton University's History Department, where I received the intellectual, emotional, and financial support that made the book possible. Julian Zelizer has been an ideal mentor, editor, and champion. Thank you also to Margot Canaday, Dirk Hartog, Kevin Kruse, and Michael Schudson for invaluable feedback on earlier versions of the project. The University of Wisconsin has been the perfect environment in which to write the book. I am especially grateful for the mentorship and friendship of Jennifer Ratner-Rosenhagen and Sue Robinson, along with the support provided by my colleagues in the School of Journalism and Mass Communication and the Institute for Research in the Humanities.

I am grateful to Lucas Graves, Donald Ritchie, and Michael Wagner for reading the book in its entirety and providing such useful comments in the final stretch. Emmanuel Felton, Elizabeth McCue, and Janie and Cappy McGarr gave me extremely helpful feedback on an early version of the manuscript. I also appreciate the work of three anonymous readers who provided comments on my proposal and manuscript, helping me better articulate the arguments of the book. Commenters at workshops over several years have helped shape my research—thank you to Robert Collins, Gary Gerstle, Nicole Hemmer, Sam Lebovic, Nicholas Lemann, and Margaret O'Mara. I feel lucky to have met the late Jim

Baughman, who championed the project and my career while I was still in graduate school.

Thank you to the many librarians and archivists who made my research fruitful, especially those at the New York Public Library, the Library of Congress, the University of Illinois, and the Wisconsin Historical Society. The Eisenhower Library and Truman Library additionally provided funding.

I was lucky to have teachers and professors in the last twenty years who encouraged me to become a historian and modeled that for me so well—thank you especially to Barton Bernstein, Estelle Freedman, Sam Freedman, Steve Kramer, and Victor Navasky.

Many friends have supported me in this years'-long process. My COVID-19 virtual writing group got me through the last year of the book project—thank you to Jen Gaddis, Wangui Muigai, and Emily Prifogle. For their friendship and patience, I am grateful to Jehan Alladina, Sarah Coleman, Sameer Dacosta, Tullia Dymarz, Randy Goldsmith, Liz Hennessy, Erin Lethlean, Claire Moses, Mary Pfotenhauer, and Eliana Stein. Thank you to Kathy Brown and to Tom and Linda Daschle for additionally hosting me so often on research trips.

Timothy Mennel at the University of Chicago Press could not have been more generous with his time and energy, helping me through every stage of drafting and editing. My thanks also to Susannah Engstrom and Mark Reschke for shepherding me through the publication process and to Sandra Hazel for taking such care with copyediting the manuscript.

I've dedicated the book to my parents, Janie and Cappy McGarr, who have been kind and enthusiastic through many years of my becoming a historian, starting with taking me to the local university's library for my very first research project when I was in high school. Thank you for making this possible.

Portions of chapter 6 appeared in "'The World's Greatest Hypocrites': White Men and Diplomatic Reporting in the Early Cold War," *Modern American History* 5, no. 2 (July 2022). Reprinted with permission.

NOTES

Introduction

1. William H. Lawrence to James Reston, memo, January 8, 1954, box 50, folder "Confidential Memoranda, January 1953–August 1959," Reston Papers.
2. Notes, January 7, 1954, box 55, folder 4, Wiggins Papers.
3. "Peiping Recognition Is Opposed by Nixon," *New York Times*, January 10, 1954; Warren Duffee (United Press), "Nixon Backs China Policy," *Washington Post*, January 10, 1954.
4. Hallin in *The "Uncensored War"* has shattered many of these myths, and he expresses skepticism that there was ever a veil lifted. The myth of a veil persists, though.
5. Talese, *The Kingdom and the Power*, 9.
6. Scotty Reston's "clerkships," an apprenticeship he ran at the *New York Times* from 1961 to 1979 for young reporters, funneled students from the *Harvard Crimson*. Of sixteen clerks, seven had gone to Harvard. Linda Greenhouse was the only woman he ever hired, in 1968–69, so he would not lose his clerk to the draft. As a Radcliffe student, Greenhouse had also written for the *Harvard Crimson*. Notes, interview with Linda Greenhouse, undated, box 2, Stacks Papers.
7. James L. Greenfield, "Editorial Notebook: Not an Anchorman in Sight," *New York Times*, July 29, 1993.
8. On the creation of a rhetorical "Atlantic Community," see Mariano, *Defining the Atlantic Community*.
9. Frankel, *The Times of My Life*, 346.
10. Frankel, 184.
11. The television reporter Roger Mudd said in a 2000 lecture that until the

U-2 incident, most journalists had been "trusting and uncritical of the government" (cited in Ritchie, *Reporting from Washington*, 220; and Schudson, *The Rise of the Right to Know*, 142).

12. See for instance Hanson Baldwin, "Notes on the Problem of Freedom vs. Security," September 6, 1962, box 1, folder 16, Daniel Papers; Chalmers Roberts, memo, June 17, 1971, box 62, folder "Reporting (1 of 2)," Roberts Papers.

13. Scholars often cite Stepp, "Then and Now," to demonstrate how much newspapers changed from the deferential 1950s and 1960s to the 1990s. Newspapers did, of course, change, as Fink and Schudson have demonstrated in their work on contextual news ("The Rise of Contextual Journalism"). But Stepp's accounting of deferential reporting practices was limited to ten local and regional newspapers, none of which had a dedicated foreign policy reporter in Washington. When he writes that newspapers of the earlier period "seem naively trusting of government, shamelessly boosterish, unembarrassedly hokey and obliging," he was referring not to foreign policy news but to local and regional reporting.

14. Herman and Chomsky use the language of filters in *Manufacturing Consent*, 2.

15. Wallace R. Deuel to Bob Lasch, April 1, 1952, box 7, folder "Post-Dispatch 1952," Deuel Papers.

16. Diary, November 19, 1954, box 4, folder "Diary Entries 1954, 1978," Reston Papers.

17. List, Assistant Secretary for Public Affairs Executive Office Subject Files, 1957–1961, box 5, RG 59. These organizations were Agence France Presse (wire service), Aftonbladet (Sweden), Davar (Israel), Die Press (Austria), France-Amerique (a US-based French newspaper), and Il Globo (an Australian-based Italian paper).

18. Beasley, *Women of the Washington Press*. See also Marzolf, *Up from the Footnote*, and Fahs, *Out on Assignment*. Marama Whyte is currently working on a book about women activists in Washington during the postwar period based on her dissertation, "The Press for Equality" (University of Sydney, 2019).

19. See especially Dean, *Imperial Brotherhood*, and Herken, *The Georgetown Set*.

20. A historical focus on famous individuals has meant a better understanding of elite columnists, such as Walter Lippmann and Joseph Alsop, the subjects of several biographies.

21. Rosten, *The Washington Correspondents*, 327.

22. Examples of works that focus on the federal government's perspective are Parry-Giles, *The Rhetorical Presidency*, and Osgood, *Total Cold War*.

23. Hallin, *The "Uncensored War,"* 117; Gans, *Deciding What's News*, 42.

24. Sociologists and historians have noted the social construction of information and the "occupational socialization" of professions, including news

reporting. For instance, see Breed, "Social Control in the Newsroom"; Darnton, "Writing News and Telling Stories"; Tuchman, *Making News*; and Herman and Chomsky, *Manufacturing Consent*. Journalism studies scholars use the concept of "boundary work" to describe a sociological understanding of knowledge production in journalism.

25. The dominant research methods have been content analysis and contemporary sociological study. For examples of content analysis, see Zaller and Chiu, "Government's Little Helper"; Herman and Chomsky, *Manufacturing Consent*; Liebovich, *The Press and the Origins of the Cold War*. For concurrent political science studies of reporters as a nonindividuated sociological group, see Cohen, *The Press and Foreign Policy*; Nimmo, *Newsgathering in Washington*; Rivers, *The Opinionmakers*; Gans, *Deciding What's News*; and Hess, *The Washington Reporters*.

26. James Reston to Paul Miller, October 11, 1951, box 99, folder "Censorship, 1951," Reston Papers.

27. On the Pentagon Papers, see Rudenstine, *The Day the Presses Stopped*.

28. Quoted in Hallin, *The "Uncensored War,"* 63.

29. Timothy Crouse explores this consequence of togetherness during the 1972 presidential campaign as "pack journalism" (*The Boys on the Bus*). Journalism studies scholars have since demonstrated the importance of the physical spaces of news production and the "conventionalized social interactions and professional rituals that define these spaces" (Caldwell, "Industrial Geography Lessons," 166).

30. For this phenomenon in business, see Laird, *Pull*.

31. See McGarr, "The Importance of Historical Perspective and Archival Methods in Political Communication Research."

32. Zelizer, "Journalists as Interpretive Communities." Physical space has also been central to journalism studies scholars. See Zelizer, *Taking Journalism Seriously*.

33. I have been influenced by the many historians of gender and sexuality who have done excellent work interrogating physical space. See, for example, Stansell, *City of Women*; Chauncey, *Gay New York*; Deutsch, *Women and the City*; and Enke, *Finding the Movement*.

34. Buckley, "Our Mission Statement." James Wechsler was an editor at the liberal New York *Post*, and when he came under Senator Joseph McCarthy's scrutiny in 1953, many of his friends and acquaintances argued over how much support they should have given Wechsler individually as well as institutionally (e.g., by the American Society of Newspaper Editors). Wechsler's wife, Nancy, told Arthur Schlesinger Jr. how hurt they were that the Alsop brothers had not come to Wechsler's defense in print. Schlesinger relayed this to Joseph Alsop, saying, "Since it is a shame to divide our side . . ." Letters between Wechsler, Joseph Alsop, and Arthur Schlesinger Jr. can be found in box 9 of the Joseph and Stewart Alsop Papers at the

Library of Congress. On Wechsler and McCarthy, see Alwood, *Dark Days in the Newsroom*, 69–75.

35. Public opinion polls tended to show support for policies like the Marshall Plan, but those polls were often flawed and did not always represent the reality (Igo, *The Averaged American*, 142–48). The America First prewar attitude remained strong after the war. In addition, many people simply did not follow international affairs: a 1950 Gallup poll showed that 45% of those polled did not even know the term *Cold War* (memo, January 31, 1951, box 4, folder "Correspondence: Deputy Asst. Sec. for Public Affairs, State Dept., 1951," Sargeant Papers).

36. See Logevall, "First among Critics."

37. Kay Halle to Arthur Schlesinger Jr., June 5, 1948, box P15, folder "Kay Halle," Schlesinger Papers.

38. Arthur Schlesinger Jr. to Joseph Alsop, June 7, 1948, box 3, chron. files, Alsop Papers.

39. Joseph Harsch to Henry Steele Commager, undated [November 1953], box 38, folder "Correspondence 1942–1953," Harsch Papers.

40. Henry Steele Commager to Joseph Harsch, November 25, 1953, box 38, folder "Correspondence 1942–1953," Harsch Papers.

Chapter One

1. Arthur Krock to Arthur Hays Sulzberger, March 2, 1932, box 270, folder 20, Sulzberger Papers.

2. Quoted in Asch and Musgrove, *Chocolate City*, 26. Congress returned Alexandria to Virginia in 1846 and absorbed Georgetown into Washington in 1871. For a history of early colonists and Native Americans in the area that became Washington, see Asch and Musgrove, 5–15.

3. Nord and others have built on Benedict Anderson's concept of "imagined communities" for newspaper readers (see especially Nord, *Communities of Journalism*).

4. *National Intelligencer and Washington (DC) Advertiser*, October 31, 1800. Chronicling America, accessed December 1, 2021, https://chronicling america.loc.gov/lccn/sn83045242/1800-10-31/ed-1/.

5. On the partisan press of the early republic, see Daniel, *Scandal and Civility*.

6. Green, *Washington*, 18–19.

7. On early boardinghouses and "fraternities," see Young, *The Washington Community*. Though not as common as they once were, men's boarding-houses continued into the twenty-first century, the best known being the "C Street" house, where Christian congressmen can live and study the Bible together.

8. Young, xii.

9. That Washington remains insular and a town that considers itself entirely separate from America—"this town"—is apparent in Leibovich's portrait of modern Washington, *This Town*.

10. Green, *Washington*, 18–19.

11. Though immigration was minimal relative to other cities, immigrant and ethnic communities still existed, as described in Cary, *Urban Odyssey*.

12. Asch and Musgrove, *Chocolate City*, 123.

13. For more on clubs and fraternal organizations as buffers coinciding with the rise of urban centers and an influx of immigrant groups, see Laird, *Pull*, 58–60, 83–91.

14. Kerber, "Separate Spheres." For women's clubs built around race distinctions and interracial networking, see Gilmore, *Gender and Jim Crow*, 190–94.

15. Laird, *Pull*, 54.

16. Laird, 2.

17. Sociologists, gender studies theorists, and others have demonstrated the importance of homosocial spaces for creating common practices and understandings. See Lipman-Blumen, "Toward a Homosocial Theory of Sex Roles," and Bird, "Welcome to the Men's Club." Lipman-Blumen has this to say about men's clubs like the Metropolitan Club: "The upper-class male club bears structural similarities to the Mafia, albeit refined by generations of affluence and culture. It has its own emphasis upon territoriality, exclusivity, dominance, and resource accumulation, preservation, and enlargement" (30).

18. Women were admitted to both the Metropolitan Club and the Cosmos Club in 1988, after the Supreme Court upheld a New York City law prohibiting discrimination at social clubs that were not "distinctly private" (*New York State Club Association Inc. v. City of New York*, 487 US 1 [1988]).

19. "The New Club," *Daily National Intelligencer* (Washington, DC) 51, no. 15959, October 13, 1863.

20. Charlick, *The Metropolitan Club of Washington*, 1.

21. For Washington "high society" during this period, see Jacob, *Capital Elites*.

22. In 1908, after forty-five years of rented quarters and cycles of decline, renewal, and ultimately prosperity, the Metropolitan Club moved into its current home at Seventeenth and H Streets.

23. Diary, June 14, 1948, box 23, folder 4, Allen Papers.

24. Gridiron Club, *Washington as It Really Is*, 9.

25. Schudson, *Discovering the News*, 69–70.

26. Quoted in Ritchie, *Press Gallery*, 92.

27. Ritchie, 109–10, 121.

28. Ritchie, 78.

29. See Summers, *The Press Gang*.

30. Dunn, *Gridiron Nights*, 3.

31. "Book of the Gridiron Club," box 79, Gridiron Club Records.

32. Ritchie, *Press Gallery*, 127.

33. Initially, the club's bylaws mandated two annual dinners, but the increased pace of newspaper work after World War II meant that the members had less time for the skit writing and rehearsals required to stage a "public" dinner, as they called their events. The president also had less time to attend such events, which had multiplied, and Eisenhower had let it be known before he took office that two Gridiron dinners a year was too much. (Referenced in Hugh Baillie to Lyle Wilson, January 6, 1953, box 2, folder 39, Merriman Smith Papers.) In January 1953, the men officially amended their bylaws so that they could host one large, white-tie dinner per year in the spring, with a second, "informal" (black-tie) dinner for members and a small group of guests in the winter.

34. Dunn, *Gridiron Nights*, 53–54.

35. References to reimbursement appear in several archival sources, including a list of men getting reimbursed in Lewis Wood to Arthur Krock, December 22, 1948, box 270, folder 18, Sulzberger Papers.

36. Richard Wilson, "The Gridiron Club," *Look*, May 11, 1948, clipped in box 106, folder "Glen Perry Scrapbook (Loose Material)," Gridiron Club Records.

37. Diary, May 18, 1956, box 23, folder "1956 May–1957," Allen Papers.

38. Lester Markel to James Reston, March 6, 1958; April 21, 1964; box 34, folder "Lester Markel," Reston Papers.

39. Diary, March 11, 1953, box 23, folder "1953 Feb–1954 Dec," Allen Papers.

40. Drag has been associated with queer identity, in popular culture as well as in history, as in Bérubé, *Coming Out Under Fire*, 67–97. At the Gridiron dinner, female characters were few, since the skits parodied politics and public policy, a male domain. When dinner participants did drag, they were distancing themselves from femininity, not embracing it, much as blackface was a way of whitening oneself. On amateur blackface as a way of proclaiming one's whiteness, see Barnes, *Darkology*.

41. "De Watermillion Hangin' on de Vine," box 14, folder "Gridiron Club, The, (1 of 2)," Ross Papers.

42. Schedule, May 4, 1955, box 270, folder 17, Sulzberger Papers.

43. Richard Nixon to Turner Catledge, November 10, 1966, box 5, folder "Nixon," series IIC, Catledge Papers.

44. Turner Catledge to Richard Nixon, November 16, 1966, box 5, folder "Nixon," series IIC, Catledge Papers.

45. Carnes, *Secret Ritual*.

46. Turner Catledge described the typical dinner in detail in a letter to Lawrence M. Williams, February 2, 1967, box 14, folder "Gridiron Club 1965," series IIC, Catledge Papers.

47. Dodge et al., *Shrdlu*, 11.

48. Wallace Deuel to Sadie Deuel, December 2, 1946, box 1, chron. files, Deuel Papers.

49. Bar Committee Report for 1953, box "Records of the Board of Governors, Minutes and Correspondence, 1950–1954," folder "Minutes, Jan 15–Feb 23, 1954," National Press Club Records.

50. Dodge et al., *Shrdlu*, 5.

51. Laird, *Pull*, 83.

52. Frank Holeman to National Press Club Archives, October 3, 1988, box 1, folder "NPC President's Files, 1956—Holeman, Frank (1988 Memo . . .)," President's Files, National Press Club Papers.

53. George Durno et al. to the Board of Governors, January 21, 1955, box 1950–1954, folder "NPC Board of Governors, 1955, Correspondence, Petition," Board of Governors Files, National Press Club Papers.

54. *Hearing on the Application of Louis R. Lautier for Admission to Senate Press Gallery and Hearing on Reports of Discrimination in Admission to Senate Restaurants and Cafeterias*, Senate, 80th Cong., 1st sess. March 18, 1947.

55. Resolution, January 15, 1955, box 1950–1954, folder "NPC Board of Governors, 1955, Correspondence, Petition," Board of Governors Files, National Press Club Papers.

56. Ethel Payne, interview by Kathleen Currie (Washington Press Club Foundation), September 8, 1987, page 42, box 41, folder 13, Payne Papers.

57. Dunnigan, *A Black Woman's Experience*, 377.

58. Robertson, *The Girls in the Balcony*.

59. Greenberg, *The Republic of Spin*, 89–90.

60. Drury, *Advise and Consent*, 370.

61. Ruth Gmeiner to Martha Strayer, February 2, 1954, box 1, folder "Professional File 1954," President's Files, Women's National Press Club Papers.

62. Hugh Baillie to Merriman Smith, March 26, 1945, box 2, folder 2, Merriman Smith Papers.

63. Anthony Leviero to Liz Carpenter, December 13, 1954, box 1, folder "Professional File 1954," President's Files, Women's National Press Club Papers.

64. Bess Furman to Martha Strayer, February 4, 1954, box 1, folder "Professional File 1954," President's Files, Women's National Press Club Papers.

65. Ruth Gmeiner to Martha Strayer, February 2, 1954, box 1, folder "Professional File 1954," President's Files, Women's National Press Club Papers.

66. Rivers, *The Opinionmakers*, 75.

67. For a review of the "diversity pays" literature—the idea that underrepresented groups bring fresh perspectives—and its opponents, see Herring, "Does Diversity Pay?"

68. Crouse, *The Boys on the Bus*, 223.

69. Kiplinger, *Washington Is Like That*, 176.

70. Appointment books, June 25, 1947, box 55, folder 14, Wiggins Papers.

71. Invitation, box 12, folder "Luncheons with Press," Office of Information, Office of Director Subject Files, 1949–53, RG 469.

72. James B. Reston to Arthur Hays Sulzberger and Turner Catledge, May 1, 1952, box 145, folder "Krock, Arthur," Reston Papers.

73. "Stag Dinner Series," Dwight D. Eisenhower, Papers as President of the United States (Ann Whitman File).

74. Script, May 7, 1955, box 45, folder "Gridiron Record, 1955," Gridiron Club Records.

75. Andrew Berding to David Lawrence, January 10, 1961, box 15, folder "Berding, Andrew H.," Lawrence Papers.

76. James S. Loeb to W. Averell Harriman, February 20, 1951, box 303, folder 8, Harriman Papers; James B. Reston to Arthur H. Sulzberger, February 11, 1955, box 270, folder 17, Sulzberger Papers.

77. Interview with Nan Robertson, ca. 1998, box 2, folder "Notes from Tape Recorded Interviews," Stacks Papers.

78. Frankfurter and Lippmann had both worked in the War Department in 1918 and lived together in Washington in a political salon known as the House of Truth (Snyder, *The House of Truth*).

79. Asch and Musgrove, *Chocolate City*, 257–60. On housing covenants, see also Thurston, *At the Boundaries of Homeownership*. For a detailed online exhibition of segregation in Washington, see the website for the exhibition *Mapping Segregation in Washington DC*, mappingsegregationdc.org (accessed December 1, 2021).

80. Landis, "Segregation in Washington," 32–34.

81. Yellin, *Racism in the Nation's Service*.

82. See, for instance, Balogh, *A Government Out of Sight*.

83. Krock and Lippmann knew each other from having both served on the Council (the policy-making board) of the New York *World* during the 1920s, but the two had a falling-out after Lippmann accused Krock of giving inside information to a Wall Street firm and prohibited him from further contributing to the editorial page. They remained civil, but according to Lippmann's biographer, "the incident caused bad feeling between the two men for years" (Steel, *Walter Lippmann and the American Century*, 201).

84. Walter Lippmann to Arthur Krock, March 25, 1932, box 38, folder "Lippmann, Walter," Krock Papers.

85. Steel, *Walter Lippmann and the American Century*, 275–76. Lippmann believed that Krock had somehow found this out and that this was one of the reasons that Krock felt competitive with him. Walter Lippmann, interview by Richard Rovere, June 30, 1964, box 17, folder 4, Rovere Papers.

86. Catledge, *My Life and the Times*, 81.

87. Brinkley, *Washington Goes to War*, 10.

88. "Pity the Poor Hostess," *Saturday Evening Post*, September 5, 1936, 82 (quoted in Brinkley, *Washington Goes to War*, 10).
89. Lombard, *While They Fought*, 13–14.
90. Rosten, *The Washington Correspondents*, 104.
91. Rosten mailed surveys to 127 Washington correspondents in spring 1936, with 107 filling out their survey and returning it. They overwhelmingly supported Roosevelt for reelection: 63.5 percent of respondents said their choice for president was Roosevelt, with 30.5 percent selecting a Republican alternative (*The Washington Correspondents*, 348). When 105 correspondents were asked to agree or disagree with the statement, "The publishers' cry of 'Freedom of the Press' in fighting the NRA code [National Recovery Administration, which imposed industry restrictions] was a ruse," 63.8 percent agreed, 24.7 percent disagreed, and 11.4 percent were uncertain (ibid., 346).
92. Roy Howard to Raymond Clapper, June 8, 1937, box 8, chron. files, Clapper Papers.
93. Raymond Clapper to Roy Howard, June 10, 1937, box 8, chron. files, Clapper Papers.
94. Arthur Krock to Arthur H. Sulzberger, October 20, 1937, folder 20, box 270, Sulzberger Papers.
95. Kiplinger, *Washington Is Like That*, 2.
96. Jack Howard to Raymond Clapper, December 10, 1941, box 33, chron. files, Clapper Papers.

Chapter Two

1. Laird, *Pull*, 22.
2. Walter Lippmann to Joseph Alsop, September 30, 1942, folder 38, box 50 (reel 40), Lippmann Papers. The midcentury Washington reporting circles provide an exception to the theory that homophobia must follow from patriarchal male bonding (Gayle Rubin, *Traffic*, 182–83, cited in Sedgwick, *Between Men*, 3). Alsop maintained his position of power there despite his homosexuality, even as other homosexuals were driven from the workforce and the city during the Lavender Scare of the late 1940s and early 1950s. See chapter 4.
3. Sherry, *In the Shadow of War*, 89.
4. C. D. Jackson to Walter Belknap, August 18, 1943, box 17, folder 1, Jackson Papers.
5. For more on interactions between influential Americans in wartime London, chief among them the broadcaster Edward R. Murrow, see Olson, *Citizens of London*.

6. Wallace Deuel to Duncan and Sadie Deuel, January 27, 1945, box 1, chron. files, Deuel Papers.

7. Directory, Association for American Correspondents in London, 1943–1944, box 58, folder "London—World War II," Reston Papers.

8. Cloud and Olson, *The Murrow Boys*, 94.

9. Joseph Harsch to Walter Lippmann, March 8, 1956 [mislabeled 1965], folder 1001 (reel 66), Lippmann Papers.

10. Quoted in Matusow, *The Evening Stars*, 53. Italics in original.

11. Diary, September 21, 1941, box 1, folder "Diaries, September 1941," Meyer Papers.

12. James Reston to Ferdinand Kuhn, October 1, 1940, box 145, folder "Kuhn, Ferdinand and Delia," Reston Papers.

13. Wallace Deuel to Sadie Deuel, February 22, 1960, box 2, chron. files, Deuel Papers.

14. James Reston to Sally Reston, September 3, 1940, box 1, folder "Correspondence," Sally Reston Papers.

15. Reston to Kuhn, October 1, 1940.

16. Cloud and Olson, *The Murrow Boys*, 94.

17. James Reston to Jim Reston, October 9, 1959, box 147, folder "Sevareid, Eric," Reston Papers.

18. Diary, May 10, 1967, box 145, folder "Kuhn, Ferdinand & Delia," Reston Papers.

19. Wallace Deuel to Duncan and Sadie Deuel, July 12, 1941, box 1, chron. files, Deuel Papers.

20. Wallace Deuel to Stuffy Walters, June 21, 1947, box 6, chron. files, Deuel Papers.

21. Joseph Harsch to Wallace Deuel, May 19, 1941, folder "Correspondence: Christian Science Monitor, 1941–1957," box 38, Harsch Papers.

22. Wallace Deuel to Sadie Deuel, August 7, 1951, box 1, chron. files, Deuel Papers.

23. Wallace Deuel to Sadie Deuel, April 11, 1954, box 2, chron. files, Deuel Papers.

24. Wallace Deuel to Sadie Deuel, April 11, 1954.

25. Thor Smith to Mary Smith, October 9, 1943, box 3, folder "Correspondence, TMS to MBS, 1943 (6)," Thor Smith Papers.

26. Thor Smith to Mary Smith, October 9, 1943.

27. Thor Smith to Mary Smith, October 13, 1943, box 3, folder "Correspondence, TMS to MBS, 1943 (6)," Thor Smith Papers.

28. Smith mentioned Willkie in letters on October 20, 1943, box 3, folder "Correspondence, TMS to MBS, 1943 (6)," and again November 10, 1943, box 3, folder "Correspondence, TMS to MBS, 1943 (7)," Thor Smith Papers. On Willkie, see Zipp, *The Idealist*, and Lewis, *The Improbable Wendell Willkie*. Reporters also discussed the ideas of the Atlanticist Clarence Streit, who,

although a fellow journalist, had begun working full time for Atlantic federation and was on the periphery of their world. On Streit, see Imlay, "Clarence Streit, Federalist Frameworks, and Wartime American Internationalism."

29. Sevareid, *Not So Wild a Dream*, 58.
30. Sevareid, 73.
31. Ira Katznelson argues in *Fear Itself* that the foreign policy of the postwar period cannot be read backward from an anticommunist Cold War, as scholars have been wont to do, but rather must be read forward, from the New Deal and the fear of fascism during the 1930s.
32. Sevareid, *Not So Wild a Dream*, 154–83.
33. Sevareid, 160.
34. John B. Oakes, interview by Susan Dryfoos, June 18, 1984, box 9, folder 6, New York Times Company, Oral History Files.
35. Travel diary, itinerary, box 150, folder "Russian Trip, June–July, 1943," Reston Papers.
36. Reston to Orvil Dryfoos, July 17, 1943, box 27, folder "Correspondence—Moscow Trip," Reston Papers.
37. Walter Karig to Charles Ross, December 20, 1944, box 40 (vol. 47), folder 1, Gridiron Club Records.
38. Arthur H. Sulzberger to James Reston, January 14, 1953, box 35, folder "Arthur Hays Sulzberger," Reston Papers.
39. James Reston to Orvil Dryfoos, July 17, 1943, box 27, folder "Correspondence—Moscow Trip," Reston Papers.
40. Sally Reston, "Girls' Town—Washington," *New York Times*, November 23, 1941.
41. James Reston to Arthur H. Sulzberger, October 2, 1952, box 35, folder "Arthur Hays Sulzberger," Reston Papers.
42. Stacks, *Scotty*, 171–74.
43. Diary, January 1, 1947, box 151, folder "JBR Journals, 1941–1970," Reston Papers.
44. Diary, May 10, 1967, box 145, folder "Kuhn, Ferdinand & Delia," Reston Papers.
45. James Reston to Jim Reston, October 9, 1959, box 147, folder "Sevareid, Eric," Reston Papers.
46. Wallace Deuel to Sadie Deuel, December 2, 1946, box 1, chron. files, Deuel Papers.
47. Reston's son served as a copyboy for the *Washington Star* the summer after Deuel's son did. This prompted Reston to tell Deuel that he and Sally would be in the Far East, so his son would need a friend (James Reston to Wallace Deuel, April 25, 1953, box 1, chron. files, Deuel Papers).
48. David Lawrence to Dwight Marvin, August 13, 1941, box 3, folder "ASNE—Washington Committee," Lawrence Papers.

49. Eric Sevareid to Paul White, July 11, 1941, reel A1, Sevareid Papers.
50. On the commission, see Bates, *An Aristocracy of Critics*.
51. Rivers and Schramm, *Responsibility in Mass Communication*, 47–52.
52. Hart, *Washington at War*, 46.
53. US Census Bureau, accessed December 1, 2021, https://www2.census.gov /library/publications/1949/demographics/P25-28.pdf and https://www2 .census.gov/library/publications/decennial/1990/population-of-states-and -counties-us-1790-1990/population-of-states-and-counties-of-the-united -states-1790-1990.pdf.
54. Brinkley, *Washington Goes to War*, 106.
55. Green, *Washington*, 481.
56. Brinkley, *Washington Goes to War*, 1–7.
57. Furman, *Washington By-Line*, 293.
58. Warren B. Francis to fellow member, November 26, 1943, box 1, folder "1943—August–Dec., n.d.," Harsch Papers.
59. See Storrs, "Attacking the Washington 'Femmocracy.'"
60. Charlick, *The Metropolitan Club of Washington*, 275.
61. Charlick, 271–75.
62. "Metropolitan Club's Annual Report of the President and Treasurer, 1948," box 4, folder "Metropolitan Club," series IIB, Catledge Papers.
63. "Metropolitan Club's Annual Report, 1959," box 44, folder "Metropolitan Club," series IIA, Catledge Papers.
64. Charlick, *The Metropolitan Club of Washington*, 284.
65. Notes, May 16, 1950, box 11, chron. files, Deuel Papers. Lippmann had written that the Schuman plan for the integration of certain industries was "bold and it is magnanimous," as well as being good for the United States, since a Franco-German partnership formed "the nucleus of a European power." Since World War II, the US government had supported a United States of Europe that might maintain the balance of power in Europe. Walter Lippmann, "The Opened Door," *New York Herald Tribune*, May 15, 1950; "A Most Important Event," *New York Herald Tribune*, May 11, 1950.
66. Notes, May 16, 1950.
67. Wallace Deuel to Duncan and Sadie Deuel, January 4, 1943, box 1, chron. files, Deuel Papers.
68. Wallace and Mary Deuel to Adlai Stevenson, September 11, 1952, box 1, chron. files, Deuel Papers.
69. Wallace Deuel to Duncan and Sadie Deuel, November 4, 1942, box 1, chron. files, Deuel Papers.
70. Elmer Davis to Eugene Meyer, April 25, 1953, box 166, folder "Clubs, Misc. Correspondence, 1921–1959, Cal-Cou," Meyer Papers.
71. Philip Graham to Mr. Phillips, May 5, 1954, box 19, folder 23, Wiggins Papers.

72. James Reston to Thomas Hamilton, March 27, 1958, box 33, folder "Thomas Hamilton," Reston Papers.
73. Stuart Symington to James Reston, November 3, 1953, box 35, folder "Stuart Symington," Reston Papers.
74. Elmer Davis to Arthur H. Sulzberger, July 18, 1942, box 224, folder 6, Sulzberger Papers.
75. Reston, *Prelude to Victory*, 237.
76. Eric Sevareid to Edward Murrow, n.d. [July or August 1942], reel A1, Sevareid Papers.
77. Wallace R. Deuel, "Our Faith and Will For Victory," *New York Times*, June 28, 1942.
78. "Readers' Choice," *Washington Post*, July 12, 1943.
79. Eugene Meyer to James Reston, August 5, 1942, box 136, folder "New York Times 1942–1959," Meyer Papers.
80. Reston, *Prelude to Victory*, ix.
81. James Reston to Arthur Krock, August 21, 1942, box 51, folder "Reston, James B.," Krock Papers.
82. James Reston to Wallace Carroll, March 29, 1954, box 99, folder "Wallace Carroll," Reston Papers.
83. "Autobiographical Notes," March 2, 1945, box 36, folder 35, Wiggins Papers.
84. "Autobiographical Notes."
85. "War of the (Mostly) Absurd," n.d., box 3, folder 6, Friendly Papers.
86. Personal log, May–June 1943, box 55, folder 1, Wiggins Papers.
87. Wallace Deuel to Duncan and Sadie Deuel, October 6 ,1945, box 1, Deuel Papers.
88. Alfred Friendly diary, September 13, 1945, box 4, folder 11, Friendly Papers.

Chapter Three

1. Draft by Ernest Lindley to the president, September 29, 1942, box 23, chron. files, Clapper Papers.
2. Deposition, 1941 [no other date given], box 183, folder "Domicile, 1939–1942," Meyer Papers.
3. The 1925 F Street Club was founded in 1933 by Laura Gross, who owned the home at that address. It was a dining club and a mainstay of Washington social life for fifty years.
4. Eugene Meyer to G. J. Rowcliff and John Lord O'Brian, May 19, 1954, box 166, folder "Clubs, Miscell Ban-Byr Corr.," Meyer Papers.
5. Jones and Tifft, *The Trust*, 215–22. See also Leff, *Buried by the* Times, 20.
6. On Jews and whiteness, see Goldstein, *The Price of Whiteness.*
7. Gridiron Club, *Washington as It Really Is*, 23.
8. Diary, July 12, 1950, box 23, folder "1950, April–December," Allen Papers.

9. Certain areas of Washington and its suburbs had restrictive covenants that contained language preventing owners from selling to "negroes or any person or persons, of negro blood or extraction, or to any person of the Semitic Race, blood or origin, or Jews, Armenians, Hebrews, Persians and Syrians, except . . . partial occupancy of the premises by domestic servants" (quoted in Justin William Moyer, "Racist Housing Covenants Haunt Property Records across the Country," *Washington Post*, October 22, 2020).

10. Raymond Clapper to Eugene Meyer, May 2, 1940, box 13, folder "Clapper, Raymond," Meyer Papers.

11. Diary, January 19, 1942, box 4, folder 10, Friendly Papers.

12. Diary, January 19, 1942.

13. Diary, January 20, 1942, box 4, folder 10, Friendly Papers.

14. Arthur Krock to E. L. James, April 25, 1940, box 39, folder 8, Sulzberger Papers.

15. Arthur Krock to Arthur Hays Sulzberger, March 28, 1941, box 39, folder 8, Sulzberger Papers.

16. Arthur Krock to Walter Lippmann, November 15, 1943, box 38, folder "Lippmann, Walter," Krock Papers.

17. Ritchie, *Reporting From Washington*, 14–16.

18. Walter Lippmann to Arthur Krock, November 17, 1943, box 38, folder "Lippmann, Walter," Krock Papers. Lippmann's attendance is noted in the Raymond Clapper Diary, September 15, 1943, box 23, chron. files, Clapper Papers.

19. Arthur Krock to Walter Lippmann, November 18, 1943, box 38, folder "Lippmann, Walter," Krock Papers.

20. "Free Press," *Washington Post*, March 12, 1944, B4.

21. See Lumsden, *Black, White and Red All Over*, 268–93.

22. See Washburn, *A Question of Sedition*.

23. Two Supreme Court cases emerging from World War I that especially limited freedom of speech were *Schenk v. United States* (1919) and *Abrams v. United States* (1919). During World War I, the federal government had also waged a well-organized propaganda and censorship operation, led by the journalist George Creel. See Capozzola, *Uncle Sam Wants You*; Vaughn, *Holding Fast the Inner Lines*; Brewer, *Why America Fights*, 46–86; and Hamilton, *Manipulating the Masses*.

24. Schudson, *Discovering the News*, 121–59. See also Greenberg, "The Ominous Clang."

25. Walter Lippmann and Charles Merz, "A Test of the News," *New Republic*, August 4, 1920, supplement.

26. For a history of the Office of Censorship, see Sweeney, *Secrets of Victory*. See also Lebovic, *Free Speech and Unfree News*, 118–37.

27. Elmer Davis, "Report to the President," box 2, folder "Davis, Elmer," Ross Papers.

28. The *New York Times'* chief military reporter, Hanson Baldwin, described general coverage in the Pacific to the editor E. L. James, October 12, 1942, box 125, folder 4, Sulzberger Papers.

29. Davis, "Report to the President."

30. Raymond McCaw to Luther Huston, November 13, 1941, box 125, folder 5, Sulzberger Papers.

31. Arthur H. Sulzberger to Arthur Krock, December 9, 1941, box 125, folder 5, Sulzberger Papers.

32. Daniel Chomsky traces Sulzberger's interventions in news stories from 1956 to 1962 in "An Interested Reader."

33. Arthur H. Sulzberger to Frank Knox, December 10, 1941, box 125, folder 5, Sulzberger Papers.

34. Arthur Krock, "Freedom of the Press Restricted for the War," *New York Times*, December 21, 1941.

35. Walter Lippmann to Arthur Krock, December 29, 1941, box 38, folder "Lippmann, Walter," Krock Papers.

36. Arthur Krock to Arthur H. Sulzberger, April 1, 1942, box 39, folder 8, Sulzberger Papers.

37. Arthur Krock to Walter Lippmann, January 10, 1942, folder 1256 (reel 72), Lippmann Papers.

38. Merriman Smith to Howard K. Smith, February 18, 1968, box 1, folder 68, Merriman Smith Papers.

39. Frank L. Kluckhohn to Lester Markel, May 27, 1942, box 125, folder 4, Sulzberger Papers.

40. Edward Murrow to Eric Sevareid, August 26, 1942, reel A1, Sevareid Papers.

41. Robert Sherwood to Wallace Carroll, quoted in Wallace Carroll to Robert Sherwood, October 3, 1942, box 28, folder "OWI—London—Carroll, Wallace 1942 (1)," Lilly Papers.

42. Diary, May 19, 1942, box 23, chron. files, Clapper Papers.

43. Washington newsmen to Stephen T. Early, Byron Price, and Elmer Davis, September 23, 1942, box 23, chron. files, Clapper Papers.

44. Diary, October 16, 1942, box 23, chron. files, Clapper Papers.

45. Summers, *Wartime Censorship*, 28–29.

46. Diary, May 19, 1942, box 23, chron. files, Clapper Papers.

47. Diary, October 30, 1942, box 23, chron. files, Clapper Papers.

48. Sen. Ralph Brewster to Guy Gannett, November 13, 1941, box OV1, Craig Papers.

49. Diary, October 30, 1942, box 23, chron. files, Clapper Papers.

50. Diary, June 30, 1942, box 23, chron. files, Clapper Papers.

51. "800,000 Troops of U.S. Army at Posts Abroad," *New York Herald Tribune*, November 1, 1942.

52. Alexander F. "Casey" Jones to Eugene Meyer, August 26, 1943, box 35, folder "Marshall, George C. 1941–45," Meyer Papers.

53. Glen Perry to Edward Bartnett, January 1, 1944, in Perry, *"Dear Bart,"* 227.

54. Turner Catledge notes, June 9, 1943, box 1, book I, Krock Papers.

55. See Slattery and Doremus, "Suppressing Allied Atrocity Stories."

56. For more on these meetings, see Perry, *"Dear Bart,"* 79–86. For the expansion of dinners after the war and value in the "caste system," see Cater, *The Fourth Branch of Government*, 130–32.

57. Diary, November 6, 1943, box 23, chron. files, Clapper Papers. According to Sweeney, Elmer Davis and Byron Price both met with King on October 14 to persuade him to release more information, which likely explains the timing of the first dinner (*Secrets of Victory*, 68).

58. Turner Catledge to Arthur Krock, February 26, 1945, box 1, book I, Krock Papers.

59. Rivers refers to this memo as being "widely read throughout the press corps" (*The Opinionmakers*, 37).

60. Friendly, "Attribution of News," 119.

61. Glen Perry to Edward Bartnett, November 7, 1942, in Perry, *"Dear Bart,"* 86.

62. Glen Perry to Edward Bartnett, November 17, 1942, in Perry, *"Dear Bart,"* 104.

63. For more on blacksheeting during the New Deal era, see Rosten, *The Washington Correspondents*, 88–91.

64. J. R. Wiggins, lecture, "Covering Washington," February 5, 1942, box 47, folder 20, Wiggins Papers.

65. Glen Perry to Edward Bartnett, November 17, 1942, in Perry, *"Dear Bart,"* 104.

66. Bert Andrews, "Maas Charges Stir Congress; Inquiry Asked," *New York Herald Tribune*, November 14, 1942.

67. Glen Perry to Edward Bartnett, November 17, 1942, in Perry, *"Dear Bart,"* 104.

68. Throughout the war, reporters were willing to limit reportage of Allied losses to those the Axis powers already knew about, so as not to provide an intelligence advantage to the enemy. For instance, after the Allies attacked Truk Island in February 1944, sustaining heavy losses for the Japanese, reporters agreed to write that only seventeen American planes had been lost, instead of the actual number of forty, because the Japanese were thought to have confirmed only seventeen (Perry, 254).

69. Memo, October 16, 1944, box 1, book I, Krock Papers.

70. James Reston to Arthur H. Sulzberger, January 7, 1945, box 35, folder "Arthur H. Sulzberger," Reston Papers.

71. Program, October 22, 1945, folder 1223 (reel 71), Lippmann Papers.

72. The Statler Hotel worked with the Secret Service and the Gridiron "to assure maximum security in a room adaptable for staging Gridiron dinner programs" (Free, *The First 100 Years!*, 43).

73. Program, October 22, 1945.
74. Program, October 22, 1945.

Chapter Four

1. For more on Truman's and Byrnes's attitudes toward the Soviet Union, see Messer, *The End of An Alliance*.
2. Joseph Alsop to James Byrnes, December 27, 1945, box 2, chron. files, Alsop Papers.
3. The concept is from Laird, *Pull*, 2–3, 23–31 passim. For more on Alsop, see Herken, *The Georgetown Set*; Almquist, *Joseph Alsop and American Foreign Policy*; and Yoder, *Joe Alsop's Cold War*.
4. For "the closet" as an invention of the US government especially through the GI Bill, see Canaday, *The Straight State*, 142, 170–71.
5. Johnson, *The Lavender Scare*, 108–12.
6. Allen Dulles to Herbert Hoover, March 27, 1957, FOIA Collection, Document Number (FOIA) /ESDN (CREST): 0005528186, Central Intelligence Agency Electronic Reading Room.
7. Alsop to Byrnes, December 27, 1945.
8. Alsop to Byrnes, December 27, 1945.
9. Laird, *Pull*, 55.
10. Alsop to Byrnes, December 27, 1945.
11. Roscoe Drummond, "State of the Nation," *Christian Science Monitor*, April 1, 1946.
12. Joseph and Stewart Alsop, "Byrnes Success on Iran Issue Seen Vindicating 'Firm' Policy," *New York Herald Tribune*, April 7, 1946.
13. Arthur Krock, "Byrnes Changes Tactics as Secretary of State," *New York Times*, April 7, 1946.
14. James F. Byrnes to Arthur Krock, April 9, 1946, box 19, folder "Byrnes, James F.," Krock Papers.
15. Arthur Krock to James Byrnes, April 10, 1946, box 19, folder "Byrnes, James F.," Krock Papers.
16. For more on communists attending press conferences remaining in 1965 as justification for "backgrounders," see Rivers, *The Opinionmakers*, 38–39, and Nimmo, *Newsgathering in Washington*, 164–65.
17. Notes, April 12, 1946, box 8, chron. files, Deuel Papers.
18. As Messer argues in *The End of an Alliance*, Byrnes had been closely associated with the Yalta Conference of February 1945, and initially that was a mark in his favor. But the Yalta Conference had become synonymous with US concessions to the Soviets, and Byrnes's usefulness as a holdover from the Roosevelt administration dwindled.

19. Memorandum of conversation, Alfred Friendly and Mark L. Chadwin, October 6, 1966, box 868, folder 3, Harriman Papers.

20. Notes, July 31, 1947, box 9, chron. files, Deuel Papers.

21. Eddie Bomar notes, November 26, 1948, box 1, folder "Background Information 1948, Nov . . . ," Hightower Papers.

22. Notes, November 26, 1948, box 10, chron. files, Deuel Papers.

23. Memo, November 26, 1948, box 3, folder "BPRNC July 29, 1948 . . . ," Office of Press Relations, RG 59.

24. See Yu and Riffe's content analysis of coverage of Chiang and Mao by the three largest-circulation US newsmagazines from 1949 to 1976. For the 1949 to 1959 period, they found that 24.1% of the coverage was favorable, 62.1% neutral, and 13.8% unfavorable ("Chiang and Mao in U.S. News Magazines").

25. R. P. Brandt to B. H. Reese, February 10, 1947, box 24, folder "St. Louis Post Dispatch Files, 1946, Oct. 23–1947, May 31," Childs Papers.

26. R. P. Brandt to B. H. Reese, March 5, 1947, box 24, folder "St. Louis Post Dispatch Files, 1946, Oct. 23–1947, May 31," Childs Papers.

27. Peter Brandt to Irving Dilliard, April 7, 1955, box 26, folder "St. Louis Post-Dispatch Files, 1955, Jan. 6–1955, n.d.," Childs Papers. The Carney incident even made it into that year's Gridiron dinner as a skit.

28. Robert J. Donovan, "U.S. Expects Red Blow at the Matsus in April," *New York Herald Tribune*, March 26, 1955.

29. Orvil Dryfoos to Arthur Sulzberger, March 21, 1955, reel 3, Dryfoos Papers.

30. Anthony Leviero, "Policy Restudied: Eisenhower May State Get-Tough Decision at Coming Talks," *New York Times*, March 26, 1955.

31. David Lawrence, "Distortion of Carney's Talk on Far East Is Reported," *New York Herald Tribune*, March 31, 1955.

32. Robert B. Carney to David Lawrence, April 5, 1955, box 21, folder "Carney, Robert B., 1955," Lawrence Papers.

33. Richard Harkness to Dwight Eisenhower, March 31, 1955, folder OF 168-B Formosa, White House Central Files, Dwight D. Eisenhower Library.

34. Wallace Deuel to Sadie Deuel, March 28, 1947, box 1, chron. files, Deuel Papers.

35. Hanson Baldwin to James Reston, April 14, 1955, box 102, folder "Hanson Baldwin," Reston Papers.

36. Series of correspondence between McCloy, Sulzberger, and Turner Catledge in box 7, folder "Sulzberger, Arthur Hays, 1955," series IIC, Catledge Papers.

37. Hanson Baldwin to Arthur Sulzberger, April 13, 1955, box 7, folder "Sulzberger, Arthur Hays, 1955," series IIC, Catledge Papers.

38. James Reston to Hanson Baldwin, April 15, 1955, box 102, folder "Hanson Baldwin," Reston Papers.

39. Chalmers Roberts to Philip Graham, December 6, 1956, box 32, folder "How to Gather Information . . . ," Roberts Papers.

40. Chalmers Roberts to Philip Graham, n.d. [stamped "Received Dec 11"], box 32, folder "How to Gather Information . . . ," Roberts Papers.

41. James Reston to Staff, April 11, 1955, box 103, folder "Office Memos," Reston Papers.

42. Peter Brandt to Irving Dilliard, April 7, 1955, box 26, folder "St. Louis Post-Dispatch Files, 1955, Jan. 6–1955, n.d.," Childs Papers.

43. Riggs, "The 'Scoops' Served at Private Washington Dinners."

44. R. P. Brandt to R. L. Crowley, June 22, 1951, box 26, folder "St. Louis Post-Dispatch Files, 1951, June 1–1951, n.d.," Childs Papers.

45. Frederic William Wile, "America's Overseas Writers," *Our World*, August 1923, clipping in folder "Formation of Overseas Writers Club," box 1, Overseas Writers Club Papers.

46. Overseas Writers members list, box 28, folder "Overseas Writers 1948," series IIC, Catledge Papers.

47. Joseph Alsop to Roscoe Drummond, February 25, 1947, box 2, chron. files, Alsop Papers.

48. Roscoe Drummond to Joseph Alsop, February 20, 1947, box 2, chron. files, Alsop Papers.

49. Joseph C. Harsch to Paul Wooton, May 1943, box 1, folder "Correspondence 1943 Jan–July," Harsch Papers.

50. Carlotta Anderson, "Overseas Writers: A Brief History," box 1, folder "Polk Case 1948," Overseas Writers Club Papers.

51. Harold Hinton to Members Overseas Writers, April 1, 1940, box 169, folder "1940—City File—Washington—General," Howard Papers.

52. Roscoe Drummond, notice to members, January, 24, 1947, box 226, folder "Washington Daily News," Howard Papers.

53. Polk, "Greece Puts Us to the Test."

54. For accounts of the Polk murder, see Keeley, *The Salonika Bay Murder*; Marton, *The Polk Conspiracy*; and Vlanton, *Who Killed George Polk?*

55. Keeley suggests that the Right had more to gain from the cover-up than the Left but that the only certainty in the case was that the "official" version— that Communists committed the murder—was fabricated (*The Salonika Bay Murder*, 323–24); Marton holds a "secret network of military, police, and intelligence operatives responsible for George Polk's murder," making it clear that the royalist Greek government, especially prime minister Constantine Tsaldaris, were primarily to blame (*The Polk Conspiracy*, 325); Vlanton writes it was likely American or Greek smugglers involved in the criminal underworld and is especially critical of Marton (*Who Killed George Polk?*, 177).

56. Associated Press, "U.S. Newsman's Bullet-Pierced Body Found," *Washington Post*, May 17, 1948. AP, "Correspondent for CBS Found Slain in Greece,"

Chicago Daily Tribune, May 17, 1948. AP, "Inquiry Ordered in Polk Death," *Los Angeles Times*, May 17, 1948.

57. Marquis W. Childs, "Washington Calling: George Polk—a Courageous Reporter," *Newsday* (Long Island), and other column subscribers, May 18, 1948.

58. Drew Pearson, "Polk Death Laid to Greek Rightists," *Washington Post*, May 20, 1948.

59. Joseph Harsch to Henry Steele Commager, undated [November 1953], box 38, folder "Correspondence 1942–1953," Harsch Papers.

60. Quoted in Marton, *The Polk Conspiracy*, 106.

61. Notes, May 26, 1948, box 9, Deuel Papers.

62. "George Polk," *Washington Post*, May 28, 1948.

63. "The George Polk Case: A Report of the Overseas Writers," folder 1722 (reel 86), Lippmann Papers.

64. Although Joseph McCarthy was not yet elected to the Senate, the Second Red Scare was well under way, with the House Un-American Activities Committee conducting investigations into domestic communism.

65. Marton, *The Polk Conspiracy*.

66. Wallace Deuel to A. T. Burch, April 23, 1948, box 6, chron. files, Deuel Papers.

67. Quoted in MacPherson, *"All Governments Lie,"* 281.

68. Wallace Deuel to Baker [Marsh], January 21, 1949, box 6, chron. files, Deuel Papers.

69. Wallace Deuel to Sadie Deuel, November 7, 1946, box 1, chron. files, Deuel Papers.

70. Steel, *Walter Lippmann and the American Century*, 486–87.

71. Harsch, *At the Hinge of History*, 229.

72. MacPherson, *"All Governments Lie,"* 281.

73. One of the only prominent Washington reporters during the 1950s actually to have been a member of the Communist Party during the 1930s was Richard Rovere, who wrote the *New Yorker*'s "Letter from Washington." He left the party over the Nazi-Soviet nonaggression pact of 1939. Though he remained progressive, his views on postwar foreign policy were very much in the mainstream, and his work often reflected the consensus of other reporters, from whom he gathered his intelligence. As he once remarked, he wrote "international affairs from the point of view of an occasional lounge-lizard in Washington and at the UN" (Richard Rovere to Charles Lichenstein, April 8, 1951, box 1, folder 3, Rovere Papers). An outsider insofar as he always kept a physical and intellectual distance from Washington, Rovere's home base was in New York's Hudson Valley. See Lane, "Richard Rovere and the American Conscience."

74. See Graves, "Blogging Back Then."

75. MacPherson, *"All Governments Lie,"* 405.

76. Rivers, in his 1965 *The Opinionmakers*, classifies *Time* magazine and Drew Pearson as "the outcasts" of the press in Washington—hated and mistrusted, yet also read by everyone. For more on Pearson, see Ritchie, *The Columnist*.

77. G. B. "Deac" Parker to Roy Howard, May 22, 1946, box 219, folder "1946 City File—Washington—Parker, George B.," Howard Papers.

78. Ed Harris, memo, January 31, 1947, box 24, folder "P. D. Memos," Childs Papers.

79. Alexander F. Jones to Drew Pearson, October 18, 1944, box 160, folder "Washington Post Comments on Column 'Wash. Merry-Go-Round' Sep 1944," Meyer Papers.

80. Stone wrote about this from the 1940s through the Dulles reign during the 1950s. See, for instance, "American Big Business and the Future of the Reich," March 19, 1945; "John Foster Dulles: In the Image of Sullivan & Cromwell," August 27, 1948 (both reprinted in Stone, *The Truman Era*).

81. Drew Pearson, "Merry-Go-Round," United Features Syndicate Release, September 29, 1944, box 160, folder "Washington Post Comments on Column 'Wash. Merry-Go-Round' Sep 1944," Meyer Papers.

82. Eugene Meyer, memo, October 17, 1944, box 160, folder "Washington Post Comments on Column 'Wash. Merry-Go-Round' Sep 1944," Meyer Papers.

83. Chalmers Roberts, oral history interview by Richard D. Challener, January 13, 1966, p. 5, John Foster Dulles Oral History Collection.

Chapter Five

1. For a triumphalist account of internationalists during the 1920s and 1930s defeating isolationism by the time of the UN charter, see Divine, *Second Chance*. For a history of the nineteenth-century foundations of US internationalism, see Ninkovich, *Global Dawn*. For "isolationism" as a straw man invented by advocates of global supremacy, see Wertheim, *Tomorrow, the World*.

2. Memo, October 10, 1939, box 274, folder 9, Sulzberger Papers.

3. Douglas, *Listening In*, 161–98; Steele, "The Great Debate."

4. Opening the New York Times Forum on Veterans, October 9, 1944, box 101, folder "Arthur Hays Sulzberger—Obituary," Reston Papers. Nikki Usher argues that the *New York Times* continues to regard itself as having an expanded role, conducting its own liberal diplomacy ("The *NYT* in Trump's America").

5. Arthur H. Sulzberger to Ruth Sulzberger, March 19, 1945, box 78, folder 7, Sulzberger Papers.

6. Peter Kihss, interview by Susan Dryfoos, February 14, 1983, box 6, folder 5, New York Times Company, Oral History Files. The political scientist Leo

Rosten in his 1937 study of Washington reporting also noted that what the *New York Times* ran in the morning affected what other newspapers ran later in the day (*The Washington Correspondents*, 95).

7. "Without Fear or Favor," *Time*, May 8, 1950, 68–77.

8. Herbert Lewis to J. R. Wiggins, November 7, 1944, box 35, folder 24, Wiggins Papers.

9. Dudziak, *War Time*, 33–62.

10. Dudziak, *War Time*.

11. See, for example, Dorman and Farhang, *The U.S. Press and Iran*; Hallin, *The "Uncensored War"*; and Zaller and Chiu, "Government's Little Helper."

12. Wells Church to Howard K. Smith, Edward R. Murrow, Winston Burdett, and John Secondari, cc: Davidson Taylor, March 23, 1948, box 50, folder 310, Murrow Papers.

13. Wallace Deuel to Duncan and Sadie Deuel, October 6, 1945, box 1, chron. files, Deuel Papers.

14. Wallace Deuel to Duncan and Sadie Deuel, December 13, 1945, box 1, chron. files, Deuel Papers.

15. Wallace Deuel to Stuffy Walters, June 25, 1947, box 6, chron. files, Deuel Papers.

16. James Reston to Arthur H. Sulzberger, January 7, 1945, box 35, folder "Arthur H. Sulzberger," Reston Papers.

17. On the League of Nations in the United States, see Knock, *To End All Wars*, and Cooper, *Breaking the Heart of the World*.

18. James Reston to Arthur H. Sulzberger, August 29, 1944, box 148, folder "Sulzberger, A. H.," Reston Papers.

19. Reston to Sulzberger, August 29, 1944.

20. Reston to Sulzberger, August 29, 1944.

21. James B. Reston, "For Use of Forces," *New York Times*, August 23, 1944.

22. Arthur H. Sulzberger to James Reston, August 23, 1944, box 148, folder "Sulzberger, A. H.," Reston Papers.

23. Kemler, "Reston of the N.Y. Times."

24. James Reston to Arthur H. Sulzberger, August 29, 1944, box 148, folder "Sulzberger, A. H.," Reston Papers.

25. Arthur H. Sulzberger to James Reston, August 23, 1944, box 148, folder "Sulzberger, A. H.," Reston Papers.

26. On press reactions to the final report, see Bates, *An Aristocracy of Critics*, 187–90.

27. Archibald MacLeish to Edward Stettinius, December 29, 1944, box 1, Records of the Assistant Secretary of State for Public Affairs and Cultural Relations (Archibald MacLeish), RG 59.

28. Walter Lippmann, "Mr. Welles and the Reason Why," *Washington Post*, December 28, 1944. For Lippmann's critiques of delaying political decisions, see, for example, "Too Little and Too Late," *Washington Post*,

October 3, 1944; "The Collapse of a Policy," *Washington Post*, December 21, 1944.

29. Arthur Krock to E. L. James, February 16, 1932, box 1, book I, Krock Papers.

30. Executive Committee of State Department Correspondents' Association to Edward Stettinius, February 15, 1945, box 1, folder "Correspondence, 1945, Feb. 16–1960, Oct. 30," Hightower Papers.

31. Michael Hogan considers "the assumption that isolationism had to be repudiated" to be one of the central shared beliefs of both conservative and liberal intellectuals during the postwar period. We cannot conflate a consensus among intellectuals with a nationally held consensus (*A Cross of Iron*, 422).

32. Rosten, *The Washington Correspondents*, 192.

33. Archibald MacLeish to Edward Stettinius, April 11, 1945, box 1, Records of the Assistant Secretary of State for Public Affairs and Cultural Relations (Archibald MacLeish), General Records of the Department of State, RG 59.

34. Archibald MacLeish to Arthur H. Sulzberger, February 20, 1945, box 1, Records of the Assistant Secretary of State for Public Affairs and Cultural Relations (Archibald MacLeish), General Records of the Department of State, RG 59.

35. Arthur Krock, "Memorandum (Private)," September 21, 1956, box 1, book II, pp. 301–4, Krock Papers.

36. Arthur Hays Sulzberger to E. L. James, telegram, April 25, 1945, box 6, folder "San Francisco Edition, 1945," series IIA, Catledge Papers.

37. E. L. James to Arthur Hays Sulzberger, telegram, April 25, 1945, folder 12, box 267, Sulzberger Papers.

38. Arthur Hays Sulzberger to E. L. James, telegram, April 26, 1945, folder 12, box 267, Sulzberger Papers.

39. Raymond McCaw to Neil MacNeil, May 17, 1945, box 6, folder "SF Edition—Interoffice 1945," series IIA, Catledge Papers.

40. Files on the facsimile edition are in box 6, folders "U.N. Conference" and "San Francisco Letters," series IIA, Catledge Papers.

41. Ben Cohen to Arthur Sulzberger, September 15, 1948, box 267, folder 10, Sulzberger Papers.

42. Edward Stettinius to Arthur Krock, July 2, 1945, box 55, folder "Stettinius, Edward R., Jr.," Krock Papers.

43. John Howe to William Benton, October 5, 1945, box 13, folder "Handling of the Press," Office Files of Assistant Secretary of State William Benton; Records of the Assistant Secretary of State for Public Affairs, 1945–1950, General Records of the Department of State, RG 59.

44. Parry-Giles emphasizes the government using journalists as propagandists in *The Rhetorical Presidency*.

45. Johnson, *The Lavender Scare*, 65–78.

46. Notes, August 18, 1945, box 8, chron. files, Deuel Papers.

47. On purges of homosexuals from the State Department, see Johnson, *The Lavender Scare*. On the Second Red Scare, see Griffith, *The Politics of Fear*.

48. E. L. James to Arthur H. Sulzberger, May 13, 1946, box 21, folder 12, Sulzberger Papers.

49. Harold Hinton to Arthur H. Sulzberger, July 15, 1948, box 33, folder 4, Sulzberger Papers.

50. "Secretary Forrestal Names Public Information Chief," press release, July 2, 1948, box 33, folder 4, Sulzberger Papers.

51. Osgood, *Total Cold War*, 2.

52. Eugene Meyer to William Benton, January 2, 1948, box 10, folder "William B. Benton," Meyer Papers.

53. Arthur Sulzberger to Paul Hoffman, April 8, 1948, box 33, folder 13, Sulzberger Papers.

54. Arthur Hays Sulzberger to Paul Hoffman, May 9, 1949, box 2, folder "Economic Cooperation Administration—1949," series IIA, Catledge Papers.

55. Transcript of Catledge memoirs taped the week of October 27, 1969, box 1, folder "New York Times: Dictated Memoirs: Miscellaneous," series IA, Catledge Papers.

56. Ferdinand Kuhn to Delia Kuhn, March 11, 1947, box 1, Kuhn Papers.

57. Alfred Friendly to Jean Friendly, August 22, 1947, box 2, folder 25, Friendly Papers.

58. Alfred Friendly diary, August 19, 1947, box 1, folder "Trip to Europe . . . ," Meyer Papers.

59. Alfred Friendly to Jean Friendly, August 23, 1947.

60. J. A. Livingston to Alfred Friendly, January 26, 1949, box 16, folder "Philadelphia Bulletin"; Office of the Director Subject Files; Files of the Office of Information; Records of U.S. Foreign Assistance Agencies, 1948–1961, RG 469.

61. Alfred Friendly to Mr. Dalton, February 7, 1949, box 16, folder "Philadelphia Bulletin"; Office of the Director Subject Files; Files of the Office of Information; Records of U.S. Foreign Assistance Agencies, 1948–1961, RG 469.

62. Wallace Deuel to Stuffy Walters, May 3, 1947, box 6, chron. files, Deuel Papers.

63. Schudson, *Discovering the News*, 160–94.

64. Stuffy Walters to Wallace Deuel, June 30, 1947, box 6, chron. files, Deuel Papers.

65. Stuffy Walters to Wallace Deuel, June 21, 1947, box 6, chron. files, Deuel Papers.

66. Wallace Deuel to Stuffy Walters, June 25, 1947, box 6, chron. files, Deuel Papers.

67. Wallace Deuel to Stuffy Walters, June 27, 1947, box 6, chron. files, Deuel Papers.

68. Wallace R. Deuel, "State Department Calls Trouble-Shooter," *Chicago Daily News*, June 11, 1947, clipped in box 37, chron. scrapbook, Deuel Papers.

69. Wallace R. Deuel, "Spruille Braden 'Tough Guy' in U.S. Diplomatic Circles," *Chicago Daily News* (et al.), February 1947, clipped in chron. scrapbook, box 37, Deuel Papers.

70. Deuel to Walters, June 27, 1947.

71. Stuffy Walters to Wallace Deuel, June 30, 1947, box 6, chron. files, Deuel Papers.

72. Wallace Deuel to Sadie Deuel, June 6, 1948, box 1, chron. files, Deuel Papers.

73. Wallace Deuel to Sadie Deuel, December 18, 1948, box 1, chron. files, Deuel Papers.

74. There was a longtime belief in Washington that Reston had written one of Vandenberg's most important speeches in 1945, but he likely had only spoken to Vandenberg about it, and he may have suggested one of the speech's treaty proposals. See Stacks, *Scotty*, 98–101.

75. James B. Reston to E. L. James, June 1, 1948, box 27, folder "Correspondence, 1948, 1954, 1956–57, 1961, 1964," Reston Papers.

76. Wallace Deuel to Sadie Deuel, June 6, 1948, box 1, chron. files, Deuel Papers.

77. Memo, Arthur Krock, June 16, 1948, box 145, folder "Krock, Arthur," Reston Papers.

78. Breed, "Social Control in the Newsroom."

79. Harold Meek to Ed Harris, August 19, 1949, box 25, folder "St. Louis Post-Dispatch Files, 1949, April 11–Dec. 2," Childs Papers.

80. Trachtenberg, *A Constructed Peace*.

81. James Reston, "Secretary Acheson: A First-Year Audit," *New York Times Magazine*, January 22, 1950, 152.

82. James Reston to Jean Monnet, March 10, 1950, box 84, folder "James B. Reston—Collection of Thoughts," Reston Papers.

83. On the Korean War strengthening NATO, see Stueck, *The Korean War*, 4–5.

84. Arthur H. Sulzberger to Arthur Krock, July 12, 1950, box 39, folder 6, Sulzberger Papers.

85. James Reston to Iphigene Bettman, July 18, 1950, box 98, folder "Gilbert and Iphigene Bettman," Reston Papers.

86. Casey, *Selling the Korean War*, 72.

87. "Text of Hoover's Address," *New York Herald Tribune*, December 21, 1950.

88. Joseph Pulitzer Jr. to B. H. Reese, December 21, 1950, box 25, folder "St. Louis Post-Dispatch Files, 1950, Nov. 21–1951, June 1," Childs Papers.

89. "Mr. Hoover's Counsel," *New York Times*, December 21, 1950.

90. "The Policy Makers, the Commander for Europe, and a Major Critic—as the Debate over Foreign Policy Grows More Intense," *New York Times*, December 24, 1950.

91. James Reston, "Hoover's Speech Raises a Fundamental Issue," *New York Times*, December 24, 1950.

92. Hoover seems to have gone further than Taft, since newspapers were quick to point out that Taft at least had called for a Monroe Doctrine for Western Europe. On Eisenhower in 1952, see Donaldson, *When America Liked Ike*, and Pickett, *Eisenhower Decides to Run*.

93. Jones and Tifft, *The Trust*, 258.

94. "Eisenhower," *New York Times*, January 7, 1952.

95. "Mr. Taft Can't Win," *New York Times*, July 1–3, 1952.

96. James Reston, "General Picks Up Speed, but He Also Loses Altitude," *New York Times*, September 24, 1952.

97. Arthur Sulzberger to James Reston, September 24, 1952, box 35, folder "Arthur Hays Sulzberger," Reston Papers.

98. Arthur H. Sulzberger to James Reston, telegram, September 19, 1952, box 35, folder "Arthur Hays Sulzberger," Reston Papers.

99. James Reston to Arthur H. Sulzberger, n.d., box 35, folder "Arthur Hays Sulzberger," Reston Papers.

100. Arthur H. Sulzberger to Sherman Adams, telegram, September 25, 1952, box 1, folder 11, Sulzberger Papers.

101. McCarthyism and the press has been explored at length, mostly relating to political and domestic coverage of the senator. See Bayley, *Joe McCarthy and the Press*; Alwood, *Dark Days in the Newsroom*; Elias, *Gossip Men*; and Fried, *A Genius for Confusion*.

102. Campbell, *Getting It Wrong*, 44–66.

103. Arthur H. Sulzberger to Sherman Adams, October 3, 1952, Name Files: Sulzberger, White House Central Files, Eisenhower Library.

104. Joseph Alsop to Isaiah Berlin, October 20, 1952, box 8, chron. files, Alsop Papers.

105. Notes, November 4, 1952, box 13, chron. files, Deuel Papers.

106. Arthur H. Sulzberger to Alfred Gruenther, "The Day before Election, 1952," box 29, folder 25, Sulzberger Papers.

107. Jones and Tifft, *The Trust*, 262.

108. Julius Ochs Adler to Dwight Eisenhower, cable, November 5, 1952, box 1, folder 14, Adler Papers.

Chapter Six

1. Joseph Harsch to Mike [unidentified], October 31, 1944, box 2, folder "Correspondence, 1944, Oct.–Dec., n.d.," Harsch Papers.

2. Joseph Harsch to Erwin "Spike" Canham, February 4, 1946, box 38, folder "Correspondence: Christian Science Monitor, 1941–1957," Harsch Papers.

3. Harsch to Mike, October 31, 1944.

4. Notes, February 23, 1946, box 8, chron. files, Deuel Papers.

5. Significant among these were Williams, *The Tragedy of American Diplomacy*, and Kolko and Kolko, *The Limits of Power*. For a thorough twentieth-century historiography of US Cold War policy, see Hurst, *Cold War US Foreign Policy*. More recent work into the twenty-first century has focused less on US diplomacy and more on the global Cold War as it played out on the ground in countries both affected by and shaping that diplomacy. See, for example, Westad, *The Global Cold War*, and McMahon, *The Cold War in the Third World*.

6. Osgood, *Total Cold War*, 123–35.

7. Borstelmann, *The Cold War and the Color Line*, 69–72.

8. Notes, February 27, 1947, box 9, chron. files, Deuel Papers.

9. Memo, March 4, 1947, box 144, folder "Dwight Eisenhower," Reston Papers.

10. Carroll Kilpatrick, memo, March 4, 1947, box 19, folder "Eisenhower, Dwight D.," Meyer Papers.

11. Kilpatrick, memo, March 4, 1947.

12. See Freeland, *The Truman Doctrine and the Origins of McCarthyism*.

13. Joseph C. Harsch, "U.S. Due to Build New Frontier in Western Europe," *Christian Science Monitor*, April 26, 1947.

14. John Campbell Ausland to Joseph Harsch, April 29, 1947, folder "Correspondence 1941–1948," box 3, Harsch Papers.

15. Fainberg, *Cold War Correspondents*, 200–206.

16. Joseph Harsch to John Campbell Ausland, May 14, 1947, folder "Correspondence 1941–1948," box 3, Harsch Papers.

17. I. F. Stone, "With Malice towards None—Except Half Mankind," January 21, 1949, reprinted in Stone, *The Truman Era*, 58–60.

18. Wall, *Inventing the "American Way,"* 163–277.

19. Readers of *Time* magazine were among those who frequently saw the black-and-white anticommunist frame, which accounts for much of the popular memory of this period as one in which ideology was more important than oil. See Foran, "Discursive Subversions," 174.

20. "American Debunker: A Close-Up of the Gridiron Club by Senator Arthur H. Vandenberg," *Liberty*, April 12, 1941, clipped in box 33, Clapper Papers.

21. Lewis Wood to Harold Talburt, April 25, 1947, box 42, folder 3, Gridiron Club Records.

22. Diary, December 15, 1946, box 19, chron. folder, Ayers Papers.

23. Barnes, "Darkology," doctoral dissertation abstract, Harvard University (2016), accessed December 1, 2021, https://dash.harvard.edu/handle/1/33493592. Her book, *Darkology*, is forthcoming.

24. Here and the next several paragraphs: "Foreign Affairs Skit," May 10, 1947, box 70, folder "Dinner Programs—May 1947," Gridiron Club Records.

25. May 10, 1947, Presidential Speech File, box 28, folder "1947, May 10, Grid-iron Dinner," Clifford Papers.

26. Notes, October 25, 1947, box 9, folder "Journal—October 1947," Deuel Papers.

27. On traditionalism versus revisionism, see Hurst, *Cold War US Foreign Policy*, 9–61.

28. On building out the propaganda apparatus, see Osgood, *Total Cold War*, 32–45.

29. See Paterson, "Foreign Aid under Wraps."

30. Macekura argues that historians, including Paterson, cited above, have unfairly "disparaged the program as exploitative, or dismissed it as insignificant" ("The Point Four Program and U.S. International Development Policy," 130).

31. "This Generation's Chance for Peace," *Washington Post*, November 23, 1947.

32. "Our Mutual Interests Dictated Marshall Plan," *Washington Post*, November 23, 1947.

33. See Wala, "Selling the Marshall Plan at Home."

34. Notes, April 28, 1948, from two sources: John Hightower, box 1, Hightower Papers; and Wallace Deuel, box 9, Deuel Papers.

35. Notes, November 4, 1949, box 10, chron. files, Deuel Papers.

36. For American attitudes about colonialism in Indonesia, see McMahon, *Colonialism and Cold War*, and Homan, "The United States and the Netherlands East Indies."

37. Arthur Krock to E. L. James, January 5, 1951, box 1, book II, pp. 234–35, Krock Papers.

38. Ferdinand Kuhn Jr., "U.S. to Seek Rare Minerals from Europe," *Washington Post*, November 14, 1947.

39. Noted in "Notes from a Wilted Cuff," *Chicago Defender*, July 8, 1944.

40. Notes, November 1946, box 3, folder 117, Nash Papers.

41. Invitation, October 31, 1951, box OV 17, Craig Papers.

42. For reintegration of the congressional press galleries in 1947, see Ritchie, *Reporting from Washington*, 35–37.

43. James Wiggins to Philip Graham, October 6, 1950, box 7, folder 2, Wiggins Papers.

44. Ethel Payne, interview by Kathleen Currie (Washington Press Club Foundation), September 17, 1987, box 41, folder 14, p. 13, Payne Papers; Emily Langer, "Simeon Booker, Intrepid Chronicler of Civil Rights Struggle for Jet and Ebony, Dies at 99," *Washington Post*, December 10, 2017.

45. Payne, interview by Currie, September 8, 1987, box 41, folder 13, p. 32, Payne Papers.

46. Payne, "Loneliness in the Capital," 153–62.

47. July 7, 1954, Dwight D. Eisenhower, "The President's News Conference Online" by Gerhard Peters and John T. Woolley, the American Presidency

Project, accessed December 1, 2021, https://www.presidency.ucsb.edu
/node/232286.

48. Payne, interview by Currie, September 8, 1987, box 41, folder 13, pp. 37–40,
Payne Papers.

49. Drew Pearson, "Pressure on Press Laid to Ike Aides," *Washington Post and
Times Herald* [and syndicated], April 27, 1955.

50. Associated Negro Press, "Africans Stay Poor while Europeans Rob Rich
Mines," *Atlanta Daily World*, September 5, 1946.

51. John Robert Badger, "World View: Looting the Levantine," *Chicago
Defender*, May 25, 1946.

52. W. O. Walker, "Down the Big Road," *Cleveland Call and Post*, October 18,
1947; "Columnists Say," *Afro-American* (Baltimore), November 1, 1947, M8.

53. White had toned down his rhetoric considerably since using the more militant language of anticolonialism and anti-imperialism during World War
II. Von Eschen, *Race against Empire*, 42.

54. Louis Lautier, "Aid Others beside Europeans—White," *Atlanta Daily World*,
February 1, 1948.

55. Alfred Friendly, "Billion Slash in Initial Aid Hinted by GOP," *Washington
Post*, January 28, 1948. Based on results in eleven white newspapers in the
digital archive ProQuest Historical Newspapers for 1948.

56. "Baruch Report on the Marshall Plan Calls on US to Mobilize for World
Peace," *New York Times*, January 20, 1948.

57. In *The "Uncensored" War*, Hallin defines the sphere of consensus as the
region that "encompasses those social objects not regarded by the journalists and most of the society as controversial" (116–17).

58. Young, "Content Analysis." "Stop communism" was ranked the fifth of nine
most common themes in the *New York Times*, beaten out by "world peace
through stabilization," "in harmony with United Nations," "help Europe
help herself," and "prevent heavy military expense" (170). So while it certainly was not ignoring communism, the *Times* did not let communism
dominate coverage of the plan.

59. Based on results in eleven white newspapers in ProQuest Historical News-
papers. Associated Press, "'Nothing for Africa' in Marshall Plan," *Christian
Science Monitor*, June 28, 1947. Associated Press, "Marshall Plan Criticized,"
New York Herald Tribune, June 28, 1947.

60. "The Marshall Plan," *Chicago Defender*, March 13, 1948.

61. See Wala, "Selling the Marshall Plan at Home."

62. "Senate Warned of Peril in Aid to Imperialism," *Chicago Tribune*, April 20,
1948. As we would expect, Black newspapers also covered the speech:
"Langer Assails U.S. Support of Colonial Rule in Africa," *Atlanta World*,
April 23, 1948; "Charges British Use Our Money to Exploit Africa," *Balti-
more Afro-American*, April 24, 1948; "U.S. $$ Enslaving Africa?," *Baltimore
Afro-American*, April 24, 1948.

63. Joe (Newman) to Bob (Mullen), October 1950, box 13, folder "Memoranda: Foster, William C.," Office of Information, Office of the Director Subject Files, 1949–53, RG 469.

64. Von Eschen, *Race against Empire*, 107–14.

65. On DuBois during this period, see Horne, *Black and Red*.

66. W. E. B. DuBois, "The Winds of Time: Marshall Plan," *Chicago Defender*, November 8, 1947.

67. One of the three spheres Hallin describes in *The "Uncensored" War*, 117.

68. Quoted in Arthur Fauset, "I Write as I See: America's Double Talk," *Philadelphia Tribune*, April 2, 1949.

69. Fauset, "I Write as I See."

70. Arthur H. Sulzberger to *Life* (not sent), October 1942, box 274, folder 8, Sulzberger Papers.

71. Von Eschen, *Race against Empire*, 183–88; Westad, *The Global Cold War*, 2.

72. Draft Foreign News Committee Report, AP Blue Book, box 1, folder 9, Wiggins Papers.

73. Chalmers Roberts, "Chou at Bandung: Great New Challenge to U.S. Diplomacy Seen," *Washington Post and Times Herald*, May 7, 1955.

74. The Reporter's History, compiled 1949 and memos through 1947, box 1, folder 1, Ascoli Papers. Also discussed in James Reston to Turner Catledge, May 3, 1954, box 23, folder "Carroll, Wallace," series IIA, Catledge Papers.

75. "Credit for Bandung," *Washington Post and Times Herald*, May 7, 1955.

76. Notes, March 1, 1955, box 20, folder 10, Wiggins Papers.

77. Seating chart, box 16, folder "Gridiron Dinner 1955," Name Series, Papers as President of the United States (Ann Whitman File).

78. "Opener," May 7, 1955, box 45, folder "Gridiron Record, 1955," Gridiron Club Records.

79. See Dudziak, *Cold War Civil Rights*, and Borstelmann, *The Cold War and the Color Line*.

80. Joseph C. Harsch, "U.S. Waters Down Anticolonialism," *Christian Science Monitor*, March 24, 1956.

81. See Yaqub, *Containing Arab Nationalism*.

82. Chalmers Roberts, notes, April 17, 1956, box 23, folder "CIA," Roberts Papers.

83. Chalmers Roberts, April 27, 1956, box 36, folder "John Foster Dulles Memos and Notes, 1952–161 (2 of 4)," Roberts Papers.

84. For an account of Suez that focuses on economic considerations, see Kunz, *The Economic Diplomacy of the Suez Crisis*. On US-Egyptian relations during this period, in addition to Yaqub, *Containing Arab Nationalism*, see Hahn, *The United States, Great Britain, and Egypt*; on the Eisenhower administration's broader Middle East policies, see Takeyh, *The Origins of the Eisenhower Doctrine*.

85. Historians have since disproved the account that the Eisenhower admin-

istration "simply confused nationalism with Communism" (Richard H. Immerman, quoted in Takeyh, *The Origins of the Eisenhower Doctrine*, xii), but this is another example where reporters on the ground in Washington could have saved the revisionists the trouble of waiting for documents to be declassified.

86. John Foster Dulles to congressional leaders, quoted in Yaqub, *Containing Arab Nationalism*, 12.

87. See Yergin, *The Prize*.

88. Joseph Harsch to Miss L. Titus, January 9, 1957, box 7, folder "Correspondence—1957, Jan.–June," Harsch Papers.

89. Arthur H. Sulzberger to Ralph Bunche, December 31, 1956, box 267, folder 8, Sulzberger Papers.

90. Joseph Harsch to Nicholas J. Conrad, undated [February 1954], folder "Correspondence, 1954, Jan.–Feb.," box 5, Harsch Papers.

91. Sulzberger to Bunche, December 31, 1956.

Chapter Seven

1. Aronson, *The Press and the Cold War*, 113.

2. Aronson, 24.

3. On Laurence, see Keever, "Top Secret"; Wellerstein, *Restricted Data*, 106–21; and Kiernan, *Atomic Bill*.

4. "Information Approved for Publication on Atomic Bombs," War Department, box 2, folder "Laurence, William L., 1946," series IIA, Catledge Papers.

5. Diary, August 7, 1945, box 19, folder "July 1, 1945–December 31, 1945," Ayers Papers.

6. Domhoff, *The Bohemian Grove and Other Retreats*, xiii.

7. This had been Mills's claim in *The Power Elite*, and the documents bear him out. Hallin in *The "Uncensored War"* (p. 21) called this "not the strongest part" of Mills's book, but in the era of Arthur Hays Sulzberger, at least, connections between media elite and other elites (government, business, and military) were indeed significant.

8. Arthur H. Sulzberger to E. L. James, August 5, 1947, box 19, folder "CIA/National Security," Reston Papers.

9. Arthur Sulzberger to Pierre Salinger, June 13, 1961, box 12, folder "Censorship, 1947–1961," series IIC, Catledge Papers.

10. Arthur H. Sulzberger to Vannevar Bush, November 12, 1947, box 19, folder "CIA/National Security," Reston Papers.

11. Arthur H. Sulzberger to Vannevar Bush, January 2, 1948, box 19, folder "CIA/National Security," Reston Papers. Friedberg in *In the Shadow of the Garrison State* demonstrates that antistatism was particularly strong during

this period, as nonstate actors girded the nation against the development of a garrison state. Katznelson in *Fear Itself* also demonstrates how a fear of totalitarianism, dating to the 1930s, influenced the postwar domestic scene.

12. Endres, "National Security Benchmark."
13. Ericson, "Building Our Own 'Iron Curtain,'" 30–31.
14. Endres, "National Security Benchmark," 1072.
15. Resolution, September 29, 1951, box 1, folder 10, Wiggins Papers.
16. Notes, box 12, folder "Press (3 of 3)," Ayers Papers.
17. "Town Meeting," April 8, 1952, box 1, folder 10, Wiggins Papers.
18. Russell Wiggins to Eugene Meyer, December 18, 1952, box 10, folder 8, Wiggins Papers.
19. Russell Wiggins to Milton Eisenhower, December 19, 1952, box 20, folder 24, Wiggins Papers.
20. Notes, April 3, 1953, box 13, chron. files, Deuel Papers.
21. Memo, April 3, 1953, accessed December 1, 2021, https://www.cia.gov /readingroom/docs/CIA-RDP70-00058R000100010051-3.pdf.
22. Notes, April 3, 1953, box 13, chron. files, Deuel Papers.
23. Notes, April 3, 1953.
24. James Reston to Turner Catledge, April 30, 1953, box 39, folder "Staff," Reston Papers.
25. Based on a ProQuest search for "Central Intelligence Agency" in the *New York Times* historical database and plotting instances of that phrase from 1945 to 1969. In 1959, there were 97 mentions of the agency by name; in 1960, 238.
26. Wallace Deuel to Harold Meek, April 6, 1953, box 26, folder "St. Louis Post-Dispatch Files, 1952, Sept. 29–1953, Sept. 14," Childs Papers.
27. Anthony Leviero to Arthur Krock, April 28, 1953, box 21, folder 2, Sulzberger Papers.
28. Wallace Deuel to Harold Meek, April 13, 1953, box 26, folder "St. Louis Post-Dispatch Files—1952, Sept. 29–1953, Sept. 14," Childs Papers.
29. "Mr. Hagerty's Press and Radio Conference," April 9, 1953, box 39, folder "James C. Hagerty's Press Conferences April through June 1953 (2)," Hagerty Papers.
30. James Reston, "Man Who Came to Dinner Stirred a Korea Policy Stew," *New York Times*, April 11, 1953.
31. Memo, June 29, 1954, box 38, folder "Memos 1951–1957," Harsch Papers.
32. "Report on Far Eastern Trip," Technical Cooperation Administration (TCA), September 24, 1953, box 99, folder "Far East Trip—1953," Reston Papers.
33. Elie Abel, "Tito's Soviet Trip Made after U.S. Cautioned on Aid," *New York Times*, September 29, 1956.
34. Elie Abel to Nat Gerstenzang, telegram, September 29, 1953, box 1, folder 1, Foreign Desk Records.

35. Turner Catledge to Arthur Sulzberger, April 21, 1953, box 21, folder "Reston," series IIA, Catledge Papers.
36. James Reston, "Clark Gets Orders," *New York Times*, April 15, 1953.
37. Associated Press, "Truce Orders Sent to Clark, U.S. Says," *New York Times*, April 16, 1953; Lindesay Parrott, "U.N. and Reds Set Truce Preliminary," *New York Times*, April 18, 1953.
38. Sydney Gruson to Manny Freedman, May 26, 1954, box 103, folder "Gruson, Sydney," Reston Papers.
39. For more on the Dulles brothers' connections to corporate America and the CIA/State Department relationship during this period, see Kinzer, *The Brothers*, and Gleijeses, *Shattered Hope*.
40. Arthur H. Sulzberger to Allen Dulles, June 30, 1954, box 30, folder 1, Sulzberger Papers.
41. Sydney Gruson to Robert Garst, July 14, 1954, box 1, folder 33, Garst Papers.
42. Gruson to Garst, July 14, 1954.
43. Arthur H. Sulzberger to Robert Garst, July 20, 1954, box 1, folder 33, Garst Papers.
44. Quoted in Tim Weiner, "Role of C.I.A. in Guatemala Told in Files of Publisher," *New York Times*, June 7, 1997.
45. James Reston to Sydney Gruson, December 12, 1956, box 103, folder "Gruson, Sydney," Reston Papers.
46. James Reston, "Washington: With the Dulles Brothers in Darkest Guatemala," *New York Times*, June 20, 1954.
47. Gleijeses, *Shattered Hope*, 369.
48. William A. Williams to Marquis Childs, January 19, 1959, box 4, folder "Correspondence—1959," Childs Papers.
49. James Reston to Robert Garst et al., August 10, 1954, box 4, folder 18, Garst Papers.
50. See Fenemore, "Victim of Kidnapping or an Unfortunate Defector?"
51. Tad Sculz, "Bonn Aide's Defection Deliberate, U.S. Officials Who Knew Him Say," *New York Times*, July 25, 1954.
52. Reston to Garst et al., August 10, 1954.
53. Associated Press, "Dr. John Lured into Red Trap: Think Security Chief Was Drugged," *Chicago Tribune*, July 27, 1954; AP, "Dr. John Possibly Drugged into E. Berlin, Official Says," *Boston Globe*, July 27, 1954.
54. Reuters, "West Germany Admits John 'Unsuited' for Post," *Christian Science Monitor*, July 27, 1954.
55. The AP reporter Don Whitehead had a byline on the story, which ran August 8, 1954; page 1F in the *Journal-Constitution*, C1 in the *Globe*. For more on the standardization of news through syndication, see Guarneri, *Newsprint Metropolis*, 194–233.
56. The *New York Times* ran the AP story August 8, 1954, but without a byline

or photos, on page C3 (an inside page), under the headline "C.I.A. and Its Spy Chief Develop Spy Plan."

57. "John Was 'Lured,' U.S. Officials Say," *New York Times*, August 10, 1954.

58. Reston to Garst et al., August 10, 1954.

59. Robert Garst to "All Concerned," August 12, 1954, box 19, folder "CIA/ National Security," Reston Papers.

60. Arthur H. Sulzberger to James Reston, August 11, 1954, box 4, folder 18, Garst Papers.

61. James Reston, "Washington: A Remarkable Coincidence in the Cold War," *New York Times*, August 15, 1954.

62. Series of memos 1953–57, box 144, folder "FOI," Reston Papers.

63. Walter Lippmann to James Reston, August 23, 1954, box 1, folder "Walter Lippmann Papers," Stacks Papers.

64. Marquis Childs, "Press Is Suspect in Administration," *Washington Post and Times Herald*, December 3, 1954.

65. Bigart was investigated by the Senate Internal Security Subcommittee (the Jenner Committee, formerly the McCarran Committee).

66. The story ran on September 16, 1955, in the *Globe and Mail* (Toronto, ON) and the *New York Times*, September 17 in the *Atlanta Constitution*. Note that searching for "Reston" as the author in ProQuest will not yield the *New York Times* story, which has been filed digitally with the author as "JamesRestonSpecial to the New York Times."

67. James Reston, "Not a Political Movement but a Love Affair," *New York Times*, September 11, 1955.

68. Elie Abel, "U.S. Held Ready to Accept Shelving of German Unity," *New York Times*, November 3, 1955.

69. Felix Belair to James Reston, November 10, 1955, box 32, folder "Felix Belair," Reston Papers.

70. US Congress, House, Subcommittee on Government Information, Committee on Government Operations, *Availability of Information from Federal Departments and Agencies*, 84th Cong., 1st sess., November 7, 1955, 25.

71. As Schudson demonstrates in *The Rise of the Right to Know*, this act, which seemed so much a product of the 1960s anti-institutionalism, in reality had its roots in the 1950s (40–63).

72. James Shepley, "How Dulles Averted War," *Life*, January 16, 1956, 70–80.

73. Mark Childs to Raymond Crowley, cable, January 11, 1956, box 27, folder "St. Louis Post-Dispatch Files, 1956, Jan. 3–1957, n.d.," Childs Papers.

74. Those terms appeared in James Reston to Turner Catledge, cable, June 25, 1956, box 37, folder "Reston," series IIA, Catledge Papers; and Felix Belair to James Reston, November 10, 1955, box 32, folder "Felix Belair," Reston Papers.

75. Childs to Crowley, January 11, 1956.

76. James Reston, "Officials and the Press: An Analysis of Their Apparent Failure to Reach Agreement on Obligations," *New York Times*, January 18, 1956.

77. Arthur Sulzberger to James Reston, January 18, 1956, box 21, folder 1, Sulzberger Papers.

78. James Reston to Arthur Sulzberger, January 20, 1956, box 21, folder 1, Sulzberger Papers.

79. Arthur Sulzberger to Robert Murphy, April 17, 1956, box 27, folder "Correspondence, 1948, 1954 . . . ," Reston Papers.

80. Eric Sevareid to John Day, September 12, 1956, box I: C4, folder "CBS Policy, 1956–57," Sevareid Papers.

81. Rowland Watts to William Worthy, December 7, 1956, box 55, Reston Papers.

82. ABC broadcast, *Edward P. Morgan and the News* (Bill Costello substituting), February 12, 1957, box I: C4, folder "CBS Policy, 1956–57," Sevareid Papers.

83. James Reston to Turner Catledge, cable, June 25, 1956, box 37, folder "Reston," series IIA, Catledge Papers; Felix Belair to James Reston, November 10, 1955, box 32, folder "Felix Belair," Reston Papers.

84. Sydney Gruson, interview by Tom Wicker, May 3, 1983, box 5, folder 7, New York Times Company, Oral History Files.

85. Paul Kennedy, "U.S. Helps Train Guatemalans at Secret Guatemalan Air-Ground Base," *New York Times*, January 10, 1961.

86. On Matthews, see DePalma, *The Man Who Invented Fidel*.

87. Herbert Matthews to Arthur H. Sulzberger et al., February 16, 1961, box 149, folder 9, Sulzberger Papers.

88. Herbert Matthews to Arthur H. Sulzberger et al., March 6, 1961, box 13, folder "Cuba 1951–1970," series IIC, Catledge Papers.

89. Arthur H. Sulzberger to James Reston, March 7, 1961, box 149, folder 9, Sulzberger Papers.

90. Orvil Dryfoos to Cyrus Sulzberger, May 11, 1961, reel 3, pp. 216–17, Dryfoos Papers.

91. On the spreading of the "suppression myth," see Campbell, *Getting It Wrong*, 83–99.

92. Schlesinger, *A Thousand Days*, 261.

93. What Daniel said in his speech and whether the *Times* had been "diligent" in its Bay of Pigs coverage remained contentious among *Times*men for at least twenty-five more years, especially as they wrote books that included contradicting narratives about what had happened. See Herbert Matthews to E. C. Daniel, March 17, 1972, and Daniel to Matthews, April 10, 1972, box 13, folder 7, Daniel Papers; and E. C. Daniel to James Reston, October 8, 1991, and Reston to Daniel, October 22, 1991, box 144, folder "Daniel, E. C.," Reston Papers.

94. C. L. Sulzberger to Orvil Dryfoos, May 15, 1961, and Dryfoos to Sulzberger, May 22, 1961, reel 3, pp. 215–17, Dryfoos Papers.

95. Wallace Deuel to Michael Deuel, May 11, 1961, box 3, chron. files, Deuel Papers.

96. Walter Lippmann, "The President in Paris," *New York Herald Tribune*, May 11, 1961.

97. Clifton Daniel to Turner Catledge, May 19, 1961, box 26, folder "National Security, 1961–1968," series IIC, Catledge Papers.

98. "C.I.A.: Maker of Policy, or Tool?" *New York Times*, April 25, 1966.

99. Harrison Salisbury to E. C. Daniel, memo, April 7, 1966, box 26, folder "National Security 1961–1968," series IIC, Catledge Papers.

100. Diary, January 19, 1966, box 145, folder "Johnson, Lyndon and Lady Bird, 1958–1995," Reston Papers.

101. Memo, September 14, 1962, box 2, folder "JFK," Dryfoos Papers.

102. Turner Catledge to Orvil Dryfoos, memo, September 10, 1962, box 13, folder "Editorial Policy (General), 1960–1966," series IIC, Catledge Papers.

103. Hanson Baldwin, "Notes on the Problem of Freedom vs. Security," September 6, 1962, box 1, folder 16, Daniel Papers.

104. Memo, September 14, 1962, box 2, folder "JFK," Dryfoos Papers.

105. Memo, September 14, 1962.

106. Robert S. Allen and Paul Scott, "Report Contradicts Government Figures on Arms Buildup in Cuba," *Los Angeles Times*, October 12, 1962.

107. David Kraslow to E. C. Daniel, June 6, 1966, box 84, folder "James B. Reston—Collection of Thoughts . . . ," Reston Papers.

108. Frankel, *High Noon in the Cold War*, 108–10.

109. "Capital's Crisis Air . . . ," *New York Times*, October 22, 1962.

110. White House memo, box I: C2, folder "CBS Correspondence, 1962," Sevareid Papers.

111. "U.S. Urges Editors to Use Care . . . ," *New York Times*, October 25, 1962.

112. Tad Szulc, interview by John F. Stacks, n.d. (ca. 1997), box 2, folder "Notes from Tape Recorded Interviews," Stacks Papers.

113. JFK to Orvil Dryfoos, October 25, 1962, box 33, folder "Orvil Dryfoos," Reston Papers.

114. "World We Live In," *Washington (DC) Evening Star*, October 31, 1962; clipping in box 1, folder "American Newspaper Publishers Association 1962," series IIB, Catledge Papers.

115. See Aronson, *The Press and the Cold War*, 178.

116. "Managing the News," *New York Times*, October 31, 1962.

117. Turner Catledge to Clifton Daniel et al., memo, March 9, 1962, box 12, folder "Censorship 1962," series IIC, Catledge Papers.

Conclusion

1. Schudson, *The Rise of the Right to Know*, 146.
2. Breed, "Social Control in the Newsroom," 335.
3. In his memoir, *First Rough Draft*, Chalmers Roberts attributes the phrase to a Philip Graham speech from 1963 (p. 2), but it likely had circulated earlier, during the 1940s.
4. Scotty Reston to Arthur Sulzberger, January 11, 1959, box 22, folder 11, Sulzberger Papers.
5. Barbie Zelizer has traced the roots of journalism in the "age of Trump" to the Cold War, arguing that then as now, the press had a black-and-white, us-versus-them "enemy formation" perspective ("Why Journalism in the Age of Trump Shouldn't Surprise Us").
6. Hallin, "The Passing of the 'High Modernism,'" 16. He derives the term from the "positivistic, technocratic, and rationalistic" high modernist art.
7. Hallin, 18.
8. Entman, *Projections of Power*, 2.
9. Wallace Carroll "through" Robert Blum, Memorandum for the Committee, March 26, 1953, box 58, folder "National Security Council, 1952–1955," Reston Papers.
10. On the rise of conservative voices in the media starting during the 1950s, see Hemmer, *Messengers of the Right*.
11. John Campbell Ausland to Joseph Harsch, April 29, 1947, folder "Correspondence 1941–1948," box 3, Harsch Papers.
12. Boyer, *By the Bomb's Early Light*, 5.
13. Walter Lippmann, "On Criticism of the Press," *Washington Post*, March 27, 1947.
14. Lebovic, *Free Speech and Unfree News*, 146–47.
15. Schudson, *Discovering the News*, 181. On *(MORE)*, see Lerner, *Provoking the Press*.
16. Schudson, *The Rise of the Right to Know*, 170–76.
17. Ritchie, *Reporting from Washington*, 45.
18. On Lippmann and Vietnam, see Logevall, "First among Critics."
19. *Times* reporters like Harrison Salisbury and David Halberstam, filing stories from Vietnam, had critical copy early in the Vietnam War. But as Hallin shows, straight-news reporting from Washington repeated the government's lies, even after editorial and opinion coverage broke sharply with the administration in 1965 (61–62, 73). Memories of deferential journalism during the war are more accurate for television than for print (Hallin, 105–210).
20. Quoted in Hess, *The Washington Reporters*, 155.
21. Memo, James Reston, December 26, 1956, box 84, folder "James B. Reston—Collection of Thoughts," Reston Papers.

22. Schudson and Fink, "The Rise of Contextual Journalism, 1950s–2000s."
23. Diary, December 24, 1952, box 23, chron. folder, Allen Papers.
24. Since this period, digital newsrooms have altered the physical spaces of reporting. See Robinson, "Convergence Crises"; Neff, "The Changing Place of Cultural Production"; and Usher, *Making News at* The New York Times.
25. Nicholas Lemann made this point to me in a comment he presented on a paper I delivered at the NYU Cold War Seminar (October 2015).
26. A recent example was in 2017, when the website Buzzfeed News published the "Russia dossier" when no other outlet had, at the same time that it had been circulating around Washington. As Seth Lipsky wrote in the *Wall Street Journal*, "The only party to this whole affair that didn't know about it, it seems, was the public" ("Did BuzzFeed Make Such a Bad Call?," January 12, 2017).
27. Leibovich, *This Town.*

ARCHIVAL COLLECTIONS

Amherst College, Archives and Special Collections (Amherst, MA)
Alfred Friendly Papers
Boston University, Howard Gotlieb Archival Research Center
Max Ascoli Papers
Columbia University, Manuscript Collections (New York City)
Ferdinand Kuhn Papers
Dwight D. Eisenhower Library (Abilene, KS)
Oliver M. Gale Papers
Alfred M. Gruenther Papers
James C. Hagerty Papers
Christian A. Herter Papers
C. D. Jackson Papers
Edward P. Lilly Papers
Carl W. McCardle Papers
Papers as President of the United States (Ann Whitman File)
Administration Series
Diary Series
Name Series
NSC Series
Stag Series
Pre-Presidential Papers
Thor M. Smith Papers
White House Central Files
Ann C. Whitman Diary Series
Georgetown University, Booth Family Center for Special Collections
(Washington, DC)
Roscoe Drummond Papers

Harry S. Truman Library (Independence, MO)

Dean G. Acheson Papers

Eben E. Ayers Papers

Clark M. Clifford Papers

Paul G. Hoffman Papers

Charles M. Hulten Papers

Joseph M. Jones Papers

Frank McNaughton Papers

Charles G. Ross Papers

Howland H. Sargeant Papers

Joseph H. Short and Beth Campbell Short Papers

Staff Members Office Files

Charles W. Jackson Files

Joseph H. Short Files

John F. Kennedy Library (Boston)

Robert H. Estabrook Papers

Kay Halle Papers

Chalmers Roberts Papers

Arthur M. Schlesinger Jr. Papers

Johns Hopkins University, Department of Rare Books and Manuscripts
(Baltimore)

William Worthy Papers

Library of Congress, Manuscripts Division (Washington, DC)

Joseph Alsop and Stewart Alsop Papers

Raymond Clapper Papers

May Craig Papers

Elmer Holmes Davis Papers

Wallace Rankin Deuel Papers

Bess Furman Papers

Gridiron Club Records

W. Averell Harriman Papers

Roy Wilson Howard Papers

Eugene Meyer Papers

Ethel L. Payne Papers

Eric Sevareid Papers

Mississippi State University, Manuscripts Division (Starkville)

Turner Catledge Papers

National Archives II (College Park, MD)

RG 59 Records of the U.S. State Department

RG 84 Records of the U.S. Foreign Service Posts

RG 286 Records of the Agency for International Development and
Predecessor Agencies

RG 469 Records of U.S. Foreign Assistance Agencies, 1948–61

National Press Club Archives (Washington, DC)

National Press Club Papers

Overseas Writers Papers

Women's National Press Club Papers

New York Public Library, Manuscripts and Archives Division (New York City)

New York Times Company Records

Julius Ochs Adler Papers

Theodore M. Bernstein Papers

Clifton Daniel Papers

Orvil Dryfoos Papers

Foreign Desk Records

Robert E. Garst Papers

General Files

National Desk Records

Oral History Files

Arthur Hays Sulzberger Papers

Princeton University, Seeley G. Mudd Manuscript Library (Princeton, NJ)

John Foster Dulles Oral History Collection

Arthur Krock Papers

David Lawrence Papers

Radcliffe Institute for Advanced Study, Arthur and Elizabeth Schlesinger Library (Cambridge, MA)

Nona Baldwin Brown Papers

Ruth Cowan Nash Papers

Tufts University, Digital Collections and Archives (Medford, MA)

Edward R. Murrow Papers

University of Illinois, University Archives, Alumni Association (Urbana-Champaign)

James B. Reston Papers

Sally Reston Papers

John F. Stacks Papers

University of Maine, Fogler Library Special Collections (Orono)

James Russell Wiggins Papers

Wisconsin Historical Society (Madison)

Robert S. Allen Papers

Marquis Childs Papers

Joseph C. Harsch Papers

John M. Hightower Papers

William H. Lawrence Papers

Richard Rovere Papers

Merriman Smith Papers

Yale University, Manuscripts and Archives (New Haven, CT)

Walter Lippmann Papers

BIBLIOGRAPHY

Allen, Craig. *Eisenhower and the Mass Media: Peace, Prosperity, and Prime-Time TV*. Chapel Hill: University of North Carolina Press, 1993.

Almquist, Leann G. *Joseph Alsop and American Foreign Policy: The Journalist as Advocate*. Lanham, MD: University Press of America, 1993.

Alsop, Joseph, and Stewart Alsop. *The Reporter's Trade*. New York: Reynal, 1958.

Alwood, Edward. *Dark Days in the Newsroom: McCarthyism Aimed at the Press*. Philadelphia: Temple University Press, 2007.

Appy, Christian G., ed. *Cold War Constructions: The Political Culture of United States Imperialism, 1945–1966*. Amherst: University of Massachusetts Press, 2000.

Aronson, James. *The Press and the Cold War*. Indianapolis: Bobbs-Merrill, 1970.

Asch, Chris Myers, and George Derek Musgrove. *Chocolate City: A History of Race and Democracy in the Nation's Capital*. Chapel Hill: University of North Carolina Press, 2017.

Balogh, Brian. *A Government Out of Sight: The Mystery of National Authority in Nineteenth-Century America*. New York: Cambridge University Press, 2009.

Barnes, Rhae Lynn. *Darkology: When the American Dream Wore Blackface*. New York: W. W. Norton, forthcoming.

Bates, Stephen. *An Aristocracy of Critics: Luce, Hutchins, Niebuhr, and the Committee That Redefined Freedom of the Press*. New Haven, CT: Yale University Press, 2020.

Baughman, James L. *The Republic of Mass Culture: Journalism, Filmmaking and Broadcasting in America since 1941*. Baltimore: Johns Hopkins University Press, 2006.

Bayley, Edwin. *Joe McCarthy and the Press*. Madison: University of Wisconsin Press, 1981.

Beasley, Maurine H. *Women of the Washington Press: Politics, Prejudice, and Persistence.* Evanston, IL: Northwestern University Press, 2012.

Beasley, Maurine H., and Sheila J. Gibbons, eds. *Taking Their Place: A Documentary History of Women and Journalism.* Washington, DC: American University Press, 1993.

Belmonte, Laura. "Promoting American Anti-imperialism in the Early Cold War." In *Empire's Twin: U.S. Anti-imperialism from the Founding Era to the Age of Terrorism,* edited by Ian Tyrell and Jay Sexton, 187–201. Ithaca, NY: Cornell University Press, 2015.

Bennett, W. Lance. "Toward a Theory of Press-State Relations in the United States." *Journal of Communication* 40, no. 2 (1990): 103–25.

Berry, Nicholas O. *Foreign Policy and the Press: An Analysis of the* New York Times *Coverage of U.S. Foreign Policy.* New York: Greenwood Press, 1990.

Bérubé, Allan. *Coming Out Under Fire: The History of Gay Men and Women in World War Two.* New York: Free Press, 1990.

Bird, Sharon R. "Welcome to the Men's Club: Homosociality and the Maintenance of Hegemonic Masculinity." *Gender and Society* 10, no. 2 (April 1996): 120–32.

Borstelmann, Thomas. *The Cold War and the Color Line: American Race Relations in the Global Arena.* Cambridge, MA: Harvard University Press, 2001.

Boyer, Paul. *By the Bomb's Early Light: American Thought and Culture at the Dawn of the Atomic Age.* Chapel Hill: University of North Carolina Press, 1994.

Bradley, Patricia. *Women and the Press: The Struggle for Equality.* Evanston, IL: Northwestern University Press, 2005.

Brands, H. W. *Cold Warriors: Eisenhower's Generation and American Foreign Policy.* New York: Columbia University Press, 1988.

Brayman, Harold. *The President Speaks Off-the-Record: From Grover Cleveland to Gerald Ford.* Princeton, NJ: Dow Jones Books, 1976.

Brazinsky, Gregg. *Winning the Third World: Sino-American Rivalry during the Cold War.* Chapel Hill: University of North Carolina Press, 2017.

Breed, Warren. "The Newspaperman, News and Society." PhD diss., Columbia University, 1952.

———. "Social Control in the Newsroom: A Functional Analysis." *Social Forces* 33, no. 4 (May 1955): 326–35.

Brewer, Susan A. *Why America Fights: Patriotism and War Propaganda from the Philippines to Iraq.* New York: Oxford University Press, 2009.

Brinkley, Alan. *The Publisher: Henry Luce and His American Century.* New York: Knopf, 2010.

Brinkley, David. *Washington Goes to War.* New York: Knopf, 1988.

Buckley, William, Jr. "Our Mission Statement." *National Review,* November 19, 1955. Accessed December 1, 2021. https://www.nationalreview.com/1955/11/our -mission-statement-william-f-buckley-jr/.

Caldwell, John T. "Industrial Geography Lessons: Socio-professional Rituals and the Borderlands of Production Culture." In *MediaSpace: Place, Scale and Cul-*

ture in a Media Age, edited by Nick Couldry and Anna McCarthy, 163–90. New York: Routledge, 2004.

Campbell, W. Joseph. *Getting It Wrong: Debunking the Greatest Myths in American Journalism*. Berkeley: University of California Press, 2016.

Canaday, Margot. *The Straight State: Sexuality and Citizenship in Twentieth-Century America*. Princeton, NJ: Princeton University Press, 2009.

Capozzola, Christopher. *Uncle Sam Wants You: World War I and the Making of the Modern American Citizen*. New York: Oxford University Press, 2008.

Carnes, Mark. *Secret Ritual and Manhood in Victorian America*. New Haven, CT: Yale University Press, 1989.

Carroll, Fred. *Race News: Black Journalists and the Fight for Racial Justice in the Twentieth Century*. Urbana: University of Illinois Press, 2017.

Cary, Francine, ed. *Urban Odyssey: A Multicultural History of Washington, D.C.* Washington, DC: Smithsonian Institution Press, 1996.

Casey, Steven. *Selling the Korean War: Propaganda, Politics, and Public Opinion in the United States, 1950–1953*. New York: Oxford University Press, 2008.

Cater, Douglass. *The Fourth Branch of Government*. Boston: Houghton Mifflin, 1959.

Catledge, Turner. *My Life and the* Times. New York: Harper and Row, 1971.

Charlick, Carl. *The Metropolitan Club of Washington: The Story of Its Men and Its Place in City and Country*. Washington, DC: Judd and Detweiler, 1964.

Chauncey, George. *Gay New York: Gender, Urban Culture, and the Making of the Gay Male World, 1890–1940*. New York: Basic Books, 2008.

Childs, Marquis. *I Write from Washington*. New York: Harper and Brothers, 1942.

Chomsky, Daniel. "'An Interested Reader': Measuring Ownership Control at the *New York Times*." *Critical Studies in Media Communication* 23, no. 1 (March 2006): 1–18.

Cloud, Stanley, and Lynne Olson. *The Murrow Boys: Pioneers on the Front Lines of Broadcast Journalism*. Boston: Houghton Mifflin, 1996.

Cohen, Bernard C. *The Press and Foreign Policy*. Princeton, NJ: Princeton University Press, 1963.

Cook, Timothy E. *Governing with the News: The News Media as a Political Institution*. Chicago: University of Chicago Press, 1998.

Cooper, John Milton, Jr. *Breaking the Heart of the World: Woodrow Wilson and the Fight for the League of Nations*. New York: Cambridge University Press, 2001.

Costigliola, Frank, and Michael J. Hogan, eds. *America in the World: The Historiography of American Foreign Relations since 1941*. New York: Cambridge University Press, 2014.

Craig, Campbell, and Fredrik Logevall. *America's Cold War: The Politics of Insecurity*. Cambridge, MA: Harvard University Press, 2009.

Crouse, Timothy. *The Boys on the Bus*. New York: Random House, 1973.

Daly, Christopher B. *Covering America: A Narrative History of a Nation's Journalism*. Amherst: University of Massachusetts Press, 2012.

Daniel, Marcus. *Scandal and Civility: Journalism and the Birth of American Democracy*. New York: Oxford University Press, 2009.

Darnton, Robert. "Writing News and Telling Stories." *Daedalus* 104, no. 2 (Spring 1975): 175–94.

Dean, Robert. *Imperial Brotherhood: Gender and the Making of Cold War Foreign Policy*. Amherst: University of Massachusetts Press, 2001.

DePalma, Anthony. *The Man Who Invented Fidel: Cuba, Castro, and Herbert L. Matthews of the* New York Times. New York: Public Affairs, 2006.

Deutsch, Sarah. *Women and the City: Gender, Space, and Power in Boston, 1870–1940*. New York: Oxford University Press, 2000.

Divine, Robert A. *Second Chance: The Triumph of Internationalism in America during World War II*. New York: Atheneum, 1967.

Dodge, Homer Joseph, et al. *Shrdlu: An Affectionate Chronicle; National Press Club, Washington, 50th Anniversary, 1908–1958*. Edited by John P. Cosgrove. [Washington, DC]: Colortone Press, 1958.

Domhoff, G. William. *The Bohemian Grove and Other Retreats: A Study in Ruling-Class Cohesiveness*. New York: Harper and Row, 1974.

Donaldson, Gary. *When America Liked Ike: How Moderates Won the 1952 Presidential Election and Reshaped American Politics*. Lanham, MD: Rowman and Littlefield, 2017.

Dorman, William A., and Mansour Farhang. *The U.S. Press and Iran: Foreign Policy and the Journalism of Deference*. Berkeley: University of California Press, 1987.

Douglas, Susan J. *Listening In: Radio and the American Imagination*. Minneapolis: University of Minnesota Press, 2004.

Drury, Allen. *Advise and Consent*. New York: Doubleday, 1959.

Dudziak, Mary. *Cold War Civil Rights: Race and the Image of American Democracy*. Princeton, NJ: Princeton University Press, 2000.

———. *War Time: An Idea, Its History, Its Consequences*. New York: Oxford University Press, 2012.

Dunn, Arthur Wallace. *Gridiron Nights: Humorous and Satirical Views of Politics and Statesmen as Presented by the Famous Dining Club*. New York: Arno Press, 1974 (1915).

Dunnigan, Alice Allison. *A Black Woman's Experience: From Schoolhouse to White House*. Philadelphia: Dorrance, 1974.

Elias, Christopher M. *Gossip Men: J. Edgar Hoover, Joe McCarthy, Roy Cohn, and the Politics of Insinuation*. Chicago: University of Chicago Press, 2021.

Endres, Kathleen. "National Security Benchmark: Truman, Executive Order 10290, and the Press." *Journalism and Mass Communication Quarterly* 67 (1990): 1071–77.

Engerman, David. *The Price of Aid: The Economic Cold War in India*. Cambridge, MA: Harvard University Press, 2018.

Enke, Finn. *Finding the Movement: Sexuality, Contested Space, and Feminist Activism*. Durham, NC: Duke University Press, 2007.

Entman, Robert M. *Projections of Power: Framing News, Public Opinion, and U.S. Foreign Policy*. Chicago: University of Chicago Press, 2004.

Ericson, Timothy L. "Building Our Own 'Iron Curtain': The Emergence of Secrecy in American Government." *American Archivist* 68, no. 1 (2005): 18–52.

Fahs, Alice. *Out on Assignment: Women and the Making of Modern Public Space*. Chapel Hill: University of North Carolina Press, 2011.

Fainberg, Diana. *Cold War Correspondents: Soviet and American Reporters on the Ideological Frontlines*. Baltimore: Johns Hopkins University Press, 2020.

Farrar, Ronald. "Harry Truman and the Press: A View from the Inside." *Journalism History* 8, no. 2 (Summer 1981): 56.

Fenemore, Mark. "Victim of Kidnapping or an Unfortunate Defector? The Strange Case of Otto John." *Cold War History* 20, no. 2 (2020): 143–60.

Ferrell, Robert H., ed. *The Diary of James C. Hagerty: Eisenhower in Mid-course, 1954–1955*. Bloomington: Indiana University Press, 1983.

Fink, Kathleen, and Michael Schudson. "The Rise of Contextual Journalism, 1950s–2000s." *Journalism* 15, no. 1 (2014): 3–20.

Foran, John. "Discursive Subversions." In *Cold War Constructions: The Political Culture of United States Imperialism, 1945–1966*, edited by Christian G. Appy, 157–82. Amherst: University of Massachusetts Press, 2000.

Fousek, John. *To Lead the Free World: American Nationalism and the Cultural Roots of the Cold War*. Chapel Hill: University of North Carolina Press, 2000.

Frankel, Max. *High Noon in the Cold War: Kennedy, Khrushchev, and the Cuban Missile Crisis*. New York: Ballantine Books, 2014.

———. *The Times of My Life: And My Life at the* Times. New York: Random House, 1999.

Free, James. *The First 100 Years! A Casual Chronicle of the Gridiron Club*. Washington: Gridiron Club, 1985.

Freeland, Richard. *The Truman Doctrine and the Origins of McCarthyism: Foreign Policy, Domestic Politics, and Internal Security, 1946–1948*. New York: Knopf, 1971.

Fried, Richard M. *A Genius for Confusion: Joseph R. McCarthy*. New York: Rowman and Littlefield, 2022.

Friedberg, Aaron. *In the Shadow of the Garrison State*. Princeton, NJ: Princeton University Press, 2011.

Friendly, Alfred. "Attribution of News: Memo to All Hands." *Nieman Reports* 53/54, no. 4/1 (Winter 1999/Spring 2000): 119–21. Orig. pub. 1958.

Furman, Bess. *Washington By-Line: The Personal History of a Newspaperwoman*. New York: Knopf, 1949.

Gaddis, John Lewis. "The Emerging Post-revisionist Synthesis on the Origins of the Cold War." *Diplomatic History* 7, no. 3 (1983): 171–90.

———. *George F. Kennan: An American Life*. New York: W. W. Norton, 2011.

———. *Strategies of Containment: A Critical Appraisal of Postwar American National Security Policy*. New York: Oxford University Press, 1982.

Gans, Herbert J. *Deciding What's News: A Study of "CBS Evening News," "NBC Nightly News,"* Newsweek *and* Time. New York: Pantheon Books, 1979.

———. *Democracy and the News*. New York: Oxford University Press, 2003.

Gardner, Lloyd. *Architects of Illusion: Men and Ideas in American Foreign Policy, 1941–1949*. Chicago: Quadrangle Books, 1970.

Gilmore, Glenda. *Gender and Jim Crow: Women and the Politics of White Supremacy in North Carolina, 1896–1920*. Chapel Hill: University of North Carolina Press, 1996.

Gleijeses, Piero. *Shattered Hope: The Guatemalan Revolution and the United States, 1944–1954*. Princeton, NJ: Princeton University Press, 1991.

Goldstein, Eric L. *The Price of Whiteness: Jews, Race, and American Identity*. Princeton, NJ: Princeton University Press, 2006.

Gorbach, Julien. "The Non-Jewish Jew: Walter Lippmann and the Pitfalls of Journalistic 'Detachment.'" *American Journalism* 37, no. 3 (2020): 321–45.

Graves, Lucas. "Blogging Back Then: Annotative Journalism in I. F. Stone's Weekly and Talking Points Memo." *Journalism* 16, no. 1 (2015): 99–118.

Green, Constance McLaughlin. *Washington: A History of the Capital*. Princeton, NJ: Princeton University Press, 2017 (1962).

Greenberg, David. "The Ominous Clang: Fears of Propaganda from World War I to World War II." In *Media Nation: The Political History of News in Modern America*, edited by Bruce Schulman and Julian Zelizer, 50–62. Philadelphia: University of Pennsylvania Press, 2017.

———. *The Republic of Spin: An Inside History of the American Presidency*. New York: W. W. Norton, 2016.

Greenfield, Meg. *Washington*. New York: Public Affairs, 2001.

Gridiron Club. *Washington as It Really Is, a Guide for Gridiron Guests; the Capitol To-Day . . .* Washington, 1906. http://hdl.handle.net/2027/loc.ark:/13960 /t8hd8486z.

Griffith, Robert. *The Politics of Fear: Joseph R. McCarthy and the Senate*. Amherst, MA: University of Massachusetts Press, 1987.

Guarneri, Julia. *Newsprint Metropolis: City Newspapers and the Making of Modern Americans*. Chicago: University of Chicago Press, 2017.

Hahn, Peter L. *The United States, Great Britain, and Egypt, 1945–1956: Strategy and Diplomacy in the Early Cold War*. Chapel Hill: University of North Carolina Press, 1991.

Halberstam, David. *The Powers That Be*. New York: Dell, 1979.

Hallin, Daniel C. "The Passing of the 'High Modernism' of American Journalism." *Journal of Communication* 42, no. 3 (Summer 1992): 14–25.

———. *The "Uncensored War": The Media and Vietnam*. New York: Oxford University Press, 1986.

Hamilton, John Maxwell. *Manipulating the Masses: Woodrow Wilson and the Birth of American Propaganda*. Baton Rouge: Louisiana State University Press, 2020.

Harsch, Joseph C. *At the Hinge of History: A Reporter's Story*. Athens, GA: University of Georgia Press, 1993.

Hart, Scott. *Washington at War, 1941–1945*. Englewood Cliffs, NJ: Prentice Hall, 1970.

Hemmer, Nicole. *Messengers of the Right: Conservative Media and the Transformation of American Politics*. Philadelphia: University of Pennsylvania Press, 2016.

Herken, Gregg. *The Georgetown Set: Friends and Enemies in Cold War Washington*. New York: Knopf, 2014.

Herman, Edward, and Noam Chomsky. *Manufacturing Consent: The Political Economy of the Mass Media*. New York: Pantheon, 1988.

Herring, Cedric. "Does Diversity Pay?: Race, Gender, and the Business Case for Diversity." *American Sociological Review* 74, no. 2 (April 2009): 208–24.

Herring, Eric, and Piers Robinson. "Too Polemical or Too Critical? Chomsky on the Study of the News Media and U.S. Foreign Policy." *Review of International Studies* 29 (2003): 555.

Hess, Stephen. *The Government/Press Connection: Press Officers and Their Offices*. Washington, DC: Brookings Institution Press, 1984.

———. *The Washington Reporters: Newswork*. Washington, DC: Brookings Institution Press, 1981.

———. *Whatever Happened to the Washington Reporters: 1978–2012*. Washington, DC: Brookings Institution Press, 2012.

Higham, John. *Strangers in the Land: Patterns of American Nativism, 1860–1925*. New Brunswick, NJ: Rutgers University Press, 1955.

Hogan, Michael. *A Cross of Iron: Harry Truman and the Origins of the National Security State*. New York: Cambridge University Press, 2000.

———. *The Marshall Plan: America, Britain, and the Reconstruction of Western Europe*. New York: Cambridge University Press, 1987.

Homan, Gerlof D. "The United States and the Netherlands East Indies: The Evolution of American Anticolonialism." *Pacific Historical Review* 53, no. 4 (November 1984): 423–46.

Horne, Gerald. *Black and Red: W. E. B. DuBois and the Afro-American Response to the Cold War*. Albany: State University Press of New York, 1985.

Hurst, Steven. *Cold War US Foreign Policy: Key Perspectives*. Edinburgh: Edinburgh University Press, 2005.

Igo, Sarah E. *The Averaged American: Survey, Citizens, and the Making of a Mass Public*. Cambridge, MA: Harvard University Press, 2007.

Imlay, Talbot. "Clarence Streit, Federalist Frameworks, and Wartime American Internationalism." *Diplomatic History* 44, no. 5 (November 2020): 808–33.

Isaacson, Walter, and Evan Thomas. *Wise Men: Six Friends and the World They Made*. New York: Simon and Schuster, 1986.

Jacob, Kathryn Allamong. *Capital Elites: High Society in Washington, D.C., after the Civil War*. Washington, DC: Smithsonian Institution Press, 1995.

Jansen, Sue Curry. *Walter Lippmann: A Critical Introduction to Media and Communication Theory*. New York: Peter Lang, 2012.

Johnson, David K. *The Lavender Scare: The Cold War Persecution of Gays and Lesbians in the Federal Government*. Chicago: University of Chicago Press, 2004.

Jones, Alex S., and Susan E. Tifft. *The Trust: The Private and Powerful Family behind the* New York Times. New York: Little, Brown, 1999.

Kaplan, Richard L. *Politics and the American Press: The Rise of Objectivity, 1865–1920*. New York: Cambridge University Press, 2002.

Katznelson, Ira. *Fear Itself: The New Deal and the Origins of Our Time*. New York: Liveright, 2013.

Kiernan, Vincent. *Atomic Bill: A Journalist's Dangerous Ambition in the Shadow of the Bomb*. Ithaca, NY: Cornell University Press, forthcoming 2022.

Keeley, Edmund. *The Salonika Bay Murder: Cold War Politics and the Polk Affair*. Princeton, NJ: Princeton University Press, 1989.

Keever, Beverly Ann Deepe. "Top Secret: Censoring the First Rough Drafts of Atomic-Bomb History." *Media History* 14, no. 2 (2008): 185–204.

Kemler, Edgar. "Reston of the N.Y. Times: Scoop Reporter at Work." *Nation*, January 7, 1956, 10.

Kerber, Linda. "Separate Spheres, Female Worlds, Woman's Place: The Rhetoric of Women's History." *Journal of American History* 75, no. 1 (June 1988): 9–39.

Kimmage, Michael. *The Abandonment of the West: The History of an Idea in American Foreign Policy*. New York: Basic Books, 2020.

Kinzer, Stephen. *The Brothers: John Foster Dulles, Allen Dulles, and Their Secret World War*. New York: Times Books, 2013.

Kiplinger, W. M. *Washington Is Like That*. New York: Harper, 1942.

Knock, Thomas J. *To End All Wars: Woodrow Wilson and the Quest for a New World Order*. Princeton, NJ: Princeton University Press, 1992.

Kolko, Gabriel, and Joyce Kolko. *The Limits of Power: The World and United States Foreign Policy, 1945–1954*. New York: Harper and Row, 1972.

Krock, Arthur. "Washington, D.C." In *We Saw It Happen: The News behind the News That's Fit to Print*, edited by Hanson W. Baldwin and Shepard Stone, 3–28. New York: Simon and Schuster, 1939.

Kunz, Diane B. *The Economic Diplomacy of the Suez Crisis*. Chapel Hill: University of North Carolina Press, 1991.

Ladd, Jonathan. *Why Americans Hate the Media and How It Matters*. Princeton, NJ: Princeton University Press, 2011.

LaFeber, Walter. *The New Empire: An Interpretation of American Expansion, 1860–1898*. Ithaca, NY: Cornell University Press, 1963.

Laird, Pamela. *Pull: Networking and Success since Benjamin Franklin*. Cambridge, MA: Harvard University Press, 2006.

Lait, Jack, and Lee Mortimer. *Washington Confidential*. New York: Crown, 1951.

Landis, Kenesaw M. "Segregation in Washington: A Report, November 1948." Chicago: National Committee on Segregation in the Nation's Capital, 1948.

Lane, Julie B. "Richard Rovere and the American Conscience." PhD diss., University of Wisconsin, 2010.

Lawrence, David. *Diary of a Washington Correspondent*. New York: H. C. Kinsey, 1942.

Lebovic, Sam. *Free Speech and Unfree News: The Paradox of Press Freedom in America*. Cambridge, MA: Harvard University Press, 2016.

Leff, Laurel. *Buried by the* Times*: The Holocaust and America's Most Important Newspaper*. New York: Cambridge University Press, 2005.

Leffler, Melvyn. *A Preponderance of Power: National Security, the Truman Administration, and the Cold War*. Stanford, CA: Stanford University Press, 1992.

———. *The Specter of Communism: The U.S. and the Origins of the Cold War, 1917–1953*. New York: Hill and Wang, 1994.

Leibovich, Mark. *This Town: Two Parties and a Funeral—Plus, Plenty of Valet Parking!—in America's Gilded Capital*. New York: Blue Rider Press, 2013.

Lerner, Kevin. *Provoking the Press: (MORE) Magazine and the Crisis of Confidence in American Journalism*. Columbia: University of Missouri Press, 2019.

Lewis, David Levering. *The Improbable Wendell Willkie: The Businessman Who Saved the Republican Party and His Country, and Conceived a New World Order*. New York: Liveright, 2018.

Liebovich, Louis. *The Press and the Origins of the Cold War, 1944–1947*. New York: Praeger, 1988.

Linsky, Martin, et al. *How the Press Affects Federal Policymaking: Six Case Studies*. New York: Norton, 1986.

Lipman-Blumen, Jean. "Toward a Homosocial Theory of Sex Roles: An Explanation of the Sex Segregations of Social Institutions." *Signs* 1, no. 3 (Spring 1976): 15–31.

Logevall, Fredrik. "First among Critics: Walter Lippmann and the Vietnam War." *Journal of American-East Asian Relations* 4, no. 4 (Winter 1995): 351–75.

Lombard, Helen. *While They Fought: Behind the Scenes in Washington, 1941–1946*. New York: Charles Scribner's Sons, 1947.

Lumsden, Linda J. *Black, White and Red All Over: A Cultural History of the Radical Press in Its Heyday, 1900–1917*. Kent, OH: Kent State University Press, 2014.

———. "The Essentialist Agenda of the 'Woman's Angle' in Cold War Washington: The Case of Associated Press Reporter Ruth Cowan." *Journalism History* 33, no. 1 (Spring 2007): 2–13.

Lundestad, Geir. *The U.S. and Western Europe since 1945: From Empire by Invitation to Transatlantic Drift*. Oxford: Oxford University Press, 2005.

Lykins, Daniel L. *From Total War to Total Diplomacy: The Advertising Council and the Construction of the Cold War Consensus*. Westport, CT: Praeger, 2003.

Macekura, Stephen. "The Point Four Program and U.S. International Development Policy." *Political Science Quarterly* 128, no. 1 (Spring 2013): 127–60.

MacPherson, Myra. *"All Governments Lie": The Life and Times of Rebel Journalist I. F. Stone*. New York: Scribner, 2008.

Marbut, F. B. *News from the Capital: The Story of Washington Reporting*. Carbondale: Southern Illinois University Press, 1971.

Mariano, Marco, ed. *Defining the Atlantic Community: Culture, Intellectuals, and Policies in the Mid-Twentieth Century*. New York: Routledge, 2010.

Marton, Kati. *The Polk Conspiracy: Murder and Coverup in the Case of CBS Correspondent George Polk*. New York: Farrar, Straus and Giroux, 1990.

Marzolf, Marion. *Up from the Footnote: A History of Women Journalists*. New York: Hastings House, 1977.

Matusow, Barbara. *The Evening Stars: The Making of the Network News Anchor*. Boston: Houghton Mifflin, 1983.

McGarr, Kathryn J. "The Importance of Historical Perspective and Archival Methods in Political Communication Research." *Political Communication* 37, no. 1 (2020): 110–16.

McGirr, Lisa. *Suburban Warriors: The Origins of the New American Right*. Princeton, NJ: Princeton University Press, 2001.

McLendon, Winzola, and Scottie Smith. *Don't Quote Me! Washington Newswomen and the Power Society*. New York: E. P. Dutton, 1970.

McMahon, Robert J. *Colonialism and the Cold War: The United States and the Struggle for Indonesian Independence, 1945–49*. Ithaca, NY: Cornell University Press, 1981.

———. "Eisenhower and Third World Nationalism: A Critique of the Revisionists." *Political Science Quarterly* 101, no. 3 (1986): 453–73.

———, ed. *The Cold War in the Third World*. New York: Oxford University Press, 2013.

Mellinger, Gwyneth. "Washington Confidential: A Double Standard Gives Way to *The People's Right to Know*." *Journalism and Mass Communications Quarterly* 92, no. 4 (2015): 857–76.

Messer, Robert. *The End of an Alliance: James F. Byrnes, Roosevelt, Truman, and the Origins of the Cold War*. Chapel Hill: University of North Carolina Press, 1982.

Mills, C. Wright. *The Power Elite*. New York: Oxford University Press, 1956.

Mills, Kay. *A Place in the News: From the Women's Page to the Front Page*. New York: Dodd, Mead, 1988.

Mindich, David T. Z. *Just the Facts: How "Objectivity" Came to Define American Journalism*. New York: New York University Press, 1998.

Moynihan, Daniel P. *Secrecy: The American Experience*. New Haven, CT: Yale University Press, 1998.

Neff, Gina. "The Changing Place of Cultural Production: The Location of Social

Networks in a Digital Media Industry." *Annals of the American Academy of Political and Social Science* 597, no. 1 (January 2005): 134–52.

Nimmo, Dan. *Newsgathering in Washington: A Study in Political Communication.* New York: Atherton Press, 1964.

Ninkovich, Frank. *Global Dawn: The Cultural Foundation of American Internationalism, 1865–1890.* Cambridge, MA: Harvard University Press, 2009.

Nord, David Paul. *Communities of Journalism: A History of American Newspapers and Their Readers.* Urbana: University of Illinois Press, 2001.

Olson, Lynne. *Citizens of London: The Americans Who Stood with Britain in Its Darkest, Finest Hour.* New York: Random House, 2010.

Osgood, Kenneth. *Total Cold War: Eisenhower's Secret Propaganda Battle at Home and Abroad.* Lawrence: University Press of Kansas, 2006.

Parker, Jason. "Cold War II: The Eisenhower Administration, the Bandung Conference, and the Reperiodization of the Postwar Era." *Diplomatic History* 30, no. 5 (November 2006): 867–92.

Parry-Giles, Shawn J. *The Rhetorical Presidency, Propaganda, and the Cold War 1945–1955.* Westport, CT: Greenwood Publishing Group, 2001.

Paterson, Thomas G. "Foreign Aid under Wraps: The Point Four Program." *Wisconsin Magazine of History* 56, no. 2 (Winter 1972–73): 119–26.

Payne, Ethel. "Loneliness in the Capital: The Black National Correspondent." In *Perspectives of the Black Press: 1974,* edited by Henry G. La Brie III, 153–61. Kennebunkport, ME: Mercer House Press, 1974.

Pearson, Drew. *Diaries, 1949–1959.* Edited by Tyler Abell. New York: Holt, Rinehart and Winston, 1974.

Perry, Glen C. H. *"Dear Bart": Washington Views of World War II.* Westport, CT: Greenwood Press, 1982.

Phillips, Cabell, et al., eds. *Dateline: Washington: The Story of National Affairs Journalism in the Life and Times of the National Press Club.* Garden City, NY: Doubleday, 1949.

Phillips-Fein, Kim. *Invisible Hands: The Businessmen's Crusade against the New Deal.* New York: W. W. Norton, 2009.

Pickett, William. *Eisenhower Decides to Run: Presidential Politics and Cold War Strategy.* Chicago: Ivan R. Dee, 2000.

"Pity the Poor Hostess." *Saturday Evening Post,* September 5, 1936, 2. Quoted in David Brinkley, *Washington Goes to War,* 10. New York: Knopf, 1988.

Plummer, Brenda Gayle, ed. *Window on Freedom: Race, Civil Rights, and Foreign Affairs.* Chapel Hill: University of North Carolina Press, 2003.

Polk, George. "Greece Puts Us to the Test." *Harper's,* December 1947, 529–36.

Porwancher, Andrew. "Objectivity's Prophet: Adolph S. Ochs and the *New York Times,* 1896–1935." *Journalism History* 36 (Winter 2011): 186–95.

Povich, Lynn. *The Good Girls Revolt: How the Women of* Newsweek *Sued Their Bosses and Changed the Workplace.* New York: Public Affairs, 2012.

Rabe, Robert A. "Reporter in a Troubled World: Marquis W. Childs and the Rise and Fall of Postwar Liberalism." PhD diss., University of Wisconsin, 2013.

Reston, James B. *Artillery of the Press*. New York: Harper and Row, 1967.

———. *Deadline: A Memoir*. New York: Random House, 1991.

———. *Prelude to Victory*. New York: A. A. Knopf, 1943.

Riggs, Robert L. "The 'Scoops' Served at Private Washington Dinners." *New Republic*, April 11, 1955, 8–9.

Ritchie, Donald A. *The Columnist: Leaks, Lies and Libel in Drew Pearson's Washington*. New York: Oxford University Press, 2021.

———. *Press Gallery: Congress and the Washington Correspondents*. Cambridge, MA: Harvard University Press, 1991.

———. *Reporting from Washington: The History of the Washington Press Corps*. New York: Oxford University Press, 2005.

Rivers, William L. *The Opinionmakers*. Boston: Beacon Press, 1965.

———. *The Other Government: Power and the Washington Media*. New York: Universe Books, 1982.

———. "The Washington Correspondents after 25 Years." *Columbia Journalism Review* 1, no. 1 (Spring 1962): 6.

Rivers, William L., and Wilbur Schramm. *Responsibility in Mass Communication*. Rev. ed. New York: Harper and Row, 1969.

Roberts, Chalmers M. *First Rough Draft: A Journalist's Journal of Our Times*. New York: Praeger, 1973.

Robertson, Nan. *The Girls in the Balcony: Women, Men, and The New York Times*. New York: Random House, 1992.

Robinson, Sue. "Convergence Crises: News Work and News Space in the Digitally Transforming Newsroom." *Journal of Communication* 61 (2011): 1122–41.

Roeder, George H. *The Censored War: American Visual Experience during World War II*. New Haven, CT: Yale University Press, 1993.

Rosten, Leo C. *The Washington Correspondents*. New York: Arno Press, 1974 (1937).

Rudenstine, David. *The Day the Presses Stopped: A History of the Pentagon Papers Case*. Berkeley: University of California Press, 1998.

Schlesinger, Arthur, Jr. *A Thousand Days: John F. Kennedy in the White House*. Boston: Houghton Mifflin, 1965.

Schroth, Raymond A. *The American Journey of Eric Sevareid*. South Royalton, VT: Steerforth Press, 1995.

Schudson, Michael. *Discovering the News: A Social History of American Newspapers*. New York: Basic Books, 1978.

———. *The Rise of the Right to Know: Politics and the Culture of Transparency, 1945–1975*. Cambridge, MA: Belknap Press of Harvard University Press, 2015.

Schulman, Bruce, and Julian Zelizer, eds. *Media Nation: The Political History of News in Modern America*. Philadelphia: University of Pennsylvania Press, 2017.

Sedgwick, Eve Kosofsky. *Between Men: English Literature and Male Homosocial Desire.* New York: Columbia University Press, 1985.

Sevareid, Eric. *Not So Wild a Dream.* New York: Knopf, 1946.

Shepley, James. "How Dulles Averted War." *Life,* January 16, 1958, 70–80.

Sherry, Michael S. *In the Shadow of War: The United States since the 1930s.* New Haven, CT: Yale University Press, 1995.

———. *Preparing for the Next War: American Plans for Postwar Defense, 1941–1945.* New Haven, CT: Yale University Press, 1977.

Shils, Edward. *The Torment of Secrecy: The Background and Consequences of American Security Policies.* Glencoe, IL: Free Press, 1956.

Sigal, Leon V. *Reporters and Officials: The Organization and Politics of Newsmaking.* Lexington, MA: D. C. Heath, 1973.

Simmons, George E. "The 'Cold War' in Large-City Dailies of the United States." *Journalism Quarterly* 25 (December 1948): 354–59, 400.

Slattery, Karen, and Mark Doremus. "Suppressing Allied Atrocity Stories: The Unwritten Clause of the World War II Censorship Code." *Journalism and Mass Communication Quarterly* 89, no. 4: 624–42.

Snyder, Brad. *The House of Truth: A Washington Political Salon and the Foundations of American Liberalism.* New York: Oxford University Press, 2017.

Sparrow, James T. *Warfare State: World War II Americans and the Age of Big Government.* New York: Oxford University Press, 2011.

Stacks, John F. *Scotty: James B. Reston and the Rise and Fall of American Journalism.* Boston: Little, Brown, 2003.

Stansell, Christine. *City of Women: Sex and Class in New York, 1789–1860.* New York: Knopf, 1986.

Steel, Ronald. *Walter Lippmann and the American Century.* Boston: Little, Brown, 1980.

Steele, Richard W. "The Great Debate: Roosevelt, the Media, and the Coming of the War, 1940–1941." *Journal of American History* 71, no. 1 (June 1984): 69–92.

Stepp, Carl Sessions. "Then and Now." *American Journalism Review* 21, no. 7 (September 1999): 60–75.

Stone, I. F. *The Best of I. F. Stone.* Edited by Karl Weber. New York: Public Affairs, 2006.

———. *The Truman Era.* London: Turnstile Press, 1953.

Storrs, Landon R. Y. "Attacking the Washington 'Femmocracy': Antifeminism in the Cold War Campaign against 'Communists in Government.'" *Feminist Studies* 33, no. 1 (Spring 2007): 118–52.

Stueck, William. *The Korean War: An International History.* Princeton, NJ: Princeton University Press, 1995.

Sulzberger, C. L. *A Long Row of Candles: Memoirs and Diaries, 1934–1954.* Toronto: Macmillan, 1969.

Summers, Mark Wahlgren. *The Press Gang: Newspapers and Politics, 1865–1878.* Chapel Hill: University of North Carolina Press, 1994.

Summers, Robert E., ed. *Wartime Censorship of Press and Radio*. New York: H. W. Wilson, 1942.

Sweeney, Michael S. *Secrets of Victory: The Office of Censorship and the American Press and Radio in World War II*. Chapel Hill: University of North Carolina Press, 2001.

Takeyh, Ray. *The Origins of the Eisenhower Doctrine: The US, Britain, and Nasser's Egypt, 1953–57*. New York: St. Martin's Press, 2000.

Talese, Gay. *The Kingdom and the Power*. New York: World, 1967.

Thurston, Chloe N. *At the Boundaries of Homeownership: Credit, Discrimination, and the American State*. New York: Cambridge University Press, 2018.

Trachtenberg, Marc. *A Constructed Peace: The Making of the European Settlement, 1945–1963*. Princeton, NJ: Princeton University Press, 1999.

Tuchman, Gaye. *Making News: A Study in the Construction of Reality*. New York: Free Press, 1978.

Usher, Nikki. *Making News at The New York Times*. Ann Arbor: University of Michigan Press, 2014.

———. "The *NYT* in Trump's America: A Failure for Liberals, a Champion for Liberalism." *Political Communication* 37, no. 4 (2020): 573–81.

Vaughn, Stephen. *Holding Fast the Inner Lines: Democracy, Nationalism, and the Committee in Public Information*. Chapel Hill: University of North Carolina Press, 1980.

Vidal, Gore. *Washington, D.C.* Boston: Little, Brown, 1967.

Vlanton, Elias. *Who Killed George Polk?: The Press Covers Up a Death in the Family*. Philadelphia: Temple University Press, 1996.

Von Eschen, Penny M. *Race against Empire: Black Americans and Anticolonialism, 1937–1957*. Ithaca, NY: Cornell University Press, 1997.

Voss, Kimberly Wilmot. "Redefining Women's News: A Case Study of Three Women's Page Editors and Their Framing of the Women's Movement." PhD diss., University of Maryland, 2004.

Voss, Kimberly Wilmot, and Lance Speere. "Way Past Deadline: The Women's Fight to Integrate the Milwaukee Press Club." *Wisconsin Magazine of History* 92, no. 1 (Autumn 2008): 28–43.

Wala, Michael. "Selling the Marshall Plan at Home: The Committee for the Marshall Plan to Aid European Recovery." *Diplomatic History* 10, no. 3 (July 1986): 247–65.

Wall, Wendy. *Inventing the "American Way": The Politics of Consensus from the New Deal to the Civil Rights Movement*. New York: Oxford University Press, 2008.

Washburn, Patrick. *A Question of Sedition: The Federal Government's Investigation of the Black Press during World War II*. New York: Oxford University Press, 1986.

Weinberg, Sidney. "What to Tell America: The Writers' Quarrel in the Office of War Information." *Journal of American History* 55 (1968): 76.

Wellerstein, Alex. *Restricted Data: The History of Nuclear Secrecy in the United States*. Chicago: University of Chicago Press, 2021.

Wertheim, Stephen. *Tomorrow, the World: The Birth of U.S. Global Supremacy*. Cambridge, MA: Harvard University Press, 2020.

Westad, Odd Arne. *The Global Cold War: Third World Interventions and the Making of Our Times*. New York: Cambridge University Press, 2005.

Whyte, Marama. "The Press for Equality: Women Journalists, Grassroots Activism, and the Feminist Fight for American Media." PhD diss., University of Sydney, 2020.

Williams, William Appleman. *The Tragedy of American Diplomacy*. Cleveland: World, 1959.

Willis, Jim. *The Media Effect: How the News Influences Politics and Government*. Westport, CT: Praeger, 2007.

Winfield, Betty Houchin. *FDR and the News Media*. New York: Columbia University Press, 1994.

Yaqub, Salim. *Containing Arab Nationalism: The Eisenhower Doctrine and the Middle East*. Chapel Hill: University of North Carolina Press, 2004.

Yellin, Eric. *Racism in the Nation's Service: Government Workers and the Color Line in Woodrow Wilson's America*. Chapel Hill: University of North Carolina Press, 2013.

Yergin, Daniel. *The Prize: The Epic Quest for Oil, Money and Power*. New York: Free Press, 1993.

———. *Shattered Peace: The Origins of the Cold War and the National Security State*. Boston: Houghton Mifflin, 1977.

Yoder, Edwin M., Jr. *Joe Alsop's Cold War: A Study of Journalistic Influence and Intrigue*. Chapel Hill: University of North Carolina Press, 1995.

Young, James Sterling. *The Washington Community: 1800–1828*. New York: Columbia University Press, 1966.

Young, Kimball. "Content Analysis of the Treatment of the Marshall Plan in Certain Representative American Newspapers." *Journal of Social Psychology* 33 (1951): 163–85.

Yu, Yang-Chou, and Daniel Riffe. "Chiang and Mao in U.S. News Magazines." *Journalism Quarterly* 66, no. 4 (December 1989): 913–19.

Zaller, John, and Dennis Chiu. "Government's Little Helper: U.S. Press Coverage of Foreign Policy Crises, 1945–1991." *Political Communication* 13 (1996): 385–405.

Zelizer, Barbie. "Journalists as Interpretive Communities." *Critical Studies in Mass Communication* 10, no. 3 (1993): 219–37.

———. *Taking Journalism Seriously: News and the Academy*. Thousand Oaks, CA: Sage, 2004.

———. "Why Journalism in the Age of Trump Shouldn't Surprise Us." In *Trump and the Media*, edited by Pablo J. Boczkowski and Zizi Papacharissi, 9–16. Cambridge, MA: MIT Press, 2018.

Zelizer, Julian. *Arsenal of Democracy: The Politics of National Security—from World War II to the War on Terrorism*. New York: Basic Books, 2010.

Zipp, Samuel. *The Idealist: Wendell Willkie's Wartime Quest for One World*. Cambridge, MA: Harvard University Press, 2020.

INDEX

Page numbers in italics refer to illustrations.